Social Problems

Social Problems

A Critical Analysis of Theories and Public Policy

Ritchie P. Lowry
Boston College

D. C. HEATH AND COMPANY
Lexington, Massachusetts   Toronto   London

International Standard Book Number: 0–669–85332–1

Library of Congress Catalog Card Number: 73–2169

Dedicated to my mother and father

Preface

Sociology is often at its best when it is myth breaking, when it turns its methodologies and theoretical perspectives to a critique of popular beliefs about human behavior that have obtained the force of dogma. Peter Berger has described this quality in the following way:

Every human society has assumptions that, most of the time, are neither challenged nor reflected upon. In other words, in every society there are patterns of thought that most people accept without question as being of the very nature of things. Alfred Schutz called the sum of these "the world-taken-for-granted," which provides the parameters and the basic programs for our everyday lives.[1]

Nowhere is this process more apparent than in the public and official views of social problems, and in the massive private and public programs designed to "solve" these problems. These views are reflected in the following kinds of beliefs: "The poor shall always be with us," "drug users are morally weak," and "homosexuals are sick." Berger points out that specific institutions and vested interests are legitimated by such taken-for-granted assumptions, and that, therefore, threats to these assumptions become threats to those who have a stake in the status quo: namely, the rich, the powerful, and the "straight." Meaningful sociology, by its very nature, keeps producing such threats:

Sociology has a built-in debunking effect. It shows up the fallaciousness of socially established interpretations of reality by demonstrating that the facts do not gibe with the "official" view or, even more simply by relativizing the latter, that is, by showing that it is only one of several possible views of society.[2]

To this extent, sociology can become an intellectually subversive occupation. Sociologists, however, are men who sometimes become as influenced by myths as the general public, and they, too, can take for granted unwarranted assumptions about social problems.

This book is a critical analysis of prevailing popular and scientific myths about contemporary social problems. It begins in Part I with a critique of popular American mythology, which short-sightedly blames evil people, irrational behavior, the collapse of moral integrity, and the like, for the multitude of current world problems—from drug use, through sexual deviance, to war and pollution. Studies that seriously question these often incorrect views are introduced to aid the analysis. Furthermore, these taken-for-granted assumptions are shown to be a consequence of major historical changes. In other words, popular myths about social problems have roots in the way in which Americans have characteristically viewed the nature of man and human behavior, particularly behavior that deviates from what is accepted as the norm or as desirable by legitimate institutions and vested interests. If adequate answers to social problems are ever to be discovered, old myths must be replaced by new, more meaningful perspectives.

This situation is further complicated by the fact that although sociologists often debunk popular mythologies, they only infrequently turn their critical talents to a needed appraisal of their own misconceptions. As members of a social system, social scientists cannot escape the influence of accepted mythology. In addition, the theoretical perspectives they devise for analyzing and ordering the world they study also frequently reflect historical biases and special misconceptions unique to the scientific community. One of the ironies of science is that, in seeking to create order out of the seeming chaos of facts available for analysis, some *preconceived* order must be assumed. The way in which this requirement results in the creation of a scientific mythology, misleading preconceptions that determine later analytical perspectives, is discussed in detail in Part II.

This book argues that sociologists have characteristically used three basic preconceptions in the study of social problems —these are deviance, disorganization, and functionalism. Each incorporates, reflects, or attempts to reconcile prevailing popular myths. Furthermore, each preconception tends to be based upon its own ethical and political presumptions about problem behavior in human societies. Sociologists, and others, must be willing to debunk their own views, while recognizing, at the same time, that some view, no matter how inadequate, is necessary for one to deal logically and intelligently with human behavior. The critiques of deviance, disorganization, and functionalism, therefore, suggest the special strengths and weaknesses of each view, both as ways of looking at various social problems and as bases for planning public policy to deal with social problems.

Therefore, in Parts II and III, using Thomas S. Kuhn's argument about the nature of scientific revolutions,[3] this book suggests that major revolutions in theoretical perspectives take place when prevailing preconceptions no longer adequately explain observed reality. This situation characterizes social scientific thinking about social problems today. The three basic preconceptions not only ineffectively describe the seeming nature of many social problems, but they also often lead to public and private solutions that create additional problems. Thus, the modern welfare bureaucracy is seen as a threat equal to poverty and unemployment; methadone maintenance to some seems to replace unapproved deviance with state-approved drug addiction; busing exacerbates ethnic tensions; and proposals for income maintenance programs and guaranteed annual wages seem to do nothing about unemployability or nonemployability for many segments of the population. As a consequence, each of the three prevailing scientific perspectives has been challenged in recent decades by alternative views that question the philosophy of and methodology used by the three traditional approaches, as well as the ethical and political values they imply. Labeling theory, conflict theory, Alvin Gouldner's concept of a reflexive sociology,[4] and a new form of behavioristic analysis of social problems are all new schools of thought competing with the old views. Theory and research concerning contemporary social problems are, therefore, in a state of turmoil and revolution, which, when coupled with the current transition in popular attitudes, leads to a situation in which solutions to problems often seem to be worse than the original problems themselves.

As a result of this situation, within the next decade or so, a new popular mythology about and a new scientific view of social problems will probably emerge. Such new views will have to meet specific requirements, if adequate resolutions of and solutions to problems are to be achieved. This book concludes in Parts III and IV by suggesting what these requirements are and how they might be met. Several introductory cautions are necessary.

First, this book obviously is not the typical discussion of problems in contemporary society. The traditional approach concentrates on particular issues (war, race, pollution, crime, narcotics use, sexual deviance, and the like) as though they were generally unrelated to one another and, more importantly, as though they were unrelated to the way in which scientists and laymen define, identify, investigate, and attempt to resolve them. The central argument of this book is that such a typical approach is precisely why contemporary society seems to be characterized by a crisis of social problems, why although we mean well we often fail in attempts at solutions.

Second, there are always risks inherent in classifying a man's work or theory according to a specific school of thought or theoretical perspective. Most social scientists utilize a mix of perspectives (deviance, disorganization, functionalism, labeling theory, conflict theory, and so on) when analyzing specific problems. Nevertheless, the approach taken in this book assumes that the major propensities of a particular theory or piece of research can be more closely identified with one perspective than with certain others. There is no attempt here to build artificial straw men for the purposes of easy criticism.

A third caution concerns the recent trend in social science for dialogues between adherents of varying perspectives to consist merely of accusations of intent. For example, functionalists have been accused by radical social scientists as being conservative handmaidens of the prevailing status quo. This book adopts the view that there is a difference between *saying that a theory* tends toward a conservative orientation and *accusing particular scholars* of being deliberately conservative. In short, this book is concerned with the consequences that flow naturally from the use of certain kinds of theories and views, no matter who uses them, not with the inner motivations of particular scientists or theorists. The traditional approach to the study of social problems has been to look at "the substance" of particular problems. The difficulty is that this "substance" is often a myth, created by the dominant popular views and scientific perspectives of a particular time and place. Until students are exposed to the necessity to challenge the traditional views, which are the unquestioned basis for almost every introductory book in the field, the study of social problems will continue to get us all into more trouble than we can handle.

My thanks to Mrs. Lorraine Bone, Mrs. Alice Close, and Mrs. Shirley Urban for the tedious and demanding task of typing, correspondence, filing, and the like. My special thanks to my students at both the graduate and undergraduate level, whose response to these kinds of ideas in my social problems course, and other courses, led to the writing of this book. I am also indebted to my colleagues at Boston College and to the sociology faculty and students at the University of Essex (England), who gave me the kind of inspiration, encouragement, and criticism so necessary for sustained, serious work. A final and most important debt of intellectual gratitude is owed to my son, Peter, who first introduced me to Thomas Kuhn's theory, which plays such a central part in this book.

RITCHIE P. LOWRY
Boston College
1972

Notes to Preface

1. Peter L. Berger, "Sociology and Freedom," *The American Sociologist,* 6 (February 1971), p. 2.
2. *Ibid.*
3. Thomas S. Kuhn, *The Structure of Scientific Revolutions,* 2nd ed. (Chicago: University of Chicago Press, 1970).
4. Alvin W. Gouldner, *The Coming Crisis of Western Sociology* (New York: Avon Books, 1970).

Contents

Tables

Diagrams

Part I

Social Problems: Prevailing Views

Social problems: Do they require acts of goodwill, social experimentation, or benign neglect?
(Dave Healey, Magnum)

1. From Do-Gooders to Antiutopians

The Crisis in Problems Theory

The late 1960's and early 1970's were years marked by increasing disillusionment over the possible use of social scientific knowledge for the resolution of major problems facing human society. This disillusionment was pronounced both within and outside of academic disciplines and included voices from the complete spectrum of political and social beliefs. Radical critics of the left, public leaders, right-wing extremists, citizens of many persuasions, and social commentators questioned the work of social and behavioral scientists, often calling it trivial, biased, meaningless, and, in some cases, dangerous. This cynicism and antiintellectual contempt of social science was expressed bluntly by one newspaper columnist:

Sociology, as we all know, is a scholarly discipline which elevates the obvious to the esoteric. A sociologist will devote several years to a study which eventually will disclose that most men and women like sex, in one form or another. A sociologist will pontificate on the inequitable distribution of wealth in language neither the rich nor the poor will understand. [These] savants who relentlessly pursue things-everyone-knew-in-the-first-place [often exceed] their own seemingly infinite capacity for revealing revealed truths.

Popular myths abound that echo this perspective. "Social science is common sense made complicated." "We know no more today about human behavior and politics than Aristotle did." "Social thinkers are parasites; it is the man of action who gets things done." Like most widely accepted stereotypes and myths, these sentiments contain partial truths, though they grossly misrepresent reality. This book considers both what is right and what is wrong with much prevailing social theory currently used to address what we consider to be major social problems. Specifically, what is the origin of the public cynicism? If this cynicism is justified, is the logical conclusion that rational, calculated solutions to social problems are unattainable? To make our knowledge more applicable to successful public policy programs, what directions should we be following? What perspectives of social problems should we be using? Cynicism in the 20th century has been a function of two major processes. The first is related to rapid social change and the resulting challenge to traditional values and ideologies. The dawn of urban industrial society in medieval Europe held out the promise to Western man of attainable utopias in the foreseeable future. Enlightenment and reason were seen as the major guiding principles for bringing about a more humane, compassionate, and just society. What actually happened during the last several hundred years is now a matter of historical record. While urbanism and industrialization resolved many of the degradations and repressions that existed in the underdeveloped feudal society, they also created new problems, which, in retrospect, seem to many to be more degrading and repressive.

The Western world fought two major wars to end war, only to find that warfare changed in nature and became potentially more devastating and all-inclusive. The great utopias of a century ago—Christianity, Capitalism, Communism—often created their own peculiar nightmares and apocalyptic visions of the future, rather than promises of salvation for man in his worldly state. Counterutopias replaced utopias as Cassandras competed in mourning a dire future for a world plagued by population crises, violence in the cities, pollution of air and water, destructive revolutionary movements, dehumanizing social institutions, ethnic and national conflict, totalitarian governments, the possibility of global nuclear wars, and the like. Even the privileged segments of the modern population judged to be lucky enough to have escaped the more obvious disadvantages of modern life are seen to be suffering their own unique forms of degradation and repression. In affluence and comfort, they are allegedly suffering from boredom and anomie, which in turn lead to suicide, narcotics addiction, aimless violence, bizarre behavior, alcoholism, and a breakdown in sexual standards. W. H. Ferry has summarized this feeling as follows:

The number of great issues to which no reasonable solution is possible appears to me to be growing almost daily. I am aware that mankind has gone on for a long time with a considerable backlog of unanswered questions or, in any case, with questions that have been at best half-answered or have been resolved in the muffled tones of compromise. But it seems that today's backlog is different in important ways. Yesterday's questions tended to be local—for example, World War I only in a limited way had global dimensions. Today's questions, on the other hand, are nearly universal in their significance. Unless we have been misled, we shall have to call the next international conflict not World War III but Space War I. There is the added sense that half-answers to today's questions cannot be satisfactory—or at least not satisfactory for very long.[1]

Against such a historical backdrop, it is not surprising that despair should be a major emotional characteristic of contemporary society, and that a new distrust of reason, ironically reminiscent of the medieval suspicions of science, has led to a hostility and fear of social scientists and social theory. Of even greater importance, however, is the second major process leading to modern cynicism, a frequently all but ignored phenomenon. Prevailing popular and scientific perspectives of social problems have not only been biased by the historical events of the last several hundred years, they have also come to be based upon their own particular misconceptions and myths. To this extent, modern skepticism of social science is not without merit. The fact that the major problems of contemporary society have appeared precisely during the same period of time as the most rapid growth of social scientific knowledge suggests the limitations of our present knowledge. Commenting on a study by the Brookings Institution, Jack Rosenthal summarizes the situation:

"Don't just do something," reads the poster in the poverty worker's

office. "Stand there." It is a wry symbol of the harsh disillusionment with Federal social programs that has increasingly infused Washington. The glory days of the Great Society, the don't-just-stand-there days, the days when it was thought that any social problem would yield to sufficient will and sufficient dollars, are over. . . . The multiplication of dollars and programs brought not solutions for such problems as welfare reform, day care and city finance but a multiplication of dilemmas. And now the dilemmas threaten to become paralyzing. . . . [The real shortage has not been money, but rather it] has been knowledge. In the last 10 years the Federal Government has been called on increasingly to do things it does not know how to do.[2]

One of the major reasons why our public and private agencies do not know how to contend with many contemporary social problems is that a good deal of social theory misrepresents the essential nature of human behavior and, thus, becomes useless, and often dangerous, as a basis for public policy. The logical conclusion, however, is not that social science is useless but rather that the knowledge generated to date must be re-examined for its biases and misrepresentations. This book, therefore, identifies the inadequacies of prevailing scientific and popular myths about social problems, indicates how these myths have become the basis for three prominent scientific paradigms or theories used to seek solutions to problems, considers the weaknesses and strengths of the three theories, and suggests alternative views and needed directions for future research and policy formulation. Before examining popular myths and scientific paradigms in detail, however, a fuller understanding of the historical origins of social problems theories is necessary.

Origins of Social-Problems Theories

The search for answers to social problems is as old as civilization. Howard Waitzkin tells the story of Plato's experience as adviser to a state leader:

At the age of forty Plato received an invitation from Dionysius, ruler of Syracuse, to serve as a consultant in establishing a utopian republic. Plato consented and traveled to Syracuse, planning to transform the society by educating its ruler. Dionysius, however, was unaware of Plato's stipulation that in order to retain one's rule as king, one must become a philosopher. Upon discovering this fact, Dionysius quarreled with Plato, arrested him, and finally sold him into slavery. Though he was ransomed by a faithful student, Plato never again tried to apply his system of social philosophy to a concrete political situation.[3]

Waitzkin points out that, like Plato, social philosophers and scientists have traditionally committed themselves to seeking rational answers to social problems. Over a century ago, August Comte (1798–1857), the father of sociology, argued that if biologists could discover laws governing the natural world, sociologists could do the same for society. These laws could then be applied to specific problems, elevating politics to the level of a science of observation.[4] Subsequently, Karl Marx (1818–1883) studied the problems of early industrial society, Emile Durkheim (1858–1917) searched for the causes of suicide, and Max Weber (1864–1920) traced the connections between the emergence of capitalism and the development of bureaucracy.[5] Thus, from the start, sociology as a discipline dealt with social problems. While recognition of this fact is important, of greater significance and interest is an understanding of the ways in which social scientists sought answers to social problems and the latent perspectives they used.

Early European and American Perspective—Science to Reformism. In reality, most of the European founders of sociology, particularly Max Weber, saw themselves as scientists first and only indirectly as problem solvers. Although they believed that scientific knowledge might be used for rational political ends, they felt that the discovery of knowledge should take place with minimal emotional and personal commitment to the subject matter. Using an ideal model of the neutral natural and physical scientist, they argued for remaining value-free, unbiased, and detached, no matter what the feelings of the social scientist might be toward the problem being analyzed. Only in this manner, they argued, could truth free of distortion be discovered. Furthermore:

It is noteworthy that some of the greatest classic figures (such as Max Weber, Emile Durkheim and Vilfredo Pareto) invested a good deal of effort in what they considered to be refutations of Marxism. Most classic sociology in Europe was a counterrevolutionary and (at least implicitly) conservative doctrine. Early American sociology had a strong reformist animus, but this was more congenial to YMCA secretaries than to revolutionaries or preachers of spiritual salvation.[6]

When sociology moved to America in the late 19th and early 20th centuries, it took on a reformist, moralistic, antiurban orientation, somewhat different than the early European perspectives, and, accordingly, the study of specific social problems developed.[7] The kinds of problems and the approach, however, were of a special nature. As Leonard Reissman points out: "The study of social problems belonged exclusively to a relatively small group of ideologically prejudiced sociologists, those who seemingly were driven by a sense of mission to identify evil and to cure it." [8] In an analysis of textbooks in the field of social disorganization in 1943, C. Wright Mills found a prevalent professional ideology: one characterized by a very low level of abstraction, the failure to consider total social structures, the use of fragmentary data and evidence, and the analysis of idiosyncratic problems with practical implications in everyday life (for example, rape in rural districts).[9] Mills suggests that this type of perspective permitted theorists to show humanitarian concern for those influenced by problem behavior, without necessitating the development of theories or programs for action that would severely threaten the established status quo or vested interests. Therefore, where early European sociology had a detached, antirevolutionary orientation, early American sociology developed a modestly involved, reformist commitment.

Changes in the American Perspective—"Involved and Revolutionary?"   Norval Glenn and David Weiner have indicated that the change resulting from the Americanization of sociology can be seen as a consequence of the predominant social origins of sociologists.[10] In addition, they indicate that sociology, particularly that part of the discipline concerned with social problems, shifted toward a third, more passionately involved, sometimes revolutionary perspective about 1950. For example, in their 1967 study of a sample of members and fellows from the American Sociological Association, they found that almost 13 percent of 429 respondents who had received their doctorates in 1947 or earlier had fathers who were clergymen. In contrast, among those who had received their doctorates between 1958 and 1967, about 7 percent had fathers who were clergymen. Among the

1947 and earlier doctorate holders, 25 percent came from the Northeastern United States and 37 percent from the North-central United States. Among the 1958 to 1967 degree holders, these proportions had shifted to 34 and 27 percent, respectively. In the 1947 and earlier group, 22 percent came from communities of less than 2500 population, and 31 percent from communities of 50,000 or more. These percentages had changed to 7 and 47 percent, respectively, for the 1958–1967 group.

In other words, early American sociologists tended to be Midwestern in origin, from small towns, influenced by religious backgrounds, and of lower middle-class standing with rapid upward mobility. From these origins came the modest and conservative reformist commitment. In contrast, later sociologists were more secular and urban. As a consequence, according to Reissman:

> By the mid-1950's the situation had changed. Research funds became available, a different breed of sociologist was attracted to and trained in the discipline, and signs of a strong ethical and scientific desire to help improve American society [and sometimes to revise it radically] appeared. Consequently, interest in the analysis of social problems multiplied, carried on a wave of new funding and new ideas about social relevance aimed at the underbelly of society. Within the decade, sociologists were involved in the failures of society: poverty, racial conflict, crime, violence, drug addiction, overpopulation, and even the international concerns of counterinsurgency.[11]

Through the century of change from European to contemporary American sociology, the academic concern for social problems appeared to be adapting to new requirements. The study of social problems began with an emphasis upon being scientific, moved to a modestly reformist orientation, and ended with emerging commitments by some scientists for an activist role in bringing about radical change. In reality, however, the adaptation was not complete, and a tension and theoretical discontinuity was developing. Although social scientists had changed in their backgrounds and interests, the theories they utilized remained indebted to original assumptions and perspectives. This dependence upon older, increasingly less applicable, theories about social problems accounts for much modern cynicism and some of the current crisis in our inability to resolve problems.

Older Theories Versus New Conditions. The European founders of social science, working at the time of the major revolutions (political, economic, communal, familial) in Western society—a period of great social upheaval and change—became interested in the central problem of accounting for those processes that maintained social order, cohesion, and stability. Disorder, dissolution, and change were typically seen as pathological and threatening states to the condition of man. When problems were studied, as in the case of Durkheim's classic analysis of suicide, they were used either as examples of social dissolution or as explanations for how society maintained "normality." The early American sociologists inherited this conservative bias and saw problems as deviations and pathologies that needed to be cured. The cure, of necessity, was in the nature of modest reform, in order not to kill the ultimate patient —the prevailing social order—to which the sociologists themselves were indebted for their rapid upward mobility. This heritage was passed on to contemporary theorists in the form of three major theoretical paradigms of social problems: *deviance, disorganization,* and *functionalism.*

Contemporary social scientists, however, found themselves dealing with a completely altered social situation. Rapid and revolutionary change, a variety of forms of deviance, and continuous conflict and dissension seemed to have become the new normalities, rather than exceptional pathologies, by the mid-20th century. This situation characterized increasing numbers of modern societies: racial and ethnic conflict in the United States, religious civil strife in Northern Ireland, a severe language conflict in Canada and Belgium, spreading drug usage in all Western nations, revolutionary upheaval and political instability in Latin America and Africa, and the like. As a consequence, older theories that focused upon the assumed natural character of social stability no longer provided adequate answers, though they were still used for analysis and as a basis for social action. Alvin Gouldner suggests one consequence of this usage of inapplicable social theory:

The crux of the issue is the lack of "fit" between new sentiments and old theories. It is precisely because of this that certain young radicals do not simply feel the old theories are "wrong" and should be criticized in detail; their more characteristic response to the older theories is a feeling of the sheer irrelevance. *Their inclination is not to disprove or argue with the old theories, but to ridicule or avoid them.*[12]

In this way, the current pessimism and antiutopianism were born. Existing theories were seen as not only irrelevant, but when used (despite their inapplicability to current problems), they seemed to create results far worse than the initial problem. In essence, a credibility gap in social science had taken place.

Compounding this situation was the tendency for modern social science to become more evangelical in its search for answers to problems, and for modern social scientists to resemble high priests or prophets of new but uncompromising utopias. Malachi Martin describes this process in the following way:

As far back in history as we can find traces of man's existence, there is evidence pointing to one perennial preoccupation of men's minds: the formulation of explanations to give meaning to the most puzzling and mysterious elements of life. . . . We find that explanations were supplied by a variety of people: priests, witch doctors, shamans, wizards, soothsayers, oracles, clerical castes, and priestly orders; and they used a variety of means to fulfill their purpose: red ocher, chicken entrails, the flight of birds, the sound of water and wind, incense, robes, gestures, sacred books, revelations, ethical systems, lists of commandments and prohibitions, sacred groups, and so on. Always it was fundamentally a question of explanation, of answering impossible questions.[13]

Martin points out that as the grip of organized religion to perform these functions has slowly weakened over recent decades, explanations offered by religious men have been rejected or ignored. Nonetheless, man's need for answers has remained. Indeed, his questioning has intensified as the problems grow worse and the traditional religious institutions seem less able to respond. As a consequence, a new breed of scientians, the practitioners of scientism, fill the role vacated by the religious institutions and supply the much-needed "explanations."

Scientians, argues Martin, have three distinguishing characteristics.[14] First, they must be scientists with impressive credentials in their fields of specialty, and the fields must be of recognized merit by the general public. Thus a Konrad Lorenz (well-known ethologist), a B. F. Skinner (noted Harvard psychologist), or a Lionel Tiger (respected paleontologist) may succeed as scientians, whereas an astrologer, theologian, or humanist, no matter how logical or rational his presentation, will not be accepted. However, though there are many capable scientists, only a few develop the second characteristic of the scientian—a sense of calling, a commitment to seeking answers to the age-old questions of mankind, a concern for ultimate questions that transcend the purely scientific. For example:

B. F. Skinner, having established that some animal behavior can be modified by environmental controls, assumes a universality for his findings and asserts that human liberty, morality, and dignity are merely behavioral traits created by environment, that there is in fact no such thing as the "inner" man. Lorenz, having catalogued the resemblances of behavior in animals and men, forthwith decides that aggression in men is the same as in animals, and that both men and animals are going about the same thing whenever resemblances occur in their behavior. He thus effectively wipes out all consideration of morality and ethics. Tiger, . . . as an extension of [his] anthropological and paleontological ruminations, [concludes] that a "biogrammer" is built into man's genes and alone determines his behavior. All else . . . is symbol and fantasy; "nature" has programmed us to act.[15]

In other words, by a "scientian leap," religious, ethical, and humanistic answers are proposed that could not have been obtained merely by being scientific, and thus a new kind of dehumanized absolutism develops.

Finally, a scientian's work leads him to proclaim the existence of a force, usually seen as an evil power, which if not properly identified and controlled will lead man to ultimate destruction. This single evil force differs according to the branch of science from which individual scientians come and may include the myth of individuality, an inherited aggressive potential, or a biologically determined intellectual capacity. "Having identified man's nemesis at last, the scientian comes bearing his new salvation: a means of control that, fortunately for us, the scientian just happens to have, and that we are told will surely deliver a saving counterforce."[16] According to Martin, the threat of scientism is that it betrays both the meaningful use of

science and the essential nature of man. It promises easy, pain-
less, and total solutions where only difficult, painful, and partial
answers may be available. Furthermore, it proposes an inhuman
or antihumane counterutopian future, where men resemble
robots and social engineering by state and private agencies is
practiced on a grand scale. The qualities of scientism have
infused much modern social-problems theory, and in part
account for the transition from the early days of dogooding to
the current antiutopian despair.

Contemporary Challenges and Needs

The contemporary situation, arising from these historical processes, is a social scientific field of inquiry marked by several
unresolved internal tensions. These tensions are reflected in the
inadequacies of prevailing theory, especially those theories used
to analyze social problems.

Conflict Between Conservative and Revolutionary Roles.　Peter
Berger has identified the first tension as a conflict between social
science as intellectually subversive and social science as intellectually conservative or supportive.[17] The conservative aspect
is evident in the fact that social science theory is a product of
its heritage, owing its formation and much of its content to the
past. Conservatism is reflected in sociology as a whole, according
to Berger, by a focus upon the imperatives of *social order, continuity,* and *triviality.* Order, which also implies social control, is
a fundamental prerequisite of the human condition, for both man
as an individual and groups as collections of individuals. Without order and control, both individuals and societies could not
and would not tolerate the resulting chaos, idiosyncracy, and
confusion of everyday life. Furthermore, Berger points out that
the imperative of continuity is closely related to order, for contemporary order is built upon routinized transitions from the
past. Individuals and social systems will react violently and re-
pressively to the threat of continual discontinuity and to the
threat of unending disorder, as recent successful political appeals
to "law-and-order" in many governments indicate. Finally, the
imperative of triviality refers to the fact that man has a limited
attention span and can tolerate only limited amounts of stimula-
tion and excitement. Daily routine, to this extent, maintains

social order and continuity and makes it possible for both individuals and social systems to function in accepted ways.

This type of perspective obviously flies in the face of much contemporary reality and revolutionary commitment. In addition, those sociologists who concentrate upon a study of order, continuity, and triviality as basic, and crucial, facts of social life, leave themselves open to the charge that they are "telling us what we knew in the first place." Ironically, social science is at the same time basically subversive, as pointed out in the Preface. Berger suggests that sociology, simply by going about its essential job, puts the prevailing order and its legitimating institutions (thus, vested interests) under critical scrutiny. The result can be the serious debunking of popular assumptions and myths and accepted ways of doing things (earning a living, making a family, rewarding the worthy, parceling out power and influence, and so on). Such debunking can imply the need for radical and revolutionary change. This dual potentiality to serve supportive and subversive roles simultaneously explains in part why social science theory frequently receives equal criticism from both the political left and the political right.

Conflict Between Descriptive Theory and Applied Research—
The Passive and Active Aspects of Modern Social Science. The second major tension characterizing modern social science is the polarity between basic descriptive theories and applied policy-oriented theories. Basic theories deal with descriptions of social life as it is, descriptions that are free of interpretation, judgment, or implications for action. In contrast, applied theories address specific social problems and issues, involve at least latent value commitments, and can be used as a basis for planning programs of social action. The early days of European scientific sociology were characterized by a concentration upon basic theory. With the development of team research and relatively massive private and public funding in the 1950's, applied research with the goal of ultimate social action became commonplace. However, both basic and applied research can be either subversive or supportive. The interrelation of these two major tensions is illustrated in Table 1–1.

Such an illustration of the four possible types of social-problems theory—*basic–supportive, basic–change, applied–sup-*

portive, and *applied–change*—leads to a better understanding of contemporary challenges and needs. The most obvious conflict in contemporary sociology is between those who advocate *basic–supportive* in contrast to those who advocate *applied–change* theories. Radical critics of the traditional discipline argue that old views duck moral and social responsibility by emphasizing the need for basic (and therefore for value-free and nonsolution-oriented) research. In addition, radical critics see older views as essentially supportive to the status quo in terms of the maintenance of prevailing social institutions, often unjust, and political power, frequently undemocratic. Traditionalists counter these arguments with the charge that applied research can easily become the tool of vested interests, those either in or out of the government, who wish to dictate what should be studied

Table 1–1

Four types of social science theories by political potential and academic classification

	Supportive	*Change*
Basic	Descriptive theory used to outline the origin and nature of social order, stability, and continuity.	Descriptive theory used to outline the origin and nature of social change, discontinuity, conflict, and instability.
Applied	Goal-oriented analytical theory used to explain how deviance, change, discontinuity, and instability can be rectified. Essentially reformist in nature.	Goal-oriented analytical theory used to explain how change can be brought about in the face of social propensities toward continuity and stability. Essentially radical and revolutionary.

ACADEMIC CLASSIFICATION

POLITICAL POTENTIAL

and how. In contrast, they claim that basic research is more likely to disclose useful truths free of social restraints. In addition to aiding in the characterization of contemporary disputes over how social problems should be studied, the typology of theories can be applied to the history of social-problems analysis. For example, most social-problems theory from the *early* American period of reform fell into the *applied–supportive* category, by concentrating upon the assumed need to eliminate the forms of problem behavior (alcohol use, rebellious behavior, divorce, and so on) from the specific individuals affected and from society as a whole. The *middle* period of development, with its stress upon the scientific nature of studying problems, rejected the overtly moralistic focus of early theory and emphasized the *basic–supportive* category. The assumption was retained that social problems, as defined by society, were disruptive to the system as a whole, but the necessity for scientific neutrality in analysis was emphasized. Only recently has work begun intensively on *basic–change* theories, since this perspective required the adoption of a new view that conflict and social instability could be as natural to the functioning of a social system as order and stability. Finally, within the last decade, *applied–change* theories have received initial attention as a result of the radical criticisms of earlier work. The contemporary situation, in which prevailing theory tends to be *basic* and *supportive* rather than *change* and *applied* in nature, is therefore marked by increasing conflict between proponents of these different perspectives.

The resulting challenge to those social scientists interested in contemporary social problems is twofold. First, prevailing theory, together with contemporary popular mythology, with their emphasis on supportive perspectives, must be re-evaluated. Both the useful and the misleading aspects of theory and mythology should be determined in order to gain a more complete understanding of the essential nature of human society, whether that nature includes normal everyday behavior or unusual problem behavior. Second, a bridge between supportive–change and basic–applied perspectives is needed, since the two dichotomous types of theory do reflect basically different but very real aspects of the human condition. The remaining chapters begin these two tasks by examining prevailing theory, as it has been used in the analysis of specific problems, and by suggesting alternative views presently being debated in the discipline. First, however, in Chapter 2, an analysis of popular myths about social problems is given, since these myths have played an important role in the creation of social theories.

Notes to Chapter 1

1. W. H. Ferry, "The Unanswerable Questions," *The Center Magazine,* 2 (July 1969), pp. 2–7.
2. Jack Rosenthal, "An Epitaph for the Great Society," *The New York Times* (May 25, 1972), p. 32.
3. Howard Waitzkin, "Truth's Search for Power: The Dilemmas of the Social Sciences," *Social Problems, 15* (Spring 1968), p. 409. Waitzkin has summarized this episode involving Plato from Will Durant's *The Story of Philosophy* (New York: Simon & Schuster, 1926), pp. 56–57.
4. August Comte, *System of Positive Polity* (London: Longmans, Green, 1877).
5. For example, see Karl Marx, *Capital* (New York: E. P. Dutton, 1930); Emile Durkheim, *Suicide,* G. Simpson, ed., J. A. Spaulding and G. Simpson, transl. (New York: The Free Press, 1951); and Max Weber, *The Protestant Ethic and the Spirit of Capitalism* (London: George Allen and Unwin, 1930).
6. Peter L. Berger, "Sociology and Freedom," *The American Sociologist, 6* (February 1971), pp. 1–2.
7. Something of the same process took place in England as well. See J. A. Barnes, *Sociology in Cambridge: An Inaugural Lecture* (London: Cambridge University Press, 1970), especially p. 2. Barnes describes the importance of what he calls the spirit of "Victorian capitalism," which emphasized a concern for the "hard facts of poverty, housing, and wages" in British sociology.
8. Leonard Reissman, "The Solution Cycle of Social Problems," *The American Sociologist, 7* (February 1972), p. 7.
9. C. Wright Mills, "The Professional Ideology of Social Pathologists," *The American Journal of Sociology, 49* (September 1943), pp. 165–166.
10. Norval D. Glenn and David Weiner, "Some Trends in the Social Origins of American Sociologists," *The American Sociologist, 4* (November 1969), pp. 291–302.
11. Leonard Reissman," "The Solution Cycle of Social Problems," *The American Sociologist, 7* (February 1972), p. 7.
12. Alvin W. Gouldner, *The Coming Crisis of Western Sociology* (New York: Avon Books, 1970), p. 7.
13. Malachi Martin, "The Scientist as Shaman," *Harper's Magazine, 244* (March 1972), p. 54.
14. *Ibid.,* pp. 54–57.
15. *Ibid.,* p. 55.
16. *Ibid.,* p. 56.
17. Peter L. Berger, "Sociology and Freedom," *The American Sociologist, 6* (February 1971), pp. 1–5.

Accident, act of God, bad luck—or man's mistakes?
(Gene Daniels, Black Star)

2. Popular Myths

As Friends of the Earth and other recently formed ecology groups have found, myths play an important role in man's frequent cruelty to other animals. For example, the belief that packs of wolves constantly roam about and attack unarmed humans, especially infants and women, persists and is depicted in late movies on television showing the suffering of early pioneers in the American West. This is true despite the fact that in the history of the North American continent there have been few, if any, recorded cases of wolves threatening innocent humans. Yet the existence of the myth enables man to kill wolves freely for sport, pelts, or simple vindictiveness. Indeed, the human belief in "wild" animals (and, therefore, in inferior, uncontrollable, and menacing animals), in contrast to "civilized" man, explains a good deal of man's wholesale destruction of other animal forms. Again, the belief persists despite accumulating evidence of substantial development in other animals (for example, the brains of porpoises, and whales, the social life of ants and apes, the balance of various species with minimal aggression in many natural states, and so on).[1]

Mythology About Social Problems

In the same manner, popular myths about social problems play an important part in man's continuing cruelty and neglect of many members of his own species. As we refer to the concept here, a myth is a partial "truth," a distortion of reality, a *selective perception* of much available evidence that permits men to make some general sense out of half-understood and incompletely observed events. To this extent, myths are useful, even in their most extreme or distorted form. For example, the belief in wild animals alerts men, particularly those in relatively undeveloped environments, to treat possibly dangerous animals with caution. In a similar manner, black stereotypes of menacing whites and white stereotypes of menacing blacks may serve to sensitize both black and white citizens to possible dangers in particular social circumstances.

The difficulty is that such views rapidly take on the character of total truths and ultimate reality. Adopting these preconceptions, which have some real basis in fact (some blacks are not safe in some white areas, and vice versa), individuals may come to see only those social and cultural stimuli that seem to reinforce the belief, or they may misinterpret environmental stimuli. To whites, a black solidarity salute is seen as a menacing gesture; ethnic pride and opposition to busing become manifestations of white racism to many blacks, just as black nationalism and community control become manifestations of black racism to many whites. By such a process, the myths of white racism and black rebelliousness are born. The more both black and white citizens act in accordance with such mythical preconceptions, the more it appears to both blacks and whites that they are inherently antagonistic to one another. In addition, the fact that some blacks and some whites are aggressive and prejudiced simply substantiates and enhances the perpetuation of the mythology. In social science this process is known as the *self-fulfilling prophecy*. One's initial preconceptions tend to become reality when only those aspects of reality that support the belief are recognized *and* when the reactions of individuals to one another are such that they sustain the preconception.

The history of interethnic relations is filled with examples of this process. Louis Wirth has described the unique role of the Jewish medieval ghetto in influencing the behavior of Jews and the prejudicial attitudes of gentiles.[2] The ghetto, which was originally a quarter for Jewish settlement in the medieval city of Venice, eventually became a recognized institution defined in custom and law. For Jews, residence in a ghetto, frequently considered a privilege and right, was accepted as a way in which traditions could be maintained through isolation from threatening social contact with strangers. At the same time, dominant interests and rulers saw ghettos as convenient devices for maintaining social control by isolating those designated as the less worthy and more threatening elements of the population. Thus, whereas ghetto residence was originally voluntary, it became compulsory through time, and relationships between Jewish and gentile neighbors became formalistic and hostile. Myths that depicted ghettos as areas of immorality and disease developed. Sometimes unapproved deviant activities, such as prostitution, were driven from majority areas of a city into minority ghettos, thereby seeming to prove the myth. Jewish ghetto residents found that close-knit, in-group ties were necessary to sustain life in such a hostile environment. From this process were born the anti-Semitic beliefs of Jewish aggressiveness, exclusivity, secretiveness, inferiority, and deviance. In the same manner, though with different particular consequences, black ghetto residents have suffered from the same type of process. Black hostilities and anxieties finally erupted collectively in the United States in the 1960's with the series of civil rebellions aimed directly at the physical ghetto; this understandable response was interpreted by many whites as proof of Negro uncontrollability and inferior behavior.[3]

Such misconceptions on the part of the participants in social interaction make appropriate understanding of the true nature of a social problem, in this case interethnic hostilities, all but impossible. The tendency to incorporate some popular mythology about social problems into the political process and to use these myths as a basis for social change or reform exacerbates an already tense situation. In 1971, Richard Block analyzed the relationship between fear of crime and support for increases in police powers, especially the power to stop and frisk suspects. Through the late 1960's and into the presidency of Richard Nixon, politicians used the issue of law-and-order to attract votes and bring about changes in the legal system (preventive detention, surveillance activities of citizens by state agencies, the replacing of liberal members of the Supreme Court by strict constitutionalists and conservatives). The assumption was that the threat of traditional crime and of violence-in-the-streets outweighed civil libertarian concerns opposing greater state police powers.

Block interviewed a sample (790) of residents of major central cities outside the American South. Respondents included both self-reported victims of crimes and those who reported no victimization, during the summer of 1966.[4] Block found no significant or large relationship between the fear of crime and support for increases in police powers among both black and white respondents in the sample. At the same time, *extreme* fear of crime was somewhat related to support for increased police powers among whites and more strongly related among blacks. When fear of the police was added as a qualifying variable, Block found whites, rather than blacks, were most likely to demand increased protection of civil liberties. There was no relationship between fear of the police and support for civil liberties among Northern urban blacks. Finally, Block reasoned that evaluations of police effectiveness might be causing these relationships, which seemed to defy much popular mythology. Among all respondents, there was only a slight relationship between fear of crime and support for police among those with similar evaluations of police effectiveness. Among blacks who rated police effectiveness as fair, there was a strong relationship between fear of crime and police support, while among other blacks there was a slight negative relationship.

Block concludes that, although fear has been used as the basis for police support by politicians and police agencies alike (the FBI consistently uses increasing crime rates as an argument for greater powers and budget), such fear is not the appropriate foundation in normal times. Citizen support, both black and white, seems to arise from good and respectful police work. Real or imagined crime waves or periods of civil disturbance cannot construct lasting support for quality policework or crime prevention. Admittedly Block's sample was relatively small, taken during a special period in recent American history, and incomplete in its representation of some critical types of respondents (for example, young black males who would be highly critical of white police). Nevertheless, the study provides sufficient basis for questioning the prevalent popular myth in which the appeal to law and order is seen as a sound political and pragmatic basis for substantial legal change. The study also illustrates the manner in which popular myths develop, although they may only have a slight relationship to reality, and how they can be provocatively questioned by social science research.

Examples and Types of Social Problems Mythology.   In the area of problem behavior, such mythology is abundant and includes the following kinds of beliefs (opposing, though equally valid, views appear in parentheses):

Violence
America is a domestically violent nation with deep cultural roots of aggression. In order to guarantee national security, the country must maintain a massive military force and bargain from strength. (Violence is not innate but rather is culturally determined. America has an important tradition of pacifism and antimilitarism. The use of force or the threat of force in bargaining situations only increases the likelihood of violent conflict.)

War
The maintenance of a large defense-related industry is necessary to support the economy. Support for our boys in warfare is necessary to maintain their morale. (Economic health can be maintained by a variety of industries exclusive of war preparation and war waging. Men in warfare do not care about issues of patriotism; they fight to stay alive.)

Crime
Modern crime is at an all-time high, and the greatest threat is violence to person. Crime is a function of lower-class standing. (In previous periods of human history, street violence and street crime have posed greater threats than they do today. Some of the most serious crimes include massive embezzlement of public monies and the promotion of drug use by upper-class respected citizens.)

Poverty
Poverty will always be with us. It is the result of the inherent unemployability of some segments of the population due to laziness,

illness, age, mental inferiority, and the like. (The definition of poverty is culturally determined and is constantly changing. The poor are most often trapped by a system that provides no alternatives.)

Deviance

Drug usage arises from feelings of alienation and uselessness induced by modern civilization. Suicide and illegitimacy are the result of a breakdown in social and cultural standards and norms. (Some drug usage is socially produced and results from close, intimate peer group ties. Some suicide, notably ritual and altruistic, is a reaffirmation of basic cultural norms. Some illegitimacy results from close emotional attachments or accepted practices in subcultures.)

Pollution

Pollution results from evil men in high places and from the operation of materialistic, capitalistic systems. (Noncapitalist societies frequently experience severe pollution problems. Automobile users, as well as automobile makers, contribute to the pollution problem.)

The following pages will deal with these types of myths, referring to the research that suggests the equal validity of opposing views. First, however, it is important to note that popular myths, such as those listed above, tend to fall into three basic types.

Popular wisdom often sees problems as *natural, inevitable, and unavoidable,* or as the result of uncontrollable accidents. A second and closely related view argues that problems exist because of *some inescapable evil in the social world.* This evil results from either the "basic" nature of man, from evil social contexts, or from consciously evil men in high and important places. Finally, popular mythology can see problems as resulting from *basic inadequacies in the people most affected by the problem.* In other words, criminals, suicide victims, the poor, homosexuals, drug users, and others are largely to blame because their own personal weaknesses result in problem behavior. The myths in the six categories of beliefs given above can be classified according to these three basic types as follows:

Social problems as accidents and inevitable—the basic aggression of Americans; the inevitability of poverty.

Social problems as a result of evil—bad lower-class people engage in crime; evil men cause pollution.

Social problems as a result of imperfections in the victims—weak people use drugs; those who are lazy are poor.

These three types of popular myths can be called the *natural theory* of social problems, the notion of *evil equals evil*, and the process of *blaming the victim*. Historically, they emerged roughly in that order.

Natural Theory—A Prescientific Popular Myth. Before the development of modern social science, the idea that social problems resulted from accidents, natural and unavoidable processes, bad luck and chance, man's inability to control the environment, or the forces of God served to make some momentary sense of misfortune for the victims and observers of catastrophe. This natural theory of social problems had its roots in both early religious and early social philosophy. The religious concept of original sin and man's inescapable destiny to face evil in this world led individuals to see war, crime, disease, alcoholism, and the like simply as extensions of the inherent evil in man and his environment. In addition, Freud's concept of the id, the unchained and potentially destructive psychic forces within men, substantiated this interpretation. Both man and nature seemed to possess an irrational character, which occasionally burst forth through constraining social and natural bonds, thus causing personal and social disasters in the form of social problems.

As modern natural and physical science developed a greater ability to control, manipulate, and constrain physical forces in the environment, and as social science seemed better able to replicate this process, earlier natural theory began to be reappraised. Vestiges, however, are still with us. Nowhere is this more obvious than in the area of ecology and the concept of natural disasters. For example, when a flood hits Rapid City, South Dakota, or an earthquake strikes areas of Southern California, the resulting loss of property and life are explained in the mass media and by public leaders in terms that reflect

natural theory (acts of God, unavoidable disasters, uncontrollable forces of nature—in other words bad luck or chance). Yet,
some ecologists maintain that there is, in reality, no such thing
as a pure natural disaster. If man did not build major urban
concentrations of population along potentially active earthquake
faults (using totally inadequate building codes and designs), or
if man did not place cities around rivers that can be expected
to crest at flood stage during heavy rains (with no provision for
excess water runoff), such "natural" disasters could not occur.
Explanations based on natural theory persist, however, because
they are comfortable and safe; they do not question the manner
in which we build cities, the way in which leaders permit codes
to be ignored, or the inability of modern man to comprehend
and respond to the most elementary facts about the forces of
nature.[5] In addition, natural theory does seem to have some
validity since unpredicted (rather than unpredictable) and little
understood (rather than unfathomable) events do sometimes
cause disasters.

　　More will be said in Chapter 3 about the concepts of
chance and probability, sometimes misused by social scientists
themselves. For the moment, however, it is important to note
that as the natural theory of social problems came under increasing scrutiny, there was a need for a new popular mythology. The concept of evil equals evil answered this need.

From Evil Equals Evil

This second type of popular myth takes one of two forms. First,
many social problems are seen as the result of inherent evil
within those affected by the problem—in other words the deviants themselves. Furthermore, this view maintains that evil
compounds evil, and that one form of deviation left unresolved
will naturally lead to another. Second, a recent version of the
myth, espoused by both the political left and right, argues that
evil individuals play a major role in social problems. In this
view, the victims are seen as helpless, the perpetrators as evil.
The political left sees evil individuals in the places of greatest
power and prestige in modern society. The political right sees
evil individuals on the extreme fringes of contemporary society.

As seen from the left, evil individuals can create major problems since they control the instruments of power, and in pursuing their own interests, they ignore the needs of the average citizen. As seen from the right, evil individuals create major problems by disrupting the normal processes of power in society and influencing the gullible to follow their destructive behavior.

Criticisms of the Evil-Equals-Evil Myth.   The trouble with both forms of the evil-equals-evil myth is that they are moral rather than scientific and sociological. They tell us something about the values and preferences of the advocates of the myth but nothing about the causes of problems or possible cures through specific social action. This is most obvious in the case of the second, and more recent, view of evil individuals. This devil theory has been used to explain pollution (selfish capitalists), war (violent political egoists), crime in the streets (irresponsible riffraff and rabble), and political disruption (conspiratorial revolutionaries). The simplistic fallacy of this view can be seen in the fact that many "good" men in similar social circumstances exhibit the same behavior as supposedly evil men. For example, most recent presidents of the United States have utilized destructive military force, albeit in somewhat different degrees, to further personal foreign policy objectives, despite individual differences in personality and philosophy (ranging from Harry Truman through Jack Kennedy and Lyndon Johnson to Richard Nixon). In other words, it is the context, not the inherent nature of the men, which plays a major role in the continued use of international violence. To be effective, exorcizing devils must come in the form of changes in the social context, the sources of problem behavior, not in the form of fruitless searches for saints to replace sinners.

The first evil-equals-evil view is a bit harder to dismiss, since it seems to possess reasonable credibility. Some evil people live in evil environments, surrounded by evil associates, and engage in a variety of evil acts. Those citizens who espouse this perspective are related to the reformists of early American sociology, for they believe that evil can be conquered by doing good. If the evil behavior, surroundings, and companions can be removed or altered, then the problem can be corrected. A

variety of seemingly humane programs that spring from this
philosophy, have been attempted. These include slum removal
or renewal, homes for wayward youth, reeducation for drug
users, and approved community organizations for former juvenile gang members. That some of these programs have been
partially effective in a few cases is evidence of the half-truth of
the myth.

The major difficulty is that the evil-equals-evil view
applies to very few instances of problem behavior. Howard
Becker and Irving Horowitz suggest that this myth is largely
false:

*[To stop fearing deviancy] requires a surrender of some common-
sense notions about the world [evil equals evil]. Most people assume,
when they see someone engaging in [abnormal] activity, that there
is worse to come. "Anyone who would do that (take dope, dress in
women's clothes, sell his body or whatever) would do anything" is
the major premise of the syllogism. "If you break one law or convention, who knows where you'll stop."* [6]

Becker and Horowitz point out that this common sense tends
to ignore contrary examples that can be found everywhere:
"professional criminals often flourish a legionnaire's patriotism;
housewives who are in every other respect conventional sometimes shoplift; homosexuals may be good family providers; some
people, who habitually use the rings from poptop cans to work
the parking meter, would not dream of taking dope, and vice
versa." [7]

Studies Contradicting the Myth—Problems of Sexual Behavior.
In other words, *deviant or evil behavior has the same basic
dynamics as normal or good behavior. It is selective and tends
to be related to specific contexts at particular times.* Recent
sociological research, especially those analyses dealing with what
is usually defined as sexually aberrant behavior, contains a number of studies illustrating this fact and questioning traditional
mythology. In 1967, the British House of Commons liberalized
laws dealing with homosexuality. The Wolfenden Report, upon

which the decision was based to legalize any type of sexual behavior between consenting adults, examined the problem from the standpoint of typical popular myths about homosexuals.[8] This report found that homosexuality exists among "all callings and at all levels of society" and is not confined to special, marginal groups pursuing only certain unusual occupations and engaging in extremely bizarre public behavior. Furthermore, the study examined the three arguments most often used to support repressive legal and moral action against homosexuals, especially male offenders: that homosexuality menaces the health of society and damages family life, and that men who engage in homosexual relations with other men may force their attentions upon younger boys.

The Wolfenden Report concludes that there is no historical evidence to substantiate the belief that homosexuality undermines society. No civilization in history has collapsed because of this problem alone. In addition, there is no evidence that male homosexuality does more or greater damage to family life than a number of other problems, some of which are not illegal or immoral in many cultures: for example, problems such as adultery, fornication, lesbian behavior, sexual incompatibility, and the like. Indeed, some research suggests that a substantial proportion of legitimate marriages where one spouse is homosexual, while not free of stress and strain, exhibit the qualities of permanence and stability. In a study of a sample of such marriages in Belgium, Larry Ross found that it is not uncommon for homosexuals of either sex to have contracted legitimate marriages with members of the opposite sex.[9] Many homosexuals, just as sexually conforming citizens, have a desire for stable family life and full integration into conventional society. Becker and Horowitz found in their study of the unique cultural acceptance of deviancy by the citizens and leaders of San Francisco that homosexuals frequently marry, have children, and hold full-time tax-paying jobs similar to straight members of the community. In addition, San Francisco politicians often make direct appeals for homosexual votes by running on platforms promising liberalized sex laws.[10]

Finally, with regard to the myth that homosexuality can

lead to child molestation, the Wolfenden Report concludes as follows:

There are those who seek as partners . . . adult males, and there are paedophiliacs, that is to say men who seek as partners boys who have not reached puberty. . . . A man who has homosexual relations with an adult partner seldom turns to boys, and vice-versa. . . . A survey of 155 prisoners diagnosed as being homosexuals on reception into Brixton prison during the period 1st January, 1954, to 31st May, 1955, indicated that 107 (69 per cent) were attracted to adults, 43 (27.7 per cent) were attracted to boys, and 5 (3.3 per cent) were attracted to both boys and adults. This last figure of 3.3 per cent is strikingly confirmed by another investigation of 200 patients outside prison. . . . Indeed, it has been put to us that to remove homosexual behavior between adult males from the listed crimes may serve to protect minors; with the law as it is, there may be some men who would prefer an adult partner but who at present turn their attention to boys because they consider that this course is less likely to lay them open to prosecution or to blackmail than if they sought other adults as their partners.[11]

Other research supports this view that sexual deviance is essentially selective, rather than a consequence of evil compounding evil. Homosexuals in prison are rarely recidivistic when released from jail; that is, when heterosexual contacts are available, those who have practiced homosexuality because of the unique features of prison life will not maintain the same behavioral pattern. At the same time, former heterosexuals are frequently forced into the homosexual relationships that predominate in the American prison. Other studies show that child molestors are not characteristically the dirty-old strangers of popular mythology. More frequently, they are close friends, neighbors, or relatives, often old and cast out from intimate social relationships, who are seeking some type of physical intimacy with others. They choose children because the relationship is "safe." It does not demand deep interpersonal involvement on an adult level.[12]

In a similar manner, pornography and prostitution exist not so much as a consequence of dirty and evil people living in the gutter underlife of contemporary society, but rather because of *dual and hypocritical views of the good people* of conventional society. *Playboy,* women's magazines, and even *The New York Times* have been called "the pious pornographers." The point is that sex sells—it is big business and it is good business. Major corporations and agencies of the federal government sometimes provide sexual entertainment, in the form of exhibitions or prostitutes, for clients and dignitaries. At the same time, participants in and promoters of this type of behavior can theoretically uphold conventional norms by zealously prosecuting a Ralph Ginsberg for representing a fundamental threat to decency. Therefore, "good" as well as "evil" can be associated with "evil."

A final example of research that questions the evil-equals-evil myth is found in those studies showing that *deviants, as well as straights, try to look conventional.* Marilyn Salutin points out, in her study of stripper morality, that "like all stigmatized people, strippers, offstage, try to negotiate a more favorable self-image. . . . They try to upgrade their occupation in a redefinition of stripping that says it is socially useful, constructive, good and generally all right to do [and by concealing] backstage information about their own personal lives that would label them as sexual deviants if known publically." [13] Salutin points out that the public face of the stripper is designed to convince others that her behavior is sexually normal and moral. Strippers maintain that they are merely entertainers and that many in the public at large are hypocritical, ignorant, or dishonest about sexual behavior. The stripper sees her occupation as openly meeting a social need in a harmless way. She interprets her low status and personal problems as resulting from the repressive nature of the public order, especially as represented by the actions of the police. Such views are not without validity or meaning.

The idea, therefore, that evil behavior leads to more evil behavior, or that evil behavior is engaged in by totally evil people, simply cannot be sustained when examined in the light of recent research. This conclusion has policy implications. The most obvious relates to the assumption that increased certainty and severity of punishment for deviant offenses will correct or inhibit the behavior of actual offenders and deter potential future offenders. This assumption, which lies behind most contemporary penology and results in severe penalties (capital punishment, long prison terms for the possession of drugs, and the like) and custodial institutions that use harsh disciplinary methods (use of caning by British teachers to control and punish students), must be questioned in the light of recent analysis.[14] We must conclude that the myth of evil equals evil, while it seems to be valid for a very few cases of problem behavior (for example, the 3 percent of males in the Wolfenden study who engaged in sexual relations with both men and boys), cannot be used as a basis for adequate across-the-board analysis and social planning. In reality, the early popular commitment to a reformist concept of evil problem behavior has eroded in recent years under the impact of new findings and knowledge and a growing concern for more humane approaches to problems. As a consequence, a recent form of popular mythology has taken its place: the process of blaming the victim.

To Blaming the Victim

Psychologist William Ryan has referred to blaming the victim as the most characteristic response to contemporary social problems on the part of most citizens, many public leaders, and some social scientists.[15] Whereas the earlier evil-equals-evil view was essentially conservative in a moralistic fashion (it simply defined most victims of problems as inferior, defective, or unfit), the view of blaming the victim seems to contain a more compassionate and humanitarian thrust. The newer mythology shifts its emphasis from individual explanations of problems to environmental causes. Racial hostilities, slum life, extreme poverty, violent and aggressive surroundings, evil companions, and the like are seen as creating circumstances into which individuals are born or introduced early in life and which create deviancy within these unfortunates. However, just as the older conservative view held that the problem behavior lay genetically within the individual, the newer view argues that the problem behavior becomes socially and culturally lodged *within the individual*. Thus, argues Ryan, the humanitarian can have it both ways:

*He can, all at the same time, concentrate his charitable interest on
the defects of the victim, condemn the vague social and environmental stresses that produced the defect (some time ago), and ignore the
continuing effect of victimizing social forces (right now). It is a
brilliant ideology for justifying a perverse form of social action designed to change, not society, as one might expect, but rather
society's victim.*[16]

Ryan gives, as an example of blaming the victim, the
recent public and private propaganda campaign concerning
lead-paint poisoning of infants living in deteriorating urban
dwellings. Newspaper, magazine, and television advertisements
have typically carried the forlorn picture of a small girl chewing
on peeling paint. The instructions given to the viewer emphasize
that if children are allowed to eat such paint (lead has an
attractive sweet taste) they can develop serious health problems, including brain damage and other conditions that may be
fatal. The campaign urges parents to discipline their children
and to seek public health care if in doubt. By this argument,
the problem of lead poisoning is seen as a function of problem
behavior *by* and *in* the victim, with whom all can express great
sympathy and concern. What the campaign ignores is the fact
that lead-based paints should be prohibited by law in tenements
and that in some cities where laws do exist, they are simply not
enforced by public leaders against slum landlords. Furthermore,
to expect a small child not to eat pleasant-tasting paint or an
unaware ghetto parent to understand the potential dangers is
totally unrealistic. The real cause of the problem is the lead
paint on the wall and the fact that its presence is illegal. A
campaign directed against this real cause, however, would call
for challenges to basic institutions and practices in contemporary society. As Ryan puts it:

*The general problem of lead poisoning, then, is more accurately
analyzed as the result of a systematic program of lawbreaking by
one interest group in the community, with the toleration and encouragement of the public authority charged with enforcing the law.
. . . To load a burden of guilt on the mother of a dead or dangerously
ill child is an egregious distortion of reality. And to do so under the*

guise of public-spirited and humanitarian service to the community is intolerable.[17]

In a similar manner, drug companies have joined the propaganda barrage against misuse of narcotics, while at the same time they seriously overproduce both retail patent drugs and physician-prescribed narcotics, at least in terms of what the population can be expected to use prudently. Large caches of drugs produced by legitimate firms have been discovered in raids upon illegitimate narcotic dealers. In addition, drug companies use advertising to persuade people to take all forms of stimulants and depressants to answer their every need—in effect, they try to legitimize drugs as a panacea—and they apply great pressure to the medical profession to test out new products on daily patients. Thus, the drug companies and those whose job it is to police them can have it both ways: they can blame the victim for becoming an addict (he should show control in his personal behavior) and demonstrate a humanitarian concern for the problem (we need educational programs so that citizens can develop the correct personal habits), while ignoring one of the major variables giving rise to the problem (covert or overt participation by legitimate companies and officials in the narcotics problem).

Blaming the Victim as an Inadequate Response to the Problem of Drugs. An especially bizarre example of this process was reported recently in an analysis of the opium trade in Laos and the complicity of American governmental agencies in that trade.[18] In contrast to the policy they followed in Vietnam, American presidents, beginning with Eisenhower, decided to wage a secret nontraditional war against Communist-backed insurgency in Laos, using the Central Intelligence Agency (CIA) and Army Green Beret units to train and equip indigenous anti-Communist guerrillas. Compared to the massive military forces committed to Vietnam, a relatively small handful of American advisers in Laos were required to select key leaders from the local population to whom they could give great military and economic power in order to run the secret war. As these leaders became successful in consolidating areas under their control, however, the war began to upset one of the traditional economic bases of the society, particularly in and around the Plain of Jars—the opium trade with Chinese merchants. Air America (the CIA air force) facilities, including planes and landing strips, began to be used to transport raw opium. Some native leaders formed their own private airlines, with assistance from the CIA and United States Agency for International Development, to continue the trade. This American complicity in the drug traffic, generally unrecognized and unacknowledged by the public leaders and the press, lasted until

President Nixon issued his declaration of war on the international heroin traffic in mid-1971 [and] the U.S. Embassy in Vientiane was finally forced to take action. Instead of trying to break up drug syndicates and purge the government leaders involved, however, the Embassy introduced legal reforms and urged a police crackdown on opium addicts [thereby blaming the victims]. A new opium law submitted to government ministries for consideration on June 8 went into effect on November 15. As a result of the new law, U.S. narcotics agents were allowed to open an office in early November— two full years after [American] GIs started using Laotian heroin in Vietnam and six months after the first large seizures were made in the United States.[19]

Also involved in the process of blaming the victim is scapegoating. Thomas Szasz has identified three characteristics that must apply when individuals seek to blame problems on scapegoats, that is, people or groups who are innocent but defenseless. Scapegoats must be politically unorganized and, therefore, defenseless; they must exhibit behavioral characteristics typically regarded as defects or diseases; and, finally, those characteristics must lend themselves to prosecution or treatment, which under the guise of humanitarian aid actually injures or harms the scapegoat.[20] Szasz refers to the manner in which Americans were told in late 1971 and early 1972 that most GI's in Vietnam smoked marijuana, large numbers used heroin, and that the narcotics problem in our armed forces had reached epidemic proportions. He warns against "making scapegoats of innocent Americans—mainly servicemen and other young persons—[and] letting guilty Americans—mainly politicians and physicians—become inquisitors in a holy war on drug addiction"[21]; for in reality we not only blame but we also punish the user of narcotics, rather than those who directly profit from the production and sale of drugs.

For example, the response of the United States Army and Congress was to establish a drug testing and "rehabilitation" program that created major problems for individual GI's. The program involved compulsory urine tests for heroin use for all personnel (these tests could not detect marijuana use). GI's voluntarily submitting themselves for treatment of addiction were guaranteed "amnesty" or exemption from court martial and possible dishonorable discharge. In many cases, compulsory hospitalization and counseling were required after detection. Immediately, difficulties arose. Those who voluntarily turned themselves in were often subject to nonjudicial punishment and harassment. Some urine tests (the reliability of this technique was still in doubt) accidentally registered positive, and non-users were stigmatized (families and friends were sometimes notified) before the error could be corrected. No adequate guarantees were formulated governing proper and secret use of medical and other data, and many users faced the prospect of lifelong difficulties after their army careers. The compulsory urine test requirement was never submitted to court for a possible self-incrimination judgment. Army counseling and advisory personnel were inadequately trained and lacked sufficient experience in dealing with the problem of drug use.[22] The program, established in the name of humanitarian treatment, successfully blamed and punished the victim, while just as successfully it ignored the real systemic roots of the problem.

Blaming the Victim as an Inadequate Response to the Housing Problem. The new popular myth of blaming the victim prevails in many problem areas beyond drug use. Michael Stegman has suggested that today's mythology of housing reform will help build castles in Spain but little else, since it is based upon a curious mixture of evil equals evil and blaming the victim.[23] He mentions four beliefs that predominate, two of which are relevent to our discussion. The first argues that evil, malevolent slumlords create and perpetuate bad housing for purely mercenary reasons. Stegman points out that, in reality, the over 6 million substandard housing units in American cities are owned by hundreds of thousands of different kinds of individuals and organizations. In addition, some research suggests that rising costs and taxes make slum property ownership far from financially rewarding, and undermaintenance is probably, for many owners, a prerequisite for not going bankrupt. The belief in evil landlords, however, can dissociate good leaders and citizens from evil intent and create the illusion of concern for slum tenants.

The second belief of housing reform, according to Stegman, argues that home ownership for the poor provides a solution to the problem. In other words, if the poor would come to resemble the nonpoor, the good citizens of society, then the evil they suffer would be eliminated. Congressional commitment to this belief led to a number of programs in the Housing Act of 1968, which provided for various forms of aid for private and group ownership and control. Stegman points out that this was a reaction against the earlier evil-equals-evil notion that gave rise to public housing, seen as a patronizing and dehumanizing dole, and a response to the belief that private ownership might prevent rioting and vandalism. Not only are these assumptions suspect, but the new housing belief projects middle-class values upon nonmiddle-class cultures:

To stimulate hopes for home ownership without moving toward reducing levels of unemployment and underemployment might be the cruelest hoax yet perpetrated on the low-income population. . . . Such a program might provide the family a piece of middle-class America, but only a little piece—a piece obtained at the cost of accepting the increased pressures that go along with internalizing middle-class values, with only a fraction of the economic resources with which to play the game.[24]

The real basis of the housing problem is not people, particularly the residents of slums; rather it is the buildings that make up the slums and the system that allows and encourages the buildings to deteriorate—a system based upon unemployment and underemployment, inadequate distribution of basic economic and social resources, and inadequate positive incentives and rewards for owners of low-income housing (plus inadequate codes and enforced regulations). The contrast between this interpretation and the concept of blaming the victim is what William Ryan has called the distinction between *universalistic* and *exceptionalistic* views of social problems:

The exceptionalist viewpoint is reflected in arrangements that are private, voluntary, remedial, special, local, and exclusive. Such arrangements imply that problems occur to specially-defined categories of persons in an unpredictable manner. The problems are unusual, even unique, they are exceptions to the rule, they occur as a result of individual defect, accident, or unfortunate circumstance and must be remedied by means that are particular and, as it were tailored to the individual case. The universalistic viewpoint, on the other hand, is reflected in arrangements that are public, legislated, promotive or preventive, general, national, and inclusive. Inherent in such a viewpoint is the idea that social problems are a function of the social arrangements of the community or the society and that, since the social arrangements are quite imperfect and inequitable, such problems are both predictable and, more important, preventable through public action. They are not unique to the individual, and the fact that they encompass individual persons does not imply that those persons are themselves defective or abnormal.[25]

The difficulty is that the exceptionalistic view is not necessarily useless or misleading in all circumstances. For example, Ryan points out that the medical care approach (applied medicine) to individuals suffering from smallpox is exceptionalist. It is designed to aid and assist only those people afflicted. On the other hand, an exceptionalistic approach would be inappropriate in massive public health programs (preventive medicine) to eliminate smallpox outbreaks among all citizens. The problem is that the exceptionalistic view has become a part of all conventional folklore about contemporary social problems, even those that are universalistic, and tends to be used in all contexts, especially in conjunction with the desire or intention to blame the victims. Once this happens, a myth, a partially real depiction of reality, has been created that makes proper analysis and action impossible. The following section and the next chapter examine the way in which social scientists and intellectuals play a part in this process.

Schlock Answers Versus New Responses

Robert Claiborne uses the concept of *schlock* social science to characterize the type of "research" and theorizing that arises from popular myths and the desire to establish public programs that result only in modest reform at best.[26] Schlock usually refers to gadgets and products that are useless, unworkable, shoddily constructed, and sometimes dangerous. Schlock includes easily broken and potentially injurious children's toys, automobiles that deteriorate rapidly, frozen pizza pies with no nutritional value, Barbie dolls that copy all of the bodily functions, and devices that crush and perfume home garbage for transportation to the community dump. As Claiborne describes it, schlock is a function of modern, urban, industrial societies, and although Claiborne claims that America seems to lead the world in the production of schlock, it is not unique to American society. Claiborne argues that it can also come in the form of software, as the content of modern television and motion pictures throughout the world so often illustrates.

As if to show that they, too, can participate in the modern capability for maintaining the affluent and wasteful society, some social scientists and their camp followers have recently joined the schlock production parade. Claiborne suggests that this is a function of the public need for quick, easy answers to a seemingly unending succession of threatening social problems, answers that are palatable and slick, but superficial. Some key word, trick phrase, or simplistic concept is sought as the basis for satisfactory explanations. Martin's scientians, referred to in Chapter 1, are kin to Claiborne's intellectual schlock producers, as both provide catchy insights in the form of concepts such as "future shock," "behavioral traits," "the naked ape," the "greening" of America, "genetic inheritance," or the "waste-makers."

Of particular interest are the possible types of response brought about by these insights to resolve the problems under analysis. Claiborne concludes that schlock social science,

whether produced by social scientists or by lay interpreters of
the discipline, leads to three equally evasive conclusions, all of
which fit the needs of those citizens who accept the natural,
evil-equals-evil, or blaming-the-victim myths about problems:

1. Nothing can be done about the problem; it is an inherent aspect
   of man and nature.
2. Nothing needs to be done about the problem; things aren't that
   bad; relax and enjoy them.
3. Nothing *much* needs to be done; a little cosmetic reform of the
   system will suffice.

In reality, each of the three popular myths we have
considered can lead to any *one* of these three responses. For
example, if one believes that poverty and its accompanying
social problems (crime, vice, lack of education, or the like) are
an unavoidable aspect of any social system, he can conclude
that nothing can be done about it, *or* that nothing need be
done (since a move to the suburbs will remove one from seeing
and experiencing the problem), *or* that moderate reform in the
nature of Head Start educational programs, job training, stricter
control of the welfare system, or tougher law enforcement will
be sufficient. In a similar manner, if one believes that drug
addiction is a result of evil, he may conclude that a certain
amount of evil is inescapable, *or* that "good people won't become
addicted," *or* that something like the United States Army's
response is appropriate. Finally, blaming the victim for law-
lessness and aggression may lead to the conclusion that some
people are going to act criminally no matter what is done, *or*
that aggression "isn't really that bad after all" (since it is a part
of rugged American individualism and the heritage of the Protestant Ethic), or that a little harsher legal response is all that is
required.

Formal public policy frequently reflects these kinds of
responses. Daniel Patrick Moynihan, President Richard Nixon's
chief domestic adviser in the late 1960's, suggested that, in the
1970's, the United States government's response to black problems and the race issue should be "benign neglect." He also
suggested that one of the major reasons for the "Negro prob-

lem" was the unusual form of the black subculture, especially the female-dominant and father-absent black family.[27] Further criticism of Moynihan's thesis will be made in Chapter 5, in an analysis of disorganization theories about social problems. In this discussion, however, it serves as a brief example of how blaming the victim and concluding that nothing much should or can be done are typical myths that relate to the despair, in-action, or hypocrisy that characterizes so much contemporary response to social problems.

The Search for a New Mythology of Social Problems. Obvi-ously, a new mythology is required, one which, as Ryan puts it, elevates concern to a universalistic level and leads to truly hu-manitarian programs of fundamental (or radical) reform of the system. The real problem, then, is where to look for such a new mythology, one more in tune with contemporary conditions and needs. Ryan has indicated a general direction. Two other social scientists, Amitai Etzioni and C. Wright Mills, provide similar signposts. Etzioni questions the prevalent approach to social problems, which assumes that "if you go out there and get the message across—persuade, propagandize, explain, campaign— people will change, that human beings are, ultimately, quite pliable." [28] He indicates that the failures characterizing local, state, and federal programs in a variety of areas would seem to contradict this reformist assumption. For example, millions of dollars spent on trying to persuade Americans not to smoke have had little, if any, effect. The government spends $16 million a year advertising desegregation to racists, world government to chauvinists, temperance to alcoholics, and drug abstention to addicts, all with obvious ineffectiveness. A Department of Health, Education, and Welfare study found that driver educa-tion, an extremely questionable program in terms of influence upon driver safety, "saves" lives at the cost of $88,000 per life (approximately 60,000 Americans are killed each year on the highways). In contrast, introducing new seat belts costs only $87 per life. Failure of educational and therapeutic approaches to heroin addiction have finally led to the methadone mainte-nance program, which initially seems to have had more success in terms of allowing the addict to function effectively in his daily life. Etzioni concludes: "What is becoming increasingly apparent is that to solve social problems by changing people is more expensive and usually less productive than approaches that *accept people as they are and seek to mend not them but the circumstances around them* [italics mine]." [29]

In a similar way, C. Wright Mills distinguishes between a *personal-troubles* and a *public-issues* approach to social problems.[30] Personal troubles occur within the individual as a result of idiosyncratic, limited experiences. Troubles are private matters, colored by the character and uniqueness of the individual. Massive social programs to eliminate personal troubles cannot succeed since they cannot possibly address the individual needs of all involved and because they ignore the larger systemic causes for many personal troubles. In contrast, public issues transcend the personal. Major societal values are involved and come under question, and social problems are seen as a consequence of institutional arrangements. Major alterations in these institutional arrangements are necessary to resolve the problems resulting in public issues.

It is obvious that what usually happens is that most citizens, public officials, the mass media, and some scientists use a personal-troubles perspective, which leads to an obsessive concern for the symptoms of a problem rather than the root causes. Thus, to solve unemployment, we either give individuals money or try to retrain them to fit available occupations rather than creating employment opportunities and situations to fit *their* needs and context. To quell urban rioting, we emphasize the need for more police and police powers rather than addressing the problems that created within individuals a feeling of helplessness, which led to their rioting. To solve the pollution crisis we ask all citizens to be neater in their personal habits rather than encouraging major changes in the styles of life and production processes that create the pollution. To resolve problems in the contemporary American family, we make divorce laws easier rather than questioning the basic roles and relationships of a family system that frequently subjugates men, women and children.

In an argument for reforming drug education programs, Richard H. De Lone, an assistant commissoner in New York City's Addiction Services Agency, combines the views of Etzioni and Mills.[31] He points out that the Federal Drug Education Act of 1970 and the 1972 Higher Education Act stand as the Nixon administration's primary contribution to educational legislation. In 1972, the U.S. Office of Education spent $13 million, and a conservative national estimate of the value of all materials, personnel, and teaching time allotted for drug education in 1972 is $100 million. In short, drug abuse education is booming in schools and communities, but for most students it is ineffective, primarily because of the assumption that one's *personal problem* can be resolved by knowledge alone. De Lone cites the growing evidence that most official drug information (in the form of pamphlets, films, or film strips) contains factual errors and misrepresentations. Some information is racially or ethnically biased (blacks are typically shown shooting heroin, never any other drug, and no black junkie is depicted kicking the habit).

After a year-long study, the National Education Association concluded that about 80 percent of drug education involved deplorable instruction, misinformation, and bias. Furthermore, De Lone refers to some evidence that suggests that there is no relationship, and in some cases, a negative relationship, between drug education and drug use and abuse. A film on the evils of heroin use can easily provide a lesson for the uninitiated, but interested, in how to obtain, prepare, and take heroin. De Lone concludes by arguing that instead of asking whether institutions (schools, families, communities, churches, agencies) can do anything by way of propaganda to prevent drug abuse, we should ask what it is about these institutions that hinders drug prevention or encourages drug abuse. In other words, properly oriented, a national drug education program would raise universalistic, social systems questions and could become the basis for major institutional reform within the school, family, community, church, or agency. But such a theoretical reorientation requires new perceptions and a new mythology about the causes and sources of social problems.

Where will a new mythology be developed that could shift the traditional approaches toward a universalistic, social-system, and public-issues consciousness? The obvious hope is that the continuing work of social scientists can provide the theoretical and empirical bases for new perspectives, rather than reflect the influence of popular mythology. The following chapters will examine the nature of prevailing social science theories about social problems in order to ascertain their usefulness and to determine how far we may be from the creation of more meaningful alternative views. More specifically, we will see how earlier theories are presently being challenged from within social science on both academic and moral grounds, particularly in the discipline of sociology. This challenge has initiated a much needed search for new conceptions of and approaches to social problems.

Notes to Chapter 2

1. See, for example, the following kinds of analysis: Konrad Lorenz, *On Aggression* (New York: Bantam Books, 1969); Ritchie P. Lowry and Robert P. Rankin, "Definitions of Culture," in *Sociology: Social Science and Social Concern*, 2nd ed. (New York: Charles Scribner's Sons, 1972), pp. 96–105; and W. M. S. Russell, "The Wild Ones," *The Listener* (November 5, 1964), pp. 710–712.

2. Louis Wirth, *The Ghetto* (Chicago: The University of Chicago Press, 1956).

3. See Robert Blauner, "Whitewash Over Watts: The Failure of the McCone Commission Report," *Transaction*, 3 (March/April 1966), p. 3; Kenneth B. Clark, *Dark Ghetto* (New York: Harper & Row, 1965); Ritchie P. Lowry and Robert P. Rankin, "Negro Riots As a Form of Communication," *Sociology: Social Science and Social Concern*, 2nd ed. (New York: Charles Scribner's Sons, 1972), p. 513; and David O. Sears and John B. McConahay, "Participation in the Los Angeles Riot," *Social Problems, 17* (Summer 1969), pp. 3–20.

4. Richard L. Block, "Support for Civil Liberties and Support for the Police," *American Behavioral Scientist, 13* (May/July 1970), pp. 781–796.

5. For a more detailed critique of this popular myth as it relates to the ecology crisis, see Ritchie P. Lowry, "Toward a Radical View of the Ecological Crisis," *Environmental Affairs, 1* (June 1971), pp. 350–359.

6. Howard S. Becker and Irving Louis Horowitz, "The Culture of Civility," *Transaction*, 7 (April 1970), p. 14.

7. *Ibid.*, pp. 14–15.

8. Sir John Wolfenden *et al.*, *Report of the Departmental Committee on Homosexual Offences and Prostitution* (London: Her Majesty's Stationery Office, 1956).

9. H. Laurence Ross, "Modes of Adjustment of Married Homosexuals," *Social Problems, 18* (Winter 1971), pp. 385–393.

10. Howard S. Becker and Irving Louis Horowitz, "The Culture of Civility," *Transaction*, 7 (April 1970), pp. 12–13.

11. Edward Sagarin and Donald E. J. MacNamara, eds., *Problems of Sex Behavior* (New York: Thomas Y. Crowell Co., 1968), pp. 131–132.

12. See Sagarin and MacNamara (*ibid.*) for an excellent compilation of these types of studies.

13. Marilyn Salutin, "Stripper Morality," *Transaction, 8* (June 1971), p. 15.

14. See, for example, Theodore G. Chiricos and Gordon P. Waldo, "Punishment and Crime: An Examination of Some Empirical Evidence," *Social Problems, 18* (Fall 1970), pp. 200–216. Some scholars maintain that statistical analysis does show a relationship between punishment and the deterrence of deviance. The problem is that this relationship may be a result of certainty (rather than severity) of punishment; the very special nature of only some kinds of deviance, or a low deviance rate, may lead to more certainty of punishment (rather than the other way around). See Charles R. Tittle, "Crime Rates and Legal Sanctions," *Social Problems, 16* (Spring 1969), pp. 409–423; and "When Punishment Prevents Crime," *Transaction, 5* (July/August 1968), pp. 7–8.

15. William Ryan, *Blaming the Victim* (New York: Pantheon Books, 1971), and "Blaming the Victim," *The Washington Monthly, 2* (January 1971), pp. 31–36.

16. William Ryan, *Blaming the Victim* (New York: Pantheon Books, 1971), p. 7.

17. William Ryan, "Blaming the Victim," *The Washington Monthly, 2* (January 1971), p. 31.

18. Alfred W. McCoy, *The Politics of Heroin in Southeast Asia* (New York: Harper & Row, 1972).

19. *Ibid.*; and "Flowers of Evil," *Harper's Magazine, 245* (July 1972), p. 53.

20. Thomas S. Szasz, "Drugs and Politics—Scapegoating 'Military Addicts': The Helping Hand Strikes Again," *Transaction, 9* (January 1972), p. 4.

21. *Ibid.*, p. 4.

22. Robert Reinhold, "Army's Drug-Testing Program Stirs Sharp Dispute," *The New York Times* (June 2, 1972), pp. 1M and 20M.

23. Michael A. Stegman, "The New Mythology of Housing," *Transaction, 7* (January 1970), pp. 55–62.

24. *Ibid.*, p. 61.

25. William Ryan, *Blaming the Victim* (New York: Pantheon Books, 1971), pp. 16–17.

26. Robert Claiborne, "Future Schlock," *The Nation* (January 25, 1971), pp. 117–120.

27. See Thomas J. Cook, "Benign Neglect: Minimum Feasible Understanding," *Social Problems, 18* (Fall 1970), pp. 145–152; Robert Heilbroner, "Benign Neglect in the United States," *Transaction, 7* (October 1970), pp. 15–22; Lee Rainwater and William L. Yancey, "Black Families and the White House," *Transaction, 3* (July/August 1966), pp. 6–11, 48–53; and William Ryan, "Mammy Observed: Fixing the Negro Family," in *Blaming the Victim* (New York: Pantheon Books, 1971), Chap. 3, pp. 61–85.

28. Amitai Etzioni, "Human Beings Are Not Very Easy to Change After All," *Saturday Review* (June 3, 1972), p. 45.

29. *Ibid.*, pp. 45–46.

30. C. Wright Mills, *The Sociological Imagination* (New York: Oxford University Press, 1959).

31. Richard H. De Lone, "The Ups and Downs of Drug-Abuse Education," *Saturday Review, 55* (December 1972), pp. 27–32.

Reliable and accurate or pseudo-scientific and biased?
(Wide World Photos)

3. Scientific Paradigms

For the last several decades, social scientists have been increasingly interested in the search for universalistic, social-system, and public-issues perspectives of social problems. The difficulty is that scientists as citizens are frequently influenced by popular beliefs, and they often create and utilize their own set of biases and myths, thereby complicating the search. These biases appear in two forms: as common *scientific fallacies* and as, what have been called, *scientific paradigms*.[1] Fallacies occur when scientists unquestioningly adopt new methods and techniques of analysis. Enthusiasm for unusual or different approaches tends to become endemic when older methods no longer seem to provide adequate answers or results in terms of the solution of either scientific or social problems. In contrast, scientific paradigms are total theoretical ways of viewing the world being studied. Like popular myths, these paradigms are half-truths, momentary stereotypes of reality, distorted and exaggerated, but useful and needed, visions of the world that the scientist is observing. They function for the scientist very much the way myths work for the layman; that is, they make some coherent sense of what would otherwise seem chaotic, accidental, and uncontrollable. In other words, without paradigms the scientist could not undertake a scientific study, but with them he runs the risk of seeing only a limited and exaggerated part of reality.

The trouble with fallacies and myths is that they become dogma and absolutes for many scientists. As a consequence, inappropriate analysis of a social problem leads to faulty conclusions. These conclusions influence the public and leaders and help sustain popular mythology. In turn, this leads to the implementation of programs for action that may not work or may create more difficult problems for the society as a whole. This chapter considers some of the more common scientific fallacies in the study of social problems, the nature and origin of scientific paradigms, and the way in which paradigms about social problems have developed.

Scientific Fallacies: The Need to Look Scientific

In criticizing fallacies utilized by historians, David Fischer points out that fallacies of factual verification are commonplace.[2] These types of fallacies also apply to scientists who study social problems. Fallacies of factual verification arise because of the stress placed upon "proof" in contemporary social science. With increasing emphasis upon making the study of man as rigorously scientific as the hard sciences, and with the ascendency of modern scientians, the need for elaborate data collection techniques, sophisticated quantitative measures, and empirical proof of complicated hypotheses has grown. Techniques, measures, and kinds of data are ideally chosen and applied by scientists in rational, logical ways. In reality, however, something different usually happens, according to Andrew Weigert:

What formal scientific criteria govern the decision-making procedure that is essential to the selection [of these scientific requirements] from among literally infinite possibilities? The decisions are sometimes made on the basis of the authority and prestige of previous users (imagine if we could say, "let us use Comte's anomie scale"!); availability; time and money at the researcher's disposal; past experience with the items; touchiness of subject matter; necessity to mislead subjects. These are real, but hardly scientific, criteria. When the study is presented for public perusal, however, the real reasons may not appear; only the telescoped rationalization will.[3]

The real reasons do not appear because they are not scientific, and the scientist, Weigert points out, cannot afford to ignore the "factual rhetoric of empiricism," or the need to prove his results in a (seemingly) scientific manner.

The Fallacy of Misplaced Precision. This situation leads to two consequences. First, the human, moral side of the subject matter, including the scientist's own biases and preferences, is ignored, though this in reality may be the most significant aspect of a study. Second, a great deal of pseudoscientific and false empiricism comes to characterize research. Fischer refers to one type of factual verification fallacy that is distinctly relevant to the study of social problems: the *fallacy of misplaced precision*.[4] The fallacy of misplaced precision involves the use of statistics and mathematical representations to prove the exactness and, therefore, obvious validity of one's findings. Otto Friedrich has called this tendency the temptation to use "imaginary numbers":

In the cloudland of higher mathematics, there is a whole area of study called "imaginary numbers." What is an imaginary number? It is a multiple of the square root of minus one. What is the good of knowing that? Imaginary numbers [are useful to mathematicians] in figuring out such problems as the flow of air or water past a curved surface like an airplane wing. In ordinary life [and in social science], imaginary numbers of a somewhat different kind seem to have become even more useful. From solemn public officials and eager corporations, from newspapers, television [and social scientists] comes a googol of seemingly definitive and unarguable statistics. They tell us, with an exactitude that appears magical, the number of heroin addicts in New York and the population of the world. By simulating reality, they assure us that facts are facts, and that life can be understood, put in order, perhaps even mastered.[5]

When it comes to analyzing social problems, the difficulty is that some numbers are used inappropriately, some are simple nonsense, others imply measurement of something that might not be quantitatively measurable, while still others obscure the fact that nonquantitative measurements or assessments may be more significant. As Friedrich points out, numbers are rarely falsified; many scientists and leaders simply create or borrow figures to give us a feeling of certainty. In other words, statistics and quantification are important if used meaningfully, but in social research they are often used inappropriately. For example, the number of narcotic addicts in New York City is impossible to measure. Not only are there serious questions of definition (who and what is an addict?) and identification, but the mere number alone does not tell us anything important (how many addicts are too many?). Yet officials of public and private agencies constantly rely upon social scientists to manufacture such numbers to influence public opinion, legislation, and social programs. Friedrich cites the example of the claim that heroin addicts in New York steal from $2 billion to $5 billion worth of goods per year to support their habit. The president of the Hudson Institute, a New York think tank, decided to check the accuracy of this imaginary number. He found that someone had multiplied an estimated 100,000 addicts by an estimated habit of $30 per day. The resulting $1.1 billion per year was then multiplied by four since thieves theoretically sell stolen goods to fences for one-quarter the real value. However, the known value of all stolen goods per year in New York does not amount to nearly that much. Therefore, either there are far fewer addicts and/or addicts steal relatively little to support their habit.[6]

Misplaced Precision and Game Theory.   An area in which imaginary numbers have been used with increasing frequency in recent years is the study of war. One of the leading exponents of misplaced precision is think-tanker Herman Kahn, author of *On Escalation*,[7] called by some the bible of nuclear deterrence. His work is not only an excellent illustration of misplaced precision but is worth consideration here since Kahn's theories played a major role in the post World War II cold war period and the ascendency of American militarism, which culminated in the Vietnam War. These historical experiences have led to much of the contemporary American crisis over resolutions to social problems, as many citizens now argue that military expenditures and influence have taken attention away from more critical social needs. In a critique of Kahn's view that a nuclear war is "survivable," Anatol Rapoport points out that warfare has mobilized contemporary scientific effort more than any other area of human endeavor.[8] World War I has been called the chemists' war; World War II, the physicists' war; and the insurgency and guerrilla engagements of Vietnam, the social scientists' war. Bringing social science methods to bear upon the problems of global warfare, Kahn argues that it would be possible for someone to "prevail" in a nuclear exchange. Rapoport points out that this view stems from Kahn's concept of warfare as essentially a logical, mathematical *game*. Furthermore, the game theory perspective does not depend for utility upon an actual playing out of the situation. In other words, game theorists apply their concepts regardless of whether generals and admirals are pushing chess pieces about a tabletop or human bodies lie in burned out cities.

Using this perspective, Kahn proposes 44 phases of international conflict ranging from the least to the most severe, thereby originating the concept of an escalation ladder in international relations:

The simplest model of an escalation ladder has only two rungs. As such it can be formalized as the so-called game of Chicken, with which Mr. Kahn begins his exposition. The designation "Chicken" derives from the game sometimes played by American youngsters on a highway. Two cars rush headlong toward each other. The first driver to swerve from the collision course is "chicken." [Richard Nixon, Lyndon Johnson, and Jack Kennedy often used the notion of the side "that blinked first" in international confrontations.] Thus victory goes to the bold.[9]

Kahn's 44 rungs is an expansion and elaboration of this two-rung notion, starting with precrisis maneuvering (rungs 1 to 3), ranging through harassing acts of violence (rung 8), conventional war (rung 12), limited nuclear war (rung 15), countercity war (rung 39), civilian devastation (rung 42), and culminating in spasm war (rung 44). Rapoport indicates that the obvious policy implication of such an analysis is that world leaders must combine brinkmanship with the necessity for measured response to threats to national security. In other words, a nation must be prepared for the possibility of nuclear devastation at various levels if the propensity toward escalation is not reversed; at the same time, leaders must take forceful actions along the way to compel the opposition to blink and turn chicken first. From such a concept, contemporary foreign policy was born, and the military actions of recent years (from Korea, through the Cuban missile crisis, to Vietnam) can be understood.

Rapoport indicates that Kahn does make one important contribution by laying to rest the traditional simplistic notion of a clear-cut peace–war dichotomy. The real world does not pose a choice between total peace or nuclear holocaust. Kahn's ladder of escalation suggests a wide range of options, including varying levels of violence, through which nation-states may wander in pursuing their national interests. This conceptualization, however, carries with it some unrealistic and dangerous implications, for, in fact, the precision and seeming logic of Kahn's ladder is imaginary. Nations do not move exactly from one rung to another. Furthermore, some of the contingencies are fictitious, in the sense that they represent situations that have never occurred and, therefore, cannot be studied "scientifically." Only two strategic nuclear devices have ever been exploded over civilian populations, and tactical nuclear weapons have never been used on the battlefield. There is, therefore, no way in which exact responses to such situations can be identified in order to build a precise theory for action.

Kahn's type of guessing game, under the guise of scientific precision, has become endemic in the study of war. Kahn and others have "calculated" potential civilian casualties in the event of a nuclear attack upon major urban populations.[10] Tables are frequently presented that correlate the increasing number of deaths and injuries that would occur with increasing megatonage of the weaponry utilized. On this basis, Kahn and others have suggested that some significant proportion of the population would survive major nuclear exchange and become the basis for continuing their culture or civilization. This type of presentation when offered in the form of tables, charts, and diagrams looks impressive and credible. The fact is that we have no way of estimating reliable physical damage to persons and property for the use of the weapons developed since Hiroshima and Nagasaki. Their power runs from 2 to over 100 times the force of the World War II devices. Furthermore, make-believe casualty diagrams, depicting injuries and deaths, cannot take into account the impact of social and psychological factors after such a bombing.[11] As a matter of fact, the imprecise nature of our knowledge about reactions to civilian bombing, whether conventional or nuclear, is reflected in the continuing contradictory assumptions of experts. Where Kahn and others have assumed that the United States could psychologically survive a nuclear war, United States Army intelligence insisted throughout the latter period of the Vietnam War that massive retaliatory bombing was the only way to force the North Vietnamese to capitulate. At the same time, Central Intelligence Agency information supported the conclusion that this bombing, engaged in by both Presidents Johnson and Nixon, was counterproductive. The will of the North Vietnamese people to continue resistance to American demands was simply being reinforced. Simultaneously, Air Force policy since the end of World War II has been built upon the assumption that present and future international conflicts of any kind will be won on the basis of either threats of massive bombing or the actual ability to inflict considerable destruction upon civilian populations and facilities during warfare. Therefore, those who employ scientific precision and game theory as a basis for planning military strategy and tactics cannot agree upon the correct outcomes. The fallacy of misplaced precision simply makes the discussion of nuclear or conventional warfare take on a dangerously misleading aspect of rationality and controllability.

Sociological and Moral Errors in the Misplaced Precision of Game Theory—Examples from the Study of War. In addition, game theorists, particularly those interested in war, typically employ one type of model, though two basic types of games are possible: The zero-sum, or competitive, and non-zero-sum, or cooperative models. A *zero-sum* game occurs where the winner's (+) and loser's (−) payoffs equal zero. In other words, one contestant's winnings are at the expense of the other contestant's losings. In contrast, a *non-zero-sum* game maximizes the propensity toward cooperation by using what has been called the

"Pareto Optimum," named for the philosopher Wilfredo Pareto.[12] The strategy in this type of game assumes that all players will both win and lose something. Thus, it is to everyone's interest to compromise and cooperate. Theories such as Kahn's tend to influence leaders to think in terms of zero-sum conditions in international relations, where a winner takes something from a loser; someone survives and someone else does not; someone prevails to the degree that someone else does not prevail. As long as nations conceive of warfare in these terms, nuclear exchange becomes more and more likely because, to attain (or maintain) the position of winner, nuclear threat at absurdly high levels must continually be escalated and unending wars of attrition (Vietnam) must be fought to force surrender of the opponent.

Finally, Kahn's pseudoscientific misplaced precision is based upon the view that a detached attitude about the genocidal by-products of nuclear war is no more reprehensible than a physician's detached attitude about serious diseases. Kahn argues that the refusal to "think about the unthinkable" is analogous to the prudish reluctance to discuss venereal disease, prostitution, or drug addiction. We must be prepared for all kinds of unthinkable (and unimaginable) contingencies,[13] especially in the area of war. This is an illustration of how the fallacy of misplaced precision can ignore the human and moral dimensions of a problem, which may be more important than the quantitative aspects. Rapoport and others have criticized Kahn's notion of thinking-about-the-unthinkable on several bases.

First, the analogy between warfare (on the one hand) and disease, earthquakes, floods, and other natural disasters (on the other) is false and inaccurate. Warfare is wholly man-made and man-conducted; diseases and other natural catastrophies are related to man and only partially the consequence of human behavior. Second, Kahn's discussion is not detached. His theory makes assumptions (often untested) about the nature and causes of war, and it creates a scenario that seems to be almost inevitable. Finally, war and its consequences are not unthinkable, particularly to contemporary decision makers who spend much time thinking about the use of military force to protect or to further national interest at the expense of other nations (the zero-sum concept). What has become really unthinkable is the concept of peace, the notion of a world based upon cooperative effort (with minimal violence and conflict), and the promotion of national interest by other than military means. In being labeled utopian, visionary, unreal, and nonviable, these latter perspectives are the true unthinkables of contemporary society, as the paucity of peace research and study so well documents.[14] In this sense, then, the Herman Kahns do not think about the unthinkable so much as they think about the unpleasant or undesirable in unthinkable ways, employing as their most popular tool the fallacy of misplaced quantitative precision.

Possible Proof and Pseudo Proof

This tendency toward misplaced precision in social science research on social problems is related to two additional fallacies of factual verification identified by Fischer: possible proof and pseudo proof.[15] Using the fallacy of *possible proof*, a scientist may "prove" something is possibly true or false. This possibility then takes on the aspect of reality and becomes for many an actuality. For example, readers of Kahn's essay may easily forget that ability to survive a nuclear conflict is only an hypothesized possibility, one that has never been tested in the real world. It is just as possible that a nation and society will not or cannot survive a nuclear exchange. *Pseudo proof* refers to presentations that employ scientific rhetoric and devices, thereby creating the impression that something has been verified, when in reality this is not the case.

Possible- and pseudo-proof fallacies have marked the recent debate over the role of intelligence, as biologically prescribed, in enhancing educational and occupational success among various class and racial groupings. Two major scientists initiated the modern public controversy. In 1969, Arthur Jensen allegedly indicated that intelligence differences among individuals were caused more by heredity than by environment and that poor and black children scored consistently lower on I.Q. tests than rich and white children. In 1971, Richard Herrnstein published an article in *The Atlantic* that suggested that I.Q. is an important and stable attribute in individuals, that I.Q. differences are mostly a result of genes, and that modern society increasingly allocates status and prestige on the basis of intelligence. Critics immediately challenged these theories on scientific and, especially, ideological grounds, since the Jensen and Herrnstein theses seemed to raise serious questions about traditional liberal mythology and could be used to support discriminatory elitist systems. What Jensen and Herrnstein had done was challenge the accepted perspective of social science that environment is crucial, and they hypothesized instead that individual differences, determined by hereditary processes, were the determining factors when it came to intelligence.[16] Jensen's research illustrates the fallacy of *possible proof*, while Herrnstein's work illustrates the fallacy of *pseudo proof*.

The Possible-Proof Fallacy in Jensen's Theory of Hereditary I.Q.
Jensen reviewed some of the evidence and the conclusions of a nationwide survey and evaluation of large, federally funded education programs (for example, Project Head Start) and found that such programs "produced no significant improvement in the measured intelligence or scholastic performance of the disadvantaged children whose educational achievements these programs were specifically intended to improve."[17] He concludes that approaches similar to those used in these programs, merely repeated and enlarged, are not likely to lead to an increase in the benefits of public education for disadvantaged citizens. He believes that a major part of this failure is the result of reluctance by leaders and scientists to take seriously the possibility of individual differences among students in developmental rates, patterns of ability, and learning styles. This reluctance is a function of liberal mythology and the tendency to label opposing views as racist. Jensen theorizes that there are two broad categories of mental abilities: intelligence (abstract reasoning) and associative learning ability. Research seems to indicate that these two types are distributed differently in various social classes and racial groupings; that is, large differences in intelligence can be found for different races and classes, but practically no differences appear for these groups in associative

learning abilities, such as memory span and rote learning. The question is: why the large differences in intelligence?

Jensen believes that the difference is a function of both environment and heredity, but that heredity plays a major role through differential selection of parent generations for different patterns of ability. He believes, too, that this is still scientifically an open question and a researchable one. In contrast, he accuses social scientists of "decreeing" on purely ideological grounds, rather than on the basis of scientific proof, that environment is the only important factor, and he presents himself as the ideal value-free man of science seeking truth, no matter how unpleasant (or unthinkable) it may be. Jensen's conclusion that hereditary factors must be crucial is based upon the following reasoning:

The fact that different racial groups in this country have widely separate geographic origins and have had quite different histories which have subjected them to different selective social and economic pressures make it highly likely that their gene pools differ for some genetically conditioned behavioral characteristics, including intelligence or abstract reasoning ability. Nearly every anatomical, physiological and biochemical system investigated shows racial differences. Why should the brain be an exception? . . . If social class intelligence differences within the Negro population have a genetic component, as in the white population, the condition I have described could create and widen the genetic intelligence differences between Negroes and whites. The social and educational implications of this trend, if it exists and persists, are enormous.[18]

It is interesting to note how many times Jensen himself has used qualifying words and phrases, such as "if," "I believe," and "highly likely." These are not precise scientific statements. On the contrary, they reflect personal judgment and interpretation and the fact that about all Jensen has done is, at best, to show that *something is possible.* In other words, hereditary factors might *possibly* be associated with intelligence, as measured by the tests used in the studies examined by Jensen. But possibility does not equal actuality. Thus those who claim that Jensen has proved the importance of genetic factors commit the fallacy of possible proof. Even Jensen's conclusion with the statement "if this trend persists" implies that a fact has been established. In short, Jensen's theory is speculative and essentially moral—in other words, flawed by the very faults that he attributes to his critics. It is not surprising, therefore, that Jensen has been attacked on political grounds.

Furthermore, *the theoretical possibility of something does not necessarily imply its probability*. For example, survivability after nuclear warfare is possible (depending upon how one manipulates the meaning of survivability), but it is not very probable. In the same manner, when one considers the array of social and environmental factors acting upon children through their most formative years, the chance that hereditary factors play a key role greatly decreases. Indeed, social scientists use the concept of "chance" to indicate probability, in contrast to possibility. Whereas the popular concept of luck implies accidental, unpatterned, and happenstance events, the scientific notion of chance relates to averages and assumes some order and pattern in events. Kahn and Jensen have not given us any precise indication of the *chances* that their particular theories and perspectives represent reality. How likely is survivability in nuclear war or genetic determination of intelligence—1 percent, 10 percent, two-out-of-three, three-out-of-four, some of the time, or most of the time?

In addition, just because some event might be possible and probable (that is, the chances of its occurrence are quite likely), it does not necessarily follow that the event is very important in explaining human behavior. For example, the world would be so altered by the devastation following a nuclear war that to talk of survivability in dispassionate, scientific ways is almost meaningless. Similarly, the multitude of social and cultural factors that have been proven to have a *probable* impact on intelligence make the *possible* existence of hereditary factors relatively unimportant, except in extreme cases, such as mental retardation. The chances are great that broken homes, extreme poverty, lack of adequate medical care, proximity to daily violence and crime, and the like, are the really important determinants of learning and achievement.

At the same time, the known genetic differences between races, to which Jensen refers, are fundamentally important because of social and cultural definitions that are most often a function of discrimination and prejudice. For example, some Negroes do possess darker skin pigmentation; but this factor is important only in so far as skin color is used by whites to discriminate against blacks or by blacks to appeal to ethnic pride. Or the fact that blacks suffer from sickle cell anemia is important socially because relatively little has been done to seek remedies or cures, since the disease does not affect whites. In addition, blacks seem to be immune to some hereditary diseases common among whites (some types of cancer). Thus, even where we know that heredity plays a role, it is not the hereditary characteristic per se that accounts for inherent superiority or inferiority. Who is most superior, the race that suffers from sickle cell anemia or the race that suffers from cancer? In other words, the social environment remains a critical factor for judging superiority and value. Furthermore, appropriate social action to remedy this problematic situation can still be based upon manipulations of the social and cultural context.

The Pseudo-Proof Fallacy in Herrnstein's Theory of I.Q. as a Basis for Social Merit. Richard Herrnstein's theory illustrates the fallacy of pseudo proof. He begins with the observation that objective intelligence tests are being used increasingly in the military, schools, professions, industries, and branches of the civil service to replace traditional bases for leadership and role selection (family, social class, influence and money, and so on). He accepts this as evidence that modern society is moving steadily toward a meritocracy, and he states that "the measurement of intelligence is psychology's most telling accomplishment to date."[19] He admits that this testing is imperfect (and perhaps imperfectable) but suggests that there has been "too much success" for it to be repudiated on technical grounds alone. After tracing in detail the history of testing from Charles Darwin through Alfred Binet to William Stern and Lewis Terman, Herrnstein agrees with Jensen's conclusion that the genetic factor is worth about 80 percent in determining human behavior, and everything else (including social environment) is worth about 20 percent.

As part of the evidence for this conclusion, he cites a

1945 study that showed the following kinds of correlations between status ranking and average I.Q. for selected occupations:[20]

Rank in List of 74 Occupations	Civilian Occupations	Average I.Q.
1	accountant	128.1
5	auditor	125.9
20	clerk–typist	116.8
35	musician	110.9
55	bartender	102.2
65	baker	97.2
74	teamster	87.7

An I.Q. of 100 indicates average intelligence compared to other individuals in one's larger cultural and social context. Within each occupation there was a range. Not-so-bright accountants and bright teamsters were far from exceptions, but Herrnstein points out that the more prestigious occupations (law, engineering, science, and public relations) seem to require a certain minimum I.Q., as reflected in average I.Q.'s, compared to the less prestigious occupations (chauffeurs, barbers, truck drivers, and lumberjacks). Similarly, in studies of individuals with I.Q.'s of 150 or greater (generally classified as genius), Western and Northern Europeans and Jews predominate, while Latins, non-Jewish Eastern Europeans, and Negroes are statistically in the minority. Finally, research shows that one's I.Q. remains essentially unchanged during one's life, and high and low I.Q.'s tend to run in families. Herrnstein concludes with the observation that:

The data on I.Q. and social-class differences show that we have been living with an inherited stratification system for some time. The signs point to more rather than less of it in the future. . . . The opportunity for social mobility across classes assumes the biological distinctiveness of each class, for the unusual offspring—whether more or less able than his (or her) closest relatives—would quickly rise above his family or sink below it, and take his place, both biologically and socially with his peers. If this is a fair picture of the future, then we should be preparing ourselves for it instead of railing against its dawning signs. Greater wealth, health, freedom, fairness, and educational opportunity are not going to give us the egalitarian society of our philosophical heritage. It will instead give us a society sharply graduated, with greater innate uniformity within families as far as inherited abilities are concerned.[21]

Apart from the startling political and moral implications in Herrnstein's conclusion, the body of his argument appears, especially to most laymen, as logical and precise. There are several serious difficulties with the kinds of suggestive pseudo data that Herrnstein employs. First, despite the extensive use of I.Q. tests (and numerous carelessly prepared and unreliable imitations) in many occupations and professions, real achievement is often a function of other factors. Military men succeed in the modern army by playing the game, not by scoring high or low on a test. Professors are promoted and receive tenure by playing by the social rules of their game. We do not select presidential candidates, among the most powerful of all modern men when they are elected, by using intelligence tests. In other words, there is much evidence that modern society is not a meritocracy when it comes to countless important and powerful roles.

Second, though the litany of scientific names from history sounds impressive, this type of information tells us nothing about the validity or usefulness of the device being used (I.Q. tests), which is the central key to Herrnstein's theory. How reliable is the information that in 1945 bakers averaged about 15 points lower in I.Q. than musicians, and how important is this difference anyway? Jerome Kagan provides some answers:

I do not contest the obvious fact that there are real differences among individuals' psychological traits—such as intelligence—that our society values. But I do suggest that, given the insufficient and controversial quality of the information relevant to the causes of these differences, it is likely that deep personal attitudes rather than logic or sound empirical data dictates one's interpretations of the documented variability in IQ.[22]

Kagan argues that I.Q. tests are culturally biased to favor some people over others; in short, they are invented, designed, and administered by white middle-class Western males, who proceed to use the device to rank order all others in the population (nonwhites, lower classes, females). The biases appear in several forms. The most important part of the test, since it has the highest correlation with total I.Q., asks individuals to define words of increasing rarity. Rarity, however, is a relative quality that depends upon one's social and cultural background. Concepts such as "shilling," "joint," "fuzz," "acid," "rock," "con," "mark," and "*gemeinschaft*" have different meanings, or none at all, depending upon one's learned (not inherited) personal experience. Caucasian middle-class test makers tend to select those concepts that reflect their own backgrounds. Most probably, black test makers could devise I.Q. tests that intelligent white suburbanites would "fail" because of unfamiliarity with the argot and experience of black ghettos.

In addition, I.Q. tests pose problems for children to resolve—for example: "What should you do if you were sent to buy a loaf of bread and the grocer said he didn't have any more?" The "correct" answer is "I would go to another store." But this is a middle-class answer that assumes there are other stores. The ghetto child, for whom there is often only one store, responds "I would go home," and receives no credit on the I.Q. test. Another set of questions asks children to group words by analogy (for example: piano with violin). This type of measure contains the same cultural and linguistic bias as the rarity section. What would middle-class white children do if they were asked to group words such as *tortilla* and *frijole*? Finally, I.Q. test items include line drawings of objects with essential elements missing, requiring the child to identify the missing element. As might be expected, the objects included apply to the dominant white middle-class society (a thermometer with mercury missing in the bulb, a hand without fingernail polish—rather than some dice with the numbers missing from one side, or a door without a double lock).

Kagan, therefore, pinpoints the pseudo-proof nature of the I.Q. test used in the hereditary argument, even though proponents of that view maintain that they are being more truly scientific than their critics. He concludes by stating that he does not deny the existence of biological differences, many of which are inherited according to social or racial groupings. But he continues in the following manner.

We do not regard inherited characteristics such as eye color or tendency to perspire as entitling anyone to special favor. Similarly, we should reflect on the wisdom of using fifteen-point differences on a culturally biased test—regardless of the magnitude of the genetic contribution to the IQ—as a weapon to sort some children into stereotyped categories that impair their ability to become mayors, teachers, or lawyers.[23]

The fact that previous programs of educational reform have failed does not prove that environmental theories are inappropriate. What is more likely is that the programs were inadequately organized, planned, and conducted. Scientists should, therefore, be concerned with the search for more adequate theoretical perspectives that will lead to more effective changes in the environment.[24]

In summary, the demand to be scientific, to be logical and precise, to present mathematically precise and sophisticated data to prove the importance and correctness of one's research, results in fallacies of verification—particularly in the fallacies of misplaced precision, possible proof, and pseudo proof. Why should this be especially true today in the study of social problems? One of the major reasons is the fact that older theories no longer provide adequate answers, and that, in the search for new perspectives, scientists frequently grasp at any device, technique, or approach that looks new and different. Why older theories are inadequate can be understood by analyzing the origin and nature of the scientific equivalent of popular myths—*scientific paradigms.*

The Origin and Nature of Scientific Paradigms

Thomas Kuhn has pointed out that major scientific theories exist to define the legitimate and accepted problems and methods of study in a given field for succeeding generations of scientists.[25]

As such, they become paradigms, which are used to prepare students for membership in a scientific community and to enable scientists committed to the same paradigms to communicate with another about important matters. In other words, to become a chemist, a student must learn the accepted chemistry theory of his day. He must learn the unique language associated with that theory, so that he can communicate with his peers. He must learn the appropriate methods of research applicable to that theory, so that he can conduct scientific experiments. In short, the daily business of science would be impossible without paradigms. Major and successful paradigms have two characteristics, according to Kuhn. First, they represent unprecedented achievements that attract committed adherents away from competing theories and modes of research. Second, they are sufficiently open ended to leave all sorts of problems for new practitioners to resolve. Examples of major paradigms from the history of the physical sciences would include Ptolemaic astronomy, Copernican astronomy, Aristotelian dynamics, Newtonian physics, and Einsteinian relativism.

There are, however, inherent problems in the way in which paradigms are used by scientists. Members of a particular school of thought and those committed to specific theories tend to become more interested in filling out the unexplained aspects of the paradigm and talking to one another than in explaining nature or questioning the paradigm. In this way, paradigms restrict the vision of scientists, though, ironically, this is necessary for science to progress. Esoteric, seemingly inconsequential, but sometimes fundamentally important problems are solved because scientists are willing to spend much time researching and theorizing about these types of issues. At the same time, however, most research never produces major novelties or breakthroughs. In other words, paradigms predetermine for scientists what class of facts they must look at, gather, and analyze; what techniques they must use in doing so (including scientific devices and apparatus); and how the facts analyzed must be related to the theory being utilized. By using paradigms, scientists, then, bias their work from the start, in very much the same way the layman biases his perspectives by adopting accepted myths.

The real fascination that paradigms hold for a scientist, according to Kuhn, is to be found in their *puzzle-solving* character. Puzzles that are unimportant in a social or moral sense may be valid subjects for study and concentration, while really critical problems may be ignored. For example, achieving world peace or curing cancer have not been considered by many scientists in recent years to be resolvable puzzles, since available paradigms offered no hope for reasonable answers. In addition, there is a prevalent view that if something cannot be reduced to puzzle form, it is not scientific (or of scientific concern); therefore paradigm members will not work on the issue involved. Indeed, those who do work on unacceptable problems may be denounced as not being a part of the fraternity. In the case of unresolvable puzzles, the problem may be explained away as metaphysical or as the province of some other scientific discipline. Thus, in the field of sociology, the sociological study of economic systems has been almost completely undeveloped since the early days of Karl Marx and Max Weber. Specifically, we do not have precise studies of poverty, the inequitable distribution of wealth, and the economic power of industrial conglomerates, because these problems have been traditionally considered the province of another field (economics), subject to natural or metaphysical forces (inequality of wealth is a basic fact of life everywhere), or not amenable to formulation in terms of puzzles acceptable to prevailing paradigms.

Finally, Kuhn points out that textbooks in a discipline tend to be a major reflection of prevailing paradigms, since they are the primary source of preparation for practitioners, laymen, and neophyte scientists. Thus, textbooks really contain the contemporary biases of a given scientific perspective. They also modify the history of a science to suit the points of view of the accepted paradigms by ignoring events, discoveries, and findings that do not fit. In so doing, they may omit critical and important information. Texts make the discipline look falsely cumulative and linear, as though a new idea builds neatly upon existing knowledge. The scientist's commitment to logic tends to make him idealize the notion of a temporal series of individual discoveries leading to a present state of knowledge. Sciences, however, do not normally progress in this way, because of the inhibiting influences of paradigms. "Discoveries" are often merely the exotic and picayune filling out of existing paradigms. When a major breakthrough is experienced, it may be a function of seemingly accidental events (or *violations by nature*) raising serious questions about existing perspectives. For example, many contemporary scientific problems were simply unknown in previous eras, since they were unknowable given the prevailing paradigms of the period (for example, an ecology or population crisis).

When Nature Contradicts Preconceptions.   Paradigms, as defined above, are therefore essentially conservative and parochial. But, asks Kuhn, if most scientific effort is not really focused upon disclosing novel facts and theories, how does discovery, paradigm change, and intellectual revolution ever take place? By analyzing the history of scientific revolutions in the natural and physical sciences, Kuhn discovered that nature (that is, events in the real world) frequently seems to violate paradigm-induced expectations. Something happens that should not, according to the preordained rules of the game. A carefully conducted laboratory experiment turns out the wrong way. Landings on the moon lead to discoveries that do not seem to coincide with preconceived notions of the nature and origin of the moon. Or, in the social sciences, individuals do not behave as expected in response to certain social programs.

When a violation by nature occurs, there are three possible responses. The most common is for paradigm adherents to attempt ingenious explanations that do not essentially alter the basic substance of their theories. The original paradigm is retained, though perhaps with minor revisions in conceptualization. Also common in science is the possibility that a violation resists even the most radical attempts at resolution. In this case, solutions may be considered unattainable, and the problem may be set aside for future generations who possess different techniques, new equipment, and revised theories. Finally, sometimes a new paradigm emerges in elementary form and begins to compete with older paradigms for a lasting place in scientific perspectives. At this point, a scientific revolution begins to take place. Recognizing that existing paradigms cannot explain the violation, some bold scientists search for novel theories, since the normal problem-solving activity of science has been interrupted. Kuhn calls this period a transition from normal to extraordinary science, which is marked by proliferating schools of thought, willingness by many scientists to try anything, overt expressions of discontent for the entire discipline, debate over fundamental assumptions, and questioning of the philosophical roots of the discipline. As in the case of political revolutions, *scientific and paradigm revolutions create emotional polarization and cannot be resolved by logic and experimentation alone.*

The Proliferation of Paradigm Revolutions. Kuhn has raised serious questions about the traditional mythology of science, which is taught to laymen and apprentices and firmly believed by most scientists. This belief sees science as always logical, continuously cumulative, and devoted to the discovery of new techniques and knowledge. The picture of science that emerges from Kuhn's analysis, however, is one of a discipline that is frequently emotional and unscientific and rarely cumulative, a discipline committed to proving preconceptions about the subject matter being studied. What, then, has caused the seeming increase in paradigm revolutions (or at least paradigm-shaking criticisms) of recent years in many scientific disciplines, including social science? Rapid social change, technological development, growing demands by the public to put science to work in the real world, and easier communication of new ideas through more available mass media have all played a role. Violations of paradigms by nature have become more commonplace. Scientists are not permitted to shelve unresolvable problems for future scholars to work upon since public opinion demands instant solutions to problems. Mavericks who will not play the game according to prevailing rules can seek out an audience for their unpopular or unacceptable views.

For example, not too many decades ago, renowned scientists were assuring man that space travel, even within our solar system, was an impossibility. And certainly few scientists conceived of the possibility of harnessing the sun's basic processes to create massive destructive or constructive force. However, existing paradigms or not, the United States and German governments mobilized scientists, only a few of whom really foresaw the scientific and social implications, to develop the atomic bomb during World War II. Because of the pressure and urgency of war, and the lack of time and opportunity to study the possible ramifications of the atomic explosion, there were still some scientists who, at the time the first experimental device was detonated, were even then not quite sure what the result would be. In fact, this was true to the extent that some even envisioned the possibility of an uncontrollable chain reaction that would destroy a good portion of the world. In the same way, increasing demands for a cure for cancer, an adequate response to poverty, a solution to the problems of ecology, and a response to the developing population crisis may not permit scientists the luxury of waiting for a natural paradigm revolution to supply new perspectives that will permit leisurely investigation of these issues in the distant future.

This is especially true in the area of social problems. What social science must do is examine the character of prevailing paradigms to determine their utility and inapplicability to the analysis and resolution of contemporary problems. That this revolutionary process, as described by Kuhn, has already begun has been referred to in the previous discussion and is evidenced by increasing debate, experimentation with new methods and techniques, growing dissatisfaction and discontent, and outright disillusionment by some within the discipline. Leonard Reissman, C. Wright Mills, and Alvin Gouldner, quoted in Chapter 1, are examples. Jensen and Herrnstein have raised serious questions about the fundamental assumptions of social environmentalists. This type of rebellious questioning stems from the fact that nature is increasingly violating traditional perspectives (Head Start programs do not work; war goes on and becomes potentially more destructive, despite the United Nations, alliances, treaties, the threat of nuclear retaliation, and the like; poverty continues amid plenty), and the old paradigms cannot supply needed responses.[26]

Scientific Paradigms About Social Problems

Earl Rubington and Martin Weinberg have traced the involvement of American sociologists with social problems.[27] They point out that the initial task was to define and identify the particular nature of social problems, a job that is not as easy as it may seem at first.

Certain events attract and hold interest. Samples of such events are armed robbery, burglary, child-molesting, drunken driving, rape, murder, suicide, divorce, race riots, pollution, and air piracy. These events and others like them make news. Their occurrence gives pause and makes people stop and think. . . . These events cause questioning because they all have the property of being troublesome. Their essential features seem to be three in number. (1) A violation of "rules" occurs. (2) The violation occurs with sufficient frequency to arouse concern among a large number of people. (3) Sufficiently alarmed, these people issue a call for action.[28]

The difficulty is, however, that social problems affect different people in different ways, while some people are not affected at all. Similarly, some of the issues considered contemporary problems were not recognized in earlier periods of history under other circumstances, and some current problems will not be considered important in the future: "What then makes a social problem? Sociologists usually consider a social problem to be *an alleged situation which is incompatible with the values of a significant number of people who agree that action is necessary to alter the situation.*" [29]

This definition by Rubington and Weinberg is an accurate and fair characterization of most of the definitions employed by social scientists in studying social problems. Such a characterization reflects the essential cultural bias of these definitions, despite attempts at qualification and generality. In other words, sociologists early in their work on social problems picked a type of definition that tended to influence their later research and theorizing. Specifically, social problems have been seen as deviations from or violations of some generally accepted, popular norm (in terms of behavior and beliefs), and they have been considered to be deviations and violations that are observable, known, and detected by significant proportions of the public.

What such a definition does is to make the analysis of hidden, latent, or potential problems all but impossible, since if the event is not recognized as a problem it will probably not be subjected to investigation. Furthermore, this definition implies that the values, or norms, being violated are the desirable, acceptable standards for belief and behavior. The action that the public demands in response to social problems is typically one that will restore the state of affairs to the way it existed before the problem occurred (and, in effect, recreate the environment that produced the problem). In this fashion, then, early sociologists tended to follow the lead and dictates of public opinion in selecting problems to be studied. It is not surprising, therefore, that social scientific attention was not devoted to the military-industrial complex until long after President Eisenhower made his famous farewell address[30]; that narcotics use did not become a central concern for many citizens until white suburban children became affected; or that recent problems such as urban disturbances and pollution were not anticipated (or the conditions leading to these events were not investigated) by social scientists until long after the events that initiated concern and response from a significant proportion of the public had occurred.

Rubington and Weinberg point out that once a social problem had been tentatively defined, social scientists next had to formulate a method and a rationale for study. Two things played a role in determining the rationale: the desire to further the discipline of sociology (and what better way of understanding the nature of human behavior than by analyzing the exceptional, unusual, or problem examples) and the wish to help mankind by solving society's problems. The method to be employed depended upon a determination of what was to be studied. The need for such determinations led to the formulation of some general perspectives, which, in turn, formed the basis for the emergence of major paradigms:

Perspectives, as orienting ideas, consist of definition, conception, and action. Having assumed the task of studying society and its problems, sociology developed a complex battery of weapons; it developed theories, methods of research, and a body of knowledge to build its own discipline while contributing in some way to the solution of social problems.[31]

Perspectives and Paradigms of Social Problems. Rubington and Weinberg suggest that five different perspectives of social problems developed roughly in the following historical sequence[32]:

1. **Social Pathology**

   The founders of sociology saw as their task knowing how a developing society would fulfill natural law and continue to progress. Sociologists specializing in social problems conceived of themselves as social reformers who were mandated to aid society toward progress. They regarded one set of social problems as the result of essentially *"sick"* people—those who were defective, delinquent, and dependent. They regarded another set of problems as essentially the result of *corrupt, greedy, and power-hungry elites* in business, industry, and government. Both types of pathological people, at the bottom and top of society, had to be rooted out in order to restore society to its natural evolution towards progress.

2. **Social Disorganization**

   In its second phase of development, American sociology made social rules, rather than individuals, the focus of inquiry into social problems. The reformism of the social-pathology view was confronted by the notion of the scientist committed to the development of the discipline. Scientists concentrated upon concepts, theories, and means of empirical research, rather than involving themselves in moral, philosophical, or critical statements. The social disorganization perspective focused upon rules and attributed social problems to breakdowns in tradition, conflict between rules, or the abuse of rules.

3. **Value Conflict**

   In a third period, the more scientific and less socially concerned branch of sociology became predominant. However, though some problems seemed to be resolvable, new ones had arisen that appeared critical and almost insoluble (the depression, the world wars). As a consequence, some sociologists began to ask whether social problems ought not be studied from the point of view of society, rather than from the point of view of sociology. This group felt that problems were endemic to society, since people could not agree about their nature or resolution. The disagreement did not result from a failure to understand the rules of society, but rather it arose from a conflict between different interests and values. This value-conflict perspective demanded a more humanistic, involved, and, sometimes, committed stance on the part of the scientist.

4. **Deviant Behavior**
As the major branches of sociology became more scientific, some in the discipline demanded the same right accorded to other developed sciences: the ability of the professional to define the problems needing study, as opposed to the sociologist's traditional reliance upon society's direction. For this group, it became important to test out the implications of theory, not just to concentrate on the solution of social ills. Social problems became defined as a departure from rules, and scientists specialized in the nature of situations where morals, norms, and laws were breached. Deviance became a major interest.

5. **Labeling Perspective**
Finally, recent labeling theory arose out of the failure of the deviant-behavior perspective to explain many aspects of social problems. Adherents of this new view questioned the methods and conceptions employed by deviant-behavior advocates. Problems were seen as resulting from the ways in which dominant society defined and identified deviance, rather than as the consequence of inherent deviant conditions within some individuals or sub-systems of society. The major emphasis for labeling theory was placed upon social definitions, and the question of why society's definition should always be considered correct was raised.

Rubington and Weinberg have identified some of the specific perspectives that are a part of three major paradigms of social problems considered in Chapters 4–6: *deviance, disorganization,* and *functionalism.* These paradigms have influenced the work of sociologists studying social problems since the earliest days of the discipline, and they still account for many of the difficulties in social programs resulting from inadequate knowledge and information. The three paradigms all have roots in the history of American and European sociology, and all are related to popular myths about social problems.

The earliest example of the deviance paradigm appeared

in the form of what Rubington and Weinberg have called the pathology perspective, which was indebted to both early reformism and the *natural myth* of social problems. Later, the pathology perspective was modified by the deviant-behavior and the labeling perspectives. As we shall see in Chapter 4, the major fallacy of the deviant-behavior paradigm, according to Robert Lauer, is the view that such behavior is somehow a violation of the normal:

This reflects a conservative strain which has pervaded sociology throughout its history. . . . The focus on stability and concomitant neglect of change assumes that static analyses can be made without coming to terms with change, and that an understanding of social change demands a prior and thorough understanding of social statics. Sociologists, then, have been far more concerned with structures than with processes. . . . Persistence and regularities have been viewed as the normal state of affairs; change has been viewed as a kind of social deviance.[33]

The second major paradigm, the notion of problem *behavior as related to disorganization*, is associated with the *popular myth that evil equals evil*. In addition, it also represents the historic conservative bias of sociology in an underlying concern for maintaining social cohesion and stability. The notion that change or deviance created crises in the social system, arose early in the development of sociology, giving rise to what Lauer calls the "fallacy of trauma":

It is not difficult to marshall evidence that seems to support the fallacy of trauma. There is, for example, some evidence that mental illness is related to social change. Certain kinds of change in conjunction with various other social and psychological factors seem to increase mental stress.[34]

Problems, like mental illness, were seen as resulting from a breakdown in the social and cultural order, a fragmenting of social bonds induced by change, conflict, and threats to the social system. The job of the social scientist was to understand these traumatic threats so that appropriate actions could be taken to reintegrate the fractured system. The view of social and cultural disorganization has been challenged recently by a new school of conflict theory.

Finally, the *functionalist paradigm* stems initially from the early *natural-theory* days of the discipline and has been used by some social scientists as an *academic equivalent to the popular myth of blaming the victim.* Essentially, the functionalist paradigm argues that problems are a result of the normal processes of a social system, as it develops, grows, and attempts to adjust to certain kinds of strains or challenges. In other words, problems are a function of the way in which society normally works and are not necessarily deviant or disorganizing. The difficulty is that such a view contains a conservative moral and political potential. The existing system, including all of its social problems, can be seen as normal, perhaps even as desirable. War, poverty, and some kinds of crime might be seen as serving the prevailing system in desirable ways. The conservative potential in this perspective has given rise in recent years to a major attack upon this important paradigm, especially from the new school of radical social science. This attack has led to a reassessment of functionalism, which might become the basis for the emergence of a modified view or a new paradigm providing more adequate perspectives for contemporary social problems.

In conclusion, scientists as citizens and men as likely to be influenced by mythology and biases as their lay counterparts, when thinking about social problems. However, scientific biases take a slightly different form than popular mythologies. First, science must contend with the propensity toward fallacies, generated by the pressures to do important, significant, and precise work. These pressures can lead to the fallacies of factual verification: that is, the fallacies of possible and pseudo proof. Second, scientists require world views, larger perspectives in the form of paradigms, to guide and organize their search for truth. They need preconceived conceptions of the nature of their subject matter to determine what should be studied, how it should be studied, and why some problems should be selected for investigation in contrast to others. These paradigms become related not only to the scientific demands of the discipline but also to the moral and political issues influencing a society. The irony is that scientific work would be impossible without paradigms, but, at the same time, paradigms often restrict, delimit, and bias the work of scientists. If rapid social change creates conditions where paradigms become less successful in providing adequate answers to both scientific and social problems and puzzles, paradigm revolutions may take place. These appear in the form of competing schools of thought and criticisms of prevailing and accepted views. This process of revolution characterizes the sociological study of social problems today. Three major paradigms have been increasingly questioned from without and within the discipline in recent years. These paradigms view problems as a function of deviant behavior, of disorganization in society, or of the natural processes of the social system. The next section of this book considers in detail the origins of the three major paradigms, the strengths and weaknesses of each, and the strengths and weaknesses of developing criticisms and competing schools of thought. On the basis of such a consideration, the search for new alternatives, for more meaningful views of contemporary social problems, can begin.

Notes to Chapter 3

1. Thomas S. Kuhn, *The Structure of Scientific Revolutions*, 2nd ed. (Chicago: University of Chicago Press, 1970).
2. David Hackett Fischer, *Historian's Fallacies: Toward a Logic of Historical Thought* (New York: Harper & Row, 1970).
3. Andrew J. Weigert, "The Immoral Rhetoric of Scientific Sociology," *The American Sociologist*, 5 (May 1970), p. 114.
4. David Hackett Fischer, *Historian's Fallacies: Toward a Logic of Historical Thought* (New York: Harper & Row, 1970), pp. 940–963.
5. Otto Friedrich, "Of Imaginary Numbers," *Time* (August 2, 1971).
6. *Ibid.*
7. Herman Kahn, *On Escalation* (New York: Frederick A. Praeger, 1965).
8. Anatol Rapoport, "Chicken a la Kahn," *The Triple Revolution: Social Problems in Depth*, Robert Perrucci and Marc Pilisuk, eds. (Boston: Little, Brown, 1968), pp. 52–65. Originally appeared in *The Virginia Quarterly Review*, 41 (Summer 1965), pp. 370–389. Also see Philip Green's *Deadly Logic: The Theory of Nuclear Deterrence* (Columbus: Ohio State University Press, 1966).

9. Anatol Rapoport, "Chicken a la Kahn," *The Triple Revolution, ibid.*, p. 55.

10. See, for example Herman Kahn, *On Thermonuclear War* (Princeton, N.J.: Princeton University Press, 1960); also, Philip Green's excellent criticism of Kahn's pseudoquantification—*Deadly Logic: The Theory of Nuclear Deterrence* (Columbus: Ohio State University Press, 1966), especially pp. 118–125.

11. See Robert A. Dentler and Phillips Cutright, *Hostage America: Human Aspects of Nuclear Attack and a Program of Prevention* (Boston: Beacon Press, 1963); Robert Jay Lifton, "Prophetic Survivors: Hiroshima and Beyond," *Social Policy, 2* (January/February 1972), pp. 8–15; and G. W. Rathjens and G. B. Kistiakowsky. "The Limitations of Strategic Arms," *Scientific American, 222* (January 1970), pp. 19–29.

12. See Clark C. Apt, *Serious Games* (New York: The Viking Press, 1970).

13. Herman Kahn, *Thinking About the Unthinkable* (New York: Horizon Press, 1962); and *On Escalation* (New York: Frederick A. Praeger, 1965).

14. For example, see Morris Janowitz, "Sociological Research on Arms Control," *The American Sociologist, 6* (June 1971), pp. 23–30; Arthur Larson, "Can Science Prevent War?," *Saturday Review* (February 20, 1965), pp. 15–17, 47; and Alan G. and Hanna Newcombe, eds., "Peace Research Reviews," *Alternative Approaches to Peace Research. Volume 4* (Oakville, Ont., Canada: Canadian Peace Research Institute, February 1972).

15. David Hackett Fischer, *Historian's Fallacies: Toward a Logic of Historical Thought* (New York: Harper & Row, 1970).

16. The following references are relevant to this discussion: David K. Cohen, "Does IQ Matter?" *Intellectual Digest, 2* (July 1972), pp. 35–38; H. J. Eysenck, "Race, Intelligence and Education," *ibid.*, pp. 33–35; Richard Herrnstein, "I.Q.," *The Atlantic, 228* (September 1971), pp. 43–64; Arthur R. Jensen, "Race and the Genetics of Intelligence: A Reply to Lewontin," *Bulletin of the Atomic Scientists, 26* (May 1970), pp. 17–23; Jerome Kagan, "The Magical Aura of the IQ," *Saturday Review* (December 4, 1971), pp. 92–93; Richard C. Lewontin, "Further Remarks on Race and the Genetics of Intelligence" and "Race and Intelligence," *Bulletin of the Atomic Scientists, 26* (May 1970) (March 1970), pp. 23–25, 2–8; Eugene Rabinowitch, "Jensen vs. Lewontin," *Bulletin of the Atomic Scientists, 26* (May 1970), pp. 25–26; and Peter Watson, "Toward a New Gauge of Intelligence," *Intellectual Digest, 2* (July 1972), pp. 38–39.

17. Arthur R. Jensen, "Race and the Genetics of Intelligence: A Reply to Lewontin," *Bulletin of the Atomic Scientists, 26* (May 1970), p. 18.

18. *Ibid.*, p. 20.

19. Richard Herrnstein, "I.Q.," *The Atlantic, 228* (September 1971), pp. 44–45.

20. *Ibid.*, p. 51.

21. *Ibid.*, p. 64.

22. Jerome Kagan, "The Magical Aura of the IQ," *Saturday Review* (December 4, 1971), p. 92.

23. *Ibid.*, p. 93.

24. For example, see John L. Horn, "Intelligence: Why It Grows, Why It Declines," *Transaction, 5* (November 1967), pp. 23–31.

25. This section is based upon Thomas S. Kuhn, *The Structure of Scientific Revolutions*, 2nd ed. (Chicago: University of Chicago Press, 1970).
26. For ideas related to Kuhn's analysis, see Robert Brown, *Explanations in Social Science* (Chicago: Aldine Publishing Company, 1963); Diana Crane, "Fashion in Science: Does It Exist?" *Social Problems, 16* (Spring 1969), pp. 433–441; Hans Mol, "The Dysfunctions of Socio-logical Knowledge," *The American Sociologist, 6* (August 1971), pp. 221–223; and Kalman Silvert, ed., *The Social Reality of Scientific Myth* (New York: American Universities Field Staff, 1969).
27. Earl Rubington and Martin S. Weinberg, *The Study of Social Problems* (New York: Oxford University Press, 1971).
28. *Ibid.*, p. xi.
29. *Ibid.*, pp. 5–6.
30. See Ritchie P. Lowry, "To Arms: Changing Military Roles and the Military-Industrial Complex," *Social Problems, 18* (Summer 1970), pp. 3–16.
31. Earl Rubington and Martin S. Weinberg, *The Study of Social Problems* (New York: Oxford University Press, 1971), p. 11.
32. *Ibid.*, especially pp. 210–214.
33. Robert H. Lauer, "The Scientific Legitimation of Fallacy: Neutralizing Social Theory," *American Sociological Review, 36* (October 1971), p. 881.
34. *Ibid.*, p. 882.

Part II

Social-Problems
Paradigms

The result of deviant people or the natural response to a deviant society?
(Wide World Photos)

4. Problems as Deviant Behavior

Social Pathology: Old and New Views

The deviancy paradigm first appeared in the form of the theory of social pathology and was based upon an organic analogy. Events were seen as problems when they interfered with the normal functioning of society, just as disease is seen as a problem because it disrupts an individual's normal bodily processes. According to Herbert Spencer and later writers, social pathologies were reflected by maladjustments in social relationships. These maladjustments developed as society progressed (a parallel was seen here between maturation of society and maturation of the human body), and some individuals and groups were unable to keep up with the growth.[1] This type of medical model led early social scientists to interpret their role as one of creating and protecting healthy individuals and societies by eliminating sickness. Social sickness constituted a violation of the expected in terms of prevailing morals, norms, and laws. Deviant behavior was, therefore, seen as sick and pathological. The earliest pathologists felt that the sickness resided within the sick; later, more humanitarian views shifted the causal emphasis to the environment. Both perspectives, however, were influenced by Darwinism to the extent that they both espoused the belief that the sick became useless or died out while the strong survived. Thus, as a result of these sociological perspectives, deviants became labeled as inherently defective, dependent, or delinquent,[2] a view similar to that taken by the naturalistic and evil-equals-evil popular myths.

As the study of society developed through its more scientific period, the influence of the pathology perspective of deviance declined, particularly because of the pronounced moral and naturalistic biases explicit in the view. Today, however, pathology is experiencing something of a revival. At the end of this chapter, and in the discussion of radical criticisms of the functionalist paradigm in Chapter 6, consideration is given to the more thoughtful scholars who are suggesting that this view, in revised form, is meaningful. For the moment, it is important to note that the older conception often remains with us in two forms: (1) the conservative view of deviants as exhibiting inherent pathological traits and (2) the liberal–radical view that deviants are essentially a manifestation of a pathological society. The first view is still reflected in the way in which some social service programs are organized and administered, and helps account for some of the contemporary failure of welfare.

The Conservative Pathology Perspective and Its Effect on the Welfare System.   David Austin describes how the pathology theory became built into early welfare programs, in spite of or contrary to the facts known about those on welfare.[3] He begins by distinguishing between minimum and optimum social services. *Optimum welfare* refers to services provided through social institutions to individuals who have needs that cannot be adequately met through the marketplace. This concept implies the providing of universal benefits to as many consumers as have unmet needs. In contrast, *minimum welfare* is the notion of a necessary evil in the form of limited services provided to a few consumers by third parties who strictly judge the eligibility of the consumers for the services. The third party, usually the welfare worker, theoretically serves public interests rather than the consumers' needs. Austin points out that though the United States has made periodic attempts to define and construct universal service systems on the principle of optimum welfare, public assistance continues to be thought of as essentially a minimum necessary evil.

This is a holdover from the last century when social services were related to charity administration by private agencies. Society distinguished between workers and idlers and reasoned that the ethic of hard work could be induced in the idlers only if public assistance was kept at the lowest possible level for all concerned (the client, the client's spouse, and the client's children). "Watchful friends" were assigned by private agencies to ensure that those who were not working would not become lazy. In the 1920's, these "friends" began to receive specialized training in schools of social work. This professionalization and the impact of the depression led to the establishment of charity administration under public auspices in the 1930's.

At first, minimum level relief programs were initiated through social security legislation for those poor considered marginal to the labor market: the elderly, the blind, and widows. In the 1950's, the totally disabled were added. At the same time, social case work developed with an emphasis upon the identification of the special psychosocial factors in dependent families. In the 1950's, treatment for these factors became important, and the idea of rehabilitation arose. Since there was no federal program for families headed by able-bodied, but unemployed men, services had to be provided through Aid to Families with Dependent Children (AFDC). However, more and more families under AFDC were headed, not by men, but by divorced, separated, and deserted wives or unmarried mothers. In most cases, these kinds of environments were considered unsuitable homes, but federal support was sustained largely by the hope of rehabilitation of AFDC cases through social case work techniques.

By the late 1960's, it was apparent that the AFDC caseloads were still growing, and the work incentive program (WIN) was initiated. As Austin indicates, the basic objective of this program was the return of dependent families with employable adults to economic self-support, including mothers in one-parent households. During the Nixon administration, additional programs—FAP (Family Assistance Program) and OFP (Opportunities for Families Plan)—still based upon the idea of making dependents employable, were attempted. Now, however, more federal power and expertise, rather than local social workers, were utilized, since politicians felt welfare had failed in part because local agencies had not stressed employability sufficiently. Thus, welfare had developed from local to federal control, but it still culminated in a minimum program based upon assumptions about the work ethic, which continued to distinguish between workers and idlers.

The story of the failure and political defeat of the Family Assistance Program in the first four years of the Nixon Administration reflects the continuing perspective of welfare as pathological. Daniel Moynihan has described how the program was actually an ironic departure for a conservative president, since it represented a limited and special type of guaranteed annual income for some poor people.[4] As a consequence, however, an unusual coalition of Northern liberals and radicals and Southern conservatives opposed the program, though for different reasons, thus making promising legislation impossible. Conservatives did not want AFDC payments raised by a factor of four or more in some Southern areas, where such an increase would seriously upset the economic basis of racism. In contrast, Moynihan maintains that liberals and radicals opposed the program since it was proposed by a conservative president.

However, what may be more significant is that President Nixon insisted upon maintaining that FAP was *not* a guaranteed income and that the program provided assistance only to the *working* poor, not to those poor receiving welfare. In other words, despite the fact that this program held some promise (it would have added many excluded poor people to the assistance rolls), its fate was assured, partly because of the political reactions identified by Moynihan, but also because its initiator and the program itself refused to confront the essential issue and relied upon an older pathology perspective. A distinction was made between those poor who worked and those who did not. Unemployment, for whatever reason, was assumed to be a result of individual pathology; therefore, no assistance could be given to those who "wouldn't" work. Furthermore, the basic concept of welfare, even some assistance for some poor who did work, was considered "bad," something to be eliminated as quickly as possible. It is not surprising, then, that such a philosophy led to opposition from several spheres and that the program was so easily abandoned even by those who proposed it. Obviously such a philosophy could not lead to the formulation and support of a program that would have emphasized full, equal, and adequate income for all citizens. Such an alternative program is impossible as long as pathology perspectives predominate and are utilized as a basis for proposing programs to resolve "the *problems* of poverty and welfare."

Austin reviews the literature of the field, which describes the ideology that has been predominant throughout history:

Social work leaders supported the use of the concept of "suitable home" to exclude "unworthy" families from [service programs] as early as the 1920's. . . . A number of states used the same principle, particularly during the 1950's, to discourage applications for AFDC or to justify the removal of families from AFDC when there was an out-of-wedlock birth.[5]

His conclusion is that professionalization of public assistance has merely resulted in the substitution of psychological definitions of defects for the moral definitions used in earlier years. Thus, an older moral pathology has simply been converted into a contemporary psychological pathology. This view of those on assistance as pathological justifies restrictive legislation, harsh welfare rules, and rigid administrative procedures.

Faulty Assumptions About Welfare in the Conservative Pathology Perspective.   On social scientific and humanitarian grounds alone, this situation would be cause for concern. However, there is an added feature. Recent research suggests that the assumptions of the pathology perspective, whether moral or psychological in nature, are faulty. The emphasis upon making dependents employable, like the early notion of the watchful friend, assumes a clearcut distinction between workers and idlers. Idlers are those who must be threatened before they will go to work, since it is presumably easier for them to be on social welfare. Austin refers to three possible criticisms of this view:

First, the poor have available to them only unskilled or

seasonal employment, for the most part. The gap between wages for this type of employment and costs of family maintenance is continuing to widen. In other words, the poor do not have to be forced to work. However, when they do work, their family income is extremely low or subject to rapid fluctuation. Welfare, then, rather than acting as a block to employability, becomes a basis for permitting families to move on their own initiative in and out of the labor market.

Second, some studies of public assistance recipients have shown that substantial proportions held some type of job before coming on welfare. In addition, many worked while receiving assistance, before the recent implementation of administrative restrictions against receiving welfare while employed.

Finally, the structure of the labor market is a major determinant of employability for the dependent. Their only employment "opportunities" are, for the most part, so-called secondary jobs, which are less attractive (low wages, poor conditions, harsh discipline, little opportunity for advancement or challenge) than the primary jobs available to the middle classes. Thus, if the notion of the work ethic is to make any sense, the elimination of dependency will require alterations in the labor market so that the dependent can have access to primary jobs.

As a matter of fact, additional research suggests that the poor do possess a strong work ethic, despite their dependency. But this ethic has different consequences for them than it does for the middle class. Leonard Goodwin interviewed families with teenage children living in the middle-income suburbs of Baltimore in 1960. He asked the husband, the wife, and the teenage son or daughter for their own work orientations and the orientations they would imagine for a woman on welfare in Baltimore, who had entered a work-training program.[6] He compared these responses with the work orientations of samples of welfare mothers enrolled in the WIN program and of welfare mothers who had teenage sons and had been on welfare the longest period of time in Baltimore. He found that both adult and teenage suburbanites draw sharp distinctions between themselves and the welfare poor. Some of these distinctions are generally appropriate. For example, not surprisingly, the poor have less confidence in themselves and tend to accept welfare more readily as a fact of life.

Some middle-class perspectives, however, were totally inappropriate. Middle-class respondents did not believe that the work ethic was strong among the poor, yet welfare women gave almost the same work ethic ratings for themselves as suburbanites did for themselves. On the other hand, the work ethic among the poor leads to increasing feelings of insecurity as the inability to succeed in the world becomes more pronounced. Suburbanites also mistakenly imagine that welfare income is inherently associated with income from quasi-illegal sources (gambling, running numbers, peddling stolen goods), which may explain the readiness of many citizens to believe in widespread welfare cheating. In short, middle-class suburbanites feel that they are fundamentally different than welfare recipients:

Middle-class suburbanites are not necessarily unsympathetic to the poor . . ., [but] they are likely to resonate to the statements of political leaders and program administrators which demand that welfare programs have strong work requirements in order that poor people can learn the value of work. . . . Middle-class persons tend to locate the problem of lower-class poverty in the psychology of the poor. Solutions, therefore, are cast in terms of getting the poor into the proper frame of mind for participating willingly in menial jobs available to them. Solutions that might involve structural changes in society, such as radical improvement in the educational and job market opportunities for lower-class persons are not even broached as part of welfare reform.[7]

In other words, unemployment continues among the poor in spite of their high commitment to the work ethic. Yet programs are designed to reeducate the poor, to remove their pathology, rather than to permit them to utilize their work commitment in positive ways or to substitute more meaningful ethics. This modern version of social pathology, the concept of inherent psychological deviance, has helped sustain unrealistic and unworkable private and public programs of assistance.

The Liberal-Radical Pathology Perspective and Its Application to Critiques of the Military-Industrial Complex. The newer liberal-radical version of pathology shifts the perspective from the inherent quality of the individual deviant to deviance which is assumed to be inherent within society as a whole, or some special subsociety within which most individuals are forced to live. The individual deviant behavior that results is seen as an extreme reaction to the larger social pathology. Recent radical critiques of the military-industrial complex typify this type of view. For example, Marc Pilisuk and Tom Hayden have theorized that American society *is a military-industrial complex* to a much greater degree than it is a society that *contains a ruling military-industrial complex.*[8] Using this theory, other radical critics have proposed, as empirical justification for this view, that the entire social system is affected by the pathology of militarism, not just a special elite or institution within the system. Jeffrey Schevitz indicates that, according to the 1967 census, there were over 2 million people employed in four war-defense industries (aircraft, electronics, instruments, and ordnance), and that this constituted 10 percent of all manufacturing workers by the 1967 census.[9] He calculates that the spending of war-defense companies for materials and services generated an additional 174,000 jobs outside of these industries and that the Department of Defense spent over $14 billion for procurement in "nondefense" industries (such as construction and petroleum), thereby creating an additional 1 million jobs. Furthermore, in 1965, before the marked military escalation in Vietnam, the federal government had 1 million civilians in defense-related agencies. These civilians, together with personnel in uniform, constituted 72 percent of all federal employment in 1965.

Thus, Schevitz estimates that there are at least 4 million jobs that are directly war-related and that contribute to the operations of the Department of Defense. In addition, these positions generate wages and salaries that create and sustain other jobs, the so-called multiplier or induced economic effect:

[A multiplier of 3.0] seems like a reasonable figure with which to work. Also (to be conservative) let us remove those in uniform from consideration in the computation of the multiplier effect. Then, the 4.1 million war-related jobs should support an equivalent of 8.2 million additional jobs for the seventy-one million people in the labor force. Thus, 12.3 million jobs, or 17.3% of the civilian labor force is directly or indirectly dependent on military spending. If we consider

the spending of those in uniform to have no employment multiplier effect and just add another three million jobs to our total of jobs dependent on military spending, over 15 million, or 20.3% of the combined civilian and military jobs are dependent on military spending.[10]

Schevitz indicates that to this quantitative analysis must be added the qualitative impact of militarization; for example, the unique dependence of scientists, engineers, and academics (all key leadership segments of contemporary society) upon the warfare state and mentality. He concludes that contemporary America is afflicted throughout by the pathology of preparation for war. Therefore, individual deviance, such as the alienation of scientists working on military-related jobs, is not a result of conflict within bureaucratized settings so much as it is a consequence of dissatisfaction, frustration, and dehumanization, arising from employment that depends upon a business committed to mass killing.

In a similar manner, Irwin Sperber suggests that the modern United States military is actually used to coopt citizens in order to preserve and expand the industrial state.[11] Overtly, the function of the military is to use the means of violence against foreign enemies to protect national interests and security. Covertly, Sperber argues, the military plays a more important role; it employs nonviolent means of cooptation both at home and abroad, particularly to protect foreign investments and to contain domestic liberation movements:

In academic and official ideological terms, America maintains its wealth and power through free enterprise, technological genius, and excellence in higher education. Despite the popularity of this optimistic world-view among most American scholars, soldiers, and citizens, the fact remains that the ruling class clearly understands its own dependence upon military institutions for social control and economic development. . . . As the ruling class recognizes, a large standing army and military conscription are essential to and characteristic of the "the American way of life". . . . The structure and policies of the American military establishment reflect and reinforce the key policies, vested interests, legitimating ideologies and sources of change in American society.[12]

Specifically, the modern American military coopts a number of potentially revolutionary segments in contemporary society. Military life is advertised to the public at large as a "one-stop service center," where youth can be awarded promising careers in business, science, public service, technology, and education, on the basis of equal opportunity for all. The youthful elite, scientists and intellectuals, are told of the promises and benefits of professionalism, involvement with modern technology, job security, and patriotic commitment. Sperber points out that the recent liberalizing of traditional military regulations plays a specially unique role. Promises of glamor, vertical mobility, and patriotic reward can persuade potential critics of American society either to select these bounties of the system or to work for peaceful reform from within. In other words, a soldier can grow hair a little longer, drink beer in the barracks, or do his own thing (smoke grass) so long as he also follows orders. Less privileged youth, who are a potential source of "trouble-making" in society because of their racial and class origins, are especially susceptible to these types of appeals. Women are appealed to by special reference in military propaganda and ideology to the adventurous life (in contrast to the dullness of female civilian life), challenging careers offering leadership and professional development, and economic opportunities that cannot possibly be matched in the civilian world (rank in the military determines salary, regardless of sex, while in the civilian world women receive less pay for equivalent work.) As Sperber puts it: "A young woman with some intellectual capacity to work with her civilian peers for the purpose of changing the institutions and professions which systematically discriminate against women is instead offered the 'challenge and opportunity to grow professionally' [and personally]." [13]

Sperber suggests that, at the same time, devices, other than positive inducements for cooptation, are employed by the military, often in the form of negative inducements, to reinforce the system. Draft avoidance has been provided for the middle class and elite by the use of student deferments, designation of certain critical civilian occupations exempted from military service or eligible for special privilege within the military, and limited, proscribed conscientious objection. In the past, this system has had two consequences. First, it rewarded the well-behaved and conforming. Second, it induced or forced others to select future careers on the basis of criteria established by the values of the prevailing system. This process is called "channeling" by those who study processes of social stratification; that is, it is by means such as those mentioned above that societies channel individuals into acceptable occupations regardless of individual needs or preferences. Thus, the military (and especially the selective service system) serves as a system of domestic social control, as a way of compelling individuals to satisfy the requirements of the system, even though these citizens might be unaware of or hostile to these requirements.

Sperber concludes by pointing out that the results of this military cooptation are, however, paradoxical:

On the one hand, it tends to lessen the opportunities for a revolutionary movement emerging in certain strata of American society, e.g., the poor, women, racial minorities. On the other hand, the process of military cooptation actually enhances the prospects for a revolutionary movement among youth as a social class, particularly from within the armed forces themselves. Black and poor white men are likely to revolt from within the military establishment not so much because they are black or poor per se . . ., but rather because they share the progressive relative deprivation characteristic of an exploited class whose members are situated in ecologically dense or crowded areas and enabled to communicate their grievances among themselves. In the short run, co-optation does inhibit or neutralize dissent, and is thus essential for the preservation of the status quo. In the long run though, the very process of co-optation itself facilitates the development of an even larger and more revolutionary class.[14]

Thus, Sperber's analysis helps explain in part the antimilitary rebelliousness of the late 1960's and early 1970's both within and without the military. This rebellion included individual and collective acts ranging from increased narcotics use, through refusal to carry out orders and fragging (trying to kill one's commanding officer), to demonstrative protests and draft evasion. These acts of deviance are perceived to be a function of and response to a pathological society, rather than a result of individual pathologies.

Weaknesses of the Radical Pathology Perspective of Militarism. There is much that is suggestive and provocative in these new views of pathology, and, as indicated above, Chapter 6 will consider these aspects in more detail. Specifically, the new view represents a type of paradigm revolution that is questioning the basic assumptions and philosophies of earlier views. The new view, however, also suffers from some of the same kinds of biases that were faults of the older view. Just as earlier pathologists assumed that there was a conscious, almost deliberate, characteristic within individual deviants, some new pathologists assume a conscious, manipulated deviance within the system. For example, older pathologists felt that if one could teach the poor to honor the work ethic, the propensity and desire toward laziness could be cured. New pathologists feel that, if one can identify and make overt the oppressive characteristics within contemporary society, more humane views will prevail through revolutionary response, and the social sickness can thus be cured.

These assumptions are based upon latent value judgments, which may not be valid. First, in the same way that research shows the poor to possess strong commitments to the work ethic despite the acceptance of welfare as a necessary fact of life, political and military leaders may possess strong commitments to equality, dissent, and freedom despite the way the system seems to work. Thus, merely changing attitudes may not be what is required, since the function of the modern military as an employment device or technique for cooptation may not be the manifest purpose of many leaders. Indeed, the willing recent abolition of the draft seems to support this conclusion. Second, as earlier views assumed an obvious unworthiness and inferiority in the acts of deviants, newer views often assume an obvious undesirability in what the system is doing and how it works. Sociologically, however, systems (be they primitive societies, medieval fiefdoms, or industrial states) do tend to channel individuals into what are considered to be important and necessary occupations. In a context of totally free and individual choice, and without some means of inducement, societies might not be able to survive specific challenges and crises, with resulting disadvantages to many (or most) citizens. In other words, there is nothing immoral or wrong per se with the social necessity for established norms, values, and preferences. Some degree of conflict is inevitable between the two primary social necessities; that is, between the conservative social system requirement for order and continuity, and the revolutionary necessity for deviance and change, referred to in Chapter 1. However, despite these theoretical weaknesses, the new pathologists, such as Schevitz and Sperber, ask a critical question about this traditional dichotomy in social life: Where in contemporary social life are we unknowingly utilizing the wrong institutions for inappropriate purposes in unacceptable ways? Specifically, is the modern military the desirable vehicle, whether through intent or accident, for guaranteeing the preservation of the modern industrial state and the control of the domestic population? That there was growing concern for this kind of issue is evidenced by the moves, in the early 1970's to abolish the draft, reform the armed services, and diminish the amount and use of both domestic and international military power—moves made even by some conservatives in the military and the federal administration.

The Deviance Paradigm

One of the most popular and persistent paradigms in social science is the concept that social problems result from violations of accepted norms in a society. This perspective arose early in the discipline and is still influential today, since its more sophisticated adherents do not express the overt bias present in the old and new theories of pathology. In addition, the deviance paradigm became popular since it encouraged much empirical research, left room for all kinds of puzzle solving, and provided a necessarily general theory for stimulating scientific work.

This paradigm saw behavior and events that depart from the expected as deviant. Whereas the older pathology view concentrated analysis upon the deviants themselves, as people who were injurious to society, the deviance paradigm shifted the scientific focus to the nature, causes, and consequences of the injurious acts.[15] Deviance theorists reasoned that some individuals had to learn deviant forms of behavior through two kinds of processes: (1) as a consequence of restricted opportunities for learning conventional behavior and (2) through increased opportunity for learning deviant ways.[16] Thus, these theorists became essentially interested in the question of why some people in society learned to be deviant, while most others learned to conform. Furthermore, this paradigm was extremely popular in social science because most deviance theorists did *not* see this form of behavior as inherently bad or undesirable. Therefore, they avoided the more obvious bias of earlier and later theories of pathology. Indeed, some negative forms of deviance (including typical problems such as crime, drug usage, violence, and sexual aberration) were sometimes seen as serving to provide society with ways of punishing transgressors, thereby reaffirming accepted norms for the majority of citizens.

In other words, some deviants can serve as *negative role models* for society in that action taken to inhibit or alter their deviance vividly demonstrates to others what is not tolerated. For example, recent federal prosecution of people like Fr. Daniel Berrigan and Dr. Daniel Ellsberg can be understood in these terms. An interesting question about Ellsberg's prosecution for disclosure of the Pentagon Papers is: Why should the government pick this individual for special legal sanction when federal officials, often including the president of the United States himself (or former Secretary of the Interior, Walter Hickel), frequently disclose or leak classified and privileged information for special political and personal reasons? Elaborate security systems of secrecy, especially those involving the military and war, can perform what some sociologists have called "boundary-maintaining" functions. The leaking of sensitive information, followed by the public prosecution of those responsible, provides leadership with a way of controlling political behavior. In this sense, the Ellsbergs serve as examples of what is and is not acceptable, how far the boundaries of appropriate behavior can be stretched, and what will happen to those who go beyond these limits.[17] In the same way, the Berrigans serve as examples of what will happen to citizens who challenge in extreme ways the accepted policies of federal leadership. For this reason, many have termed these cases examples of political trials rather than prosecution for legal crimes. To this extent, then, conventional society often depends upon some observable deviance for the perpetuation of conventionality, and squares and straights can become dependent upon the existence of at least some hippies and freaks.

In addition, deviance theorists argued that some deviants could become *positive role models*. Positive deviance is behavior that varies significantly from the accepted but that, because of the peculiar situation, is rewarded in exceptional ways. For example, the hero in battle who becomes an expert in killing the enemy is given medals and public recognition, or the religious prophet who denounces materialism is admired despite his opposition to accepted norms. Emile Durkheim, one of the founders of sociology, was the first to develop this view in his study of suicide.[18] He distinguished between altruistic suicide, on the one hand, and anomic and egoistic suicide, on the other. Through an examination of suicide rates in different cultural contexts in the 1800's, Durkheim found that variations for this deviant act by social characteristics of groups were great. Protestants tended to have higher rates than Catholics; servants tended to take their own lives on the death of their masters; career military professionals showed a propensity toward suicide; and high rates of divorce and separation were correlated with high rates of suicide. Durkheim hypothesized that, whereas the typical view of suicide saw this form of deviance as a consequence of a breakdown or weakening of accepted norms or inherent pathologies within individuals, some suicides actually resulted from *a strong commitment to special norms, a kind of positive deviance*. Thus, egoistic suicide among Protestants is a result of their greater individual dependence upon personal strengths in contrast to Catholic commitment to group norms. A military officer, on the other hand, may altruistically take his life because this is the accepted way of saving face or the honorable and heroic thing to do. Or, those who are divorced and separated become lonely and dissociated from prevailing norms (a state of anomie), but servants take their lives altruistically because of a desire to honor and serve their master even after death. During World War II, Japanese Kamikazi pilots committed altruistic suicide by diving planes onto United States naval ships; more recently Buddhist monks set themselves afire in South Vietnam to protest the war and the tyranny of the Saigon government.

However, despite the attempts by deviance theorists to avoid the more blatant biases of the pathology perspective, the deviancy paradigm contains its own special assumptions. Expected behavior, accepted norms, and conformity to conventionality become the standard against which all other behavior must be measured to determine if it is deviant. Though deviancy was not necessarily seen as inherently bad, it was seen as disruptive, or injurious to the orderly functioning of the social system. Both positive and negative forms of deviance create crises, threats, problems, and challenges. Therefore, deviance should be corrected, diminished, or, at the very least, held to a minimum. These kinds of assumptions in the paradigm have become the basis for increasing criticism of the deviancy view in recent years, as we will see at the end of this chapter.

The general nature of the deviance paradigm illustrates Kuhn's concept of the successful scientific perspective. Its focus upon the special nature of deviant subgroups in society creates a context within which social scientists can propose all kinds of theories, conduct a variety of empirical studies, solve a number of challenging puzzles, and recommend a number of programs of action to resolve the problems being analyzed.

A Continuum of Deviant Behavior.   For example, Ruth Cavan suggests that laws are of little help or use when applied to juvenile delinquency, since they tend to be specific norms applicable essentially to adult criminal offenses. This situation is amply reflected by the confusion and variation that characterizes the way in which different states and legal jurisdictions define and deal with juvenile delinquents. She proposes a view that conceives of behavior as ranging along *a continuum from extreme underconformity to extreme overconformity,*[19] as illustrated in Diagram 4–1. The distribution of general human behavior patterns, with regard to its qualitative and quantitative aspects, tends to resemble a bell-shaped, or normal, curve. Most

Diagram 4–1

A representation of the distribution of general behavior patterns, ranging from the negative-deviance extreme (underconformity) to the positive-deviance extreme (overconformity.) *

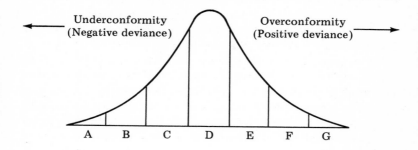

A - Underconforming contraculture
B - Extreme underconformity
C - Minor and tolerated underconformity
D - Range of normal conforming behavior
E - Minor and tolerated overconformity
F - Extreme overconformity
G - Overconforming contraculture

* After Ruth S. Cavan, "The Concepts and Contraculture as Applied to Delinquency," *The Sociological Quarterly*, 2 (October 1961).

people conform and fall within area D, though infrequently they may engage in minor under- or overconformity (areas C and E). This type of behavior is considered conventional and acceptable, that is, within the boundaries of permissability. Those whose behavior falls into areas B and C represent marginal deviants. In the case of juveniles, underconformers (area B) tend to get into trouble with teachers, their parents, or police. If boys, they tend to commit acts of vandalism, smoke pot and use alcohol, or engage in minor theft and dangerous driving. If girls, they engage in sexual promiscuity or become truants and runaways. However, this type of behavior, though deemed as deviant by conventional standards, is considered amenable to programs of action and rehabilitation; thus society responds to extreme under- or overconformity with special laws.

remedial educational programs, parent–child community action, and the like.

In contrast, those whose behavior falls within areas A and G represent more than merely extreme deviants. These are individuals who have either *totally rejected accepted norms* and stand in complete opposition to them (underconformity) or have *compulsively adopted some accepted norms* in extreme forms (overconformity). Because of the extreme nature of their response, they build their own distinct contracultures with unique values and patterns of behavior. Illustrations of under-conforming contracultures (area A) include: youth gangs where stealing, aggressiveness, and violence are rewarded and praised; and hippie subcultures where sexual freedom, the rejection of traditional religion and materialism, and the experimental use of hallucinogens are the norm.[20] In contrast, but similarly, over-conforming contracultures (area G) come in the form of youth who become "grinds" or "brains" and have to be encouraged to "have fun like normal people"; peaceful but committed and activist conscientious objectors to war; and superpatriotic groups and members of evangelical religious cults and idealistic utopian communities. Though the deviance paradigm assumes behavior in the contracultures to be as much a result of learning as are the other types of deviance, the implication is that social action must be different depending upon the type of deviant behavior. In addition, Cavan's theory takes into account the *relative* aspect of behavior judgment not present in pathology perspectives—that is, her theory recognizes that what is deviance to one group in society may not be deviance to another. Thus, the deviancy paradigm is amenable to humanitarian and liberal interpretations of problem behavior.

Theory of Deviance as Conflict Between Means and Ends. Robert Merton has supplied another typology based upon the notion of a *conflict between means and ends.*[21] Some individuals become frustrated when they lack the means for obtaining culturally accepted goals, while others reject the goals of society while automatically accepting the means, and still others reject both the means and the goals. Utilizing this concept, Merton proposes five alternative forms of behavior, four of which can be used to describe types of deviance (see Table 4–1).

Table 4–1

The acceptance and rejection of societal means and goals associated with five types of behavior*

	Acceptance $(+)$ or Rejection $(-)$ of	
Type of Behavior	*Means*	*Goals*
Conforming	$+$	$+$
Innovating	$-$	$+$
Ritualism	$+$	$-$
Retreatism	$-$	$-$
Rebellion	$+/-$	$+/-$

* After Robert K. Merton, *Social Theory and Social Structure*, rev. ed. (New York: The Free Press, 1964), p. 140.

Conformists obviously accept both the goals of society and the means considered appropriate for obtaining those goals, whereas those who reject both means and goals tend to become retreatists. Retreatism can result in a variety of different kinds of problem behavior: psychoneurosis, vagrancy, alcoholism, narcotics use, living in isolation, becoming a tramp or hermit, and the like. In contrast, ritualists give up striving for goals, which they may feel are unattainable, and they content themselves with conformity to respectable behavior. Indeed, such a commitment to conventionality may become extreme and exaggerated and result in Cavan's contraculture, to the extent that the over-conforming behavior goes far beyond typical and expected patterns. Ultrapatriots, who insist upon rigid commitment to the use and expression of nationalistic symbols, and bureaucrats, who adhere to the rules no matter what the practical situation demands, are examples. Innovators accept the goals but feel that prevailing means are ineffective or useless. Civil disobedience, disruptive behavior, or bizarre protest may be seen as the only way in which the goals of freedom, equality, and justice can be achieved. Criminals also frequently express the innovative perspective, arguing that what they are doing is essentially what everyone else is doing in the daily rat race (striving for economic and prestige awards), but that conventional means are unavailable to them. Finally, rebels are deviants who reject old means and goals but seek to create new ones. Critics of the contemporary American political system, the

Women's Liberation Movement, and groups advocating a new sexual morality have all been influenced on occasion by the rebellion perspective.

The Theory of Differential Association—Examples from Delinquency and Accident Research. To adherents of the deviance paradigm, the obvious remedy for social problems lies in re-socialization, through training, education, or propaganda. If deviance is learned, then it must be unlearned and conventional behavior must be relearned. Edwin Sutherland's *theory of differential association* gave full expression to this view.[22] He argued that an individual becomes delinquent when conditions favorable to the development and acceptance of normative violation outweigh conditions unfavorable to such violations. Criminal behavior, then, arises as a consequence of contacts with criminal subcultures and isolation from anticriminal influences. Involved in this process are both the individual and the nature of the situation. For example, a sociable, gregarious, and active boy in the suburbs may become a member of a scout troop, whereas a psychotic, introverted, and isolated boy in the same context may drift into forms of deviant behavior. In contrast, the active boy in city ghettos will be drawn to delinquent subcultures, whereas an isolated boy in that context will stay at home and out of trouble.[23] For the last several decades, this theory has encouraged a variety of studies of the learning processes involved in deviant behavior,[24] and it has become the basis for community action programs in urban ghettos to provide youth with nondelinquent alternatives. It has also become the basis for recognizing that many of our prisons create crime rather than acting as a deterrent or rehabilitator.[25] This latter recognition is reflected in the fact that the known and estimated recidivism rate (those who repeat as criminals after release from prison) generally runs from 60 to 70 percent.

The concept of learning as an important element in deviant behavior has led some social scientists to utilize the paradigm in provocative ways to examine unusual kinds of social problems. For example, Edward Suchman has analyzed *accidents as a form of deviance.*[26] He points out that though accidents are a major cause of injury and death, research in this area has generally neglected the behavioral aspects. Little is known about the nature and causes of accidents, despite the fact that they are the leading cause of death for people between the ages of 1 and 34 years of age and account for more than one-half the deaths in the 15- to 24-year-old age group. He suggests that this is undoubtedly a function of the fatalistic view of accidents, the natural popular myth of social problems, which sees these kinds of events as chance occurrences beyond scientific control.

Suchman, however, indicates that accident statistics clearly reveal accidental injury and death are not distributed by chance among subgroups in society. Furthermore, accidents can be classified as a kind of social pathology and, thereby, subjected to analysis using the deviance perspective. For example, automobiles, which constitute the single most important agent of accidental deaths and injuries in the United States, can be seen in some cases as deadly weapons, and those who utilize them for this purpose reflect an underlying social pathology. Thus, automobile accidents, like homicide or suicide, may typify the socialization of aggression. Some research suggests that children in families with higher cohesion and belief in tradition are less likely to have various types of accidents than children from families that are not well-integrated. In other words, accidents can be a result of an opportunity context, where anti-accident learning is less available than proaccident learning. Those scholars who attribute part of the high rate of childhood accidents to a strong emphasis upon aggression and violence in the mass media are arguing that the propensity towards accidents is taught through some of the major socializing agencies of contemporary society.

Suchman hypothesizes that to the extent to which society has institutionalized certain safe modes of behavior, departures from this norm can be viewed as deviant. For some individuals, repeated accidents may be a symptom of individual deviance in the form of what Merton has termed the rejection of conventional means and/or goals. For example, studies show that individuals who are accident prone are more likely to have court records of law violations than individuals with few accidents. National Safety Council statistics show that three out of four fatal automobile accidents involve serious violations of traffic laws. What may be significant behaviorally is not the accident per se but rather the deviance in the form of the violation. Furthermore, many traffic laws do not work well in controlling behavior, and, therefore, some violations are treated by police and citizens as "folk crimes," that is, deviance that is ignored or condoned. This suggests a pathological condition within society as a whole. Finally, Suchman refers to studies that demonstrate the anti-social nature of some accident repeaters. One study of taxicab drivers found that repeaters were more likely to have records of disciplinary problems, being fired from the job, and bootlegging (taking on other employment) on the job. In addition, they were more likely to have had police and juvenile court records and to have been AWOL (Absent Without Leave) while in military service. Thus, the driver's behavior in his cab reflected the same aggressiveness, impulsiveness, lack of social concern, and disrespect for authority that characterized his personal life in other contexts.[27]

Critiques of Deviance

As Thomas Kuhn pointed out, one of the ironies of a successful scientific paradigm is that some of the reasons for its popularity and usefulness can also become over time bases for increasing criticism and discontent with the paradigm. This is certainly true of the deviancy perspective. Its generality and its tendency to create a multitude of puzzles to be resolved accounted for the popularity of the paradigm for many decades. At the same time, this generality and the persistence of many unanswered puzzles has led to increasing attacks upon the paradigm in recent years, so much so that we may, quite possibly, be witnessing the beginnings of a paradigm revolution. Criticisms of the deviance paradigm generally fall into three categories: those that maintain that implicit value judgments may be built into the perspective; those that question the view that deviants are uniquely aberrant; and those that criticize the assumptions that deviance is easy to identify and that most people agree as to which acts are deviant.

Bias and Value Judgments in the Deviance Paradigm. The first criticism raises questions about the deviance paradigm's implicit value judgments, in spite of many careful qualifications offered by advocates of the perspective. Some critics have claimed that the deviance paradigm substitutes for sociologists, in slightly more sophisticated language, the conventional wisdom that "some people are no damn good," or, in other words, the notion that evil can lead to evil or that evil must lead to evil. This view is evident in the learning and socialization emphasis of the paradigm. Despite attempts by deviance adherents to argue that this form of behavior can serve larger social purposes, and is, therefore, not necessarily bad, the paradigm still views deviant behavior as *disruptive*, as something which must be *contained or controlled*, and as *correctable* by the reeducation of the individual deviants. In addition, negative deviance is sometimes seen as bad, while positive deviance may be seen as "not quite so bad."

Essentially, the propensity toward value judgment has become built into the deviance paradigm and is, therefore, difficult to avoid no matter how careful its practitioners may be. Such judgments are integral to the nature of a paradigm that defines problem behavior as those acts that deviate from some generally accepted, normal, or widely approved norm. Many who use the paradigm must, therefore, adopt society's definitions of what constitutes deviant behavior. In a consideration of deviant behavior theory and criminology in Britain, Stan Cohen points out that this dependence often makes theory generated strangely non- or antisociological.[28] For example, studies of crime as deviance must assume that something is wrong with the criminal, rather than focus upon the larger society. At the same time, deviance theory leads to the assumption that, because deviant behavior exists, social control is necessary. It is just as possible sociologically to assume that deviant behavior arises because of certain types of social control; this latter assumption, however, calls for a different paradigm or perspective.

In a similar manner, Alexander Liazos has pointed to the problems inherent in traditional deviance theory.[29] He recognizes that new theory differs from older pathology views in that it is based upon more extensive and detailed research; provides a needed theoretical framework for analysis; has abandoned the small-town morality, which assumed that all deviance was necessarily bad; and has become more solidly related to basic sociological perspectives of human behavior, whether deviant or normal. However, Liazos argues that the *deviance paradigm is still essentially microsociological*; it focuses upon the deviant himself rather than upon the larger social system. This focus leads to a concentration upon dramatic forms of individual deviance (prostitution, homosexuality, and juvenile delinquency), which Liazos characterizes as the "sociology of nuts, sluts, and perverts." The difficulty is that covert, latent, and elitist or systemic forms of deviant behavior are almost totally ignored (racism, sexism, exploitation, war, and the like). In other words, a fundamental concern for the nature of power in contemporary society and the role that power plays in social problems is totally absent. Concepts such as victimization, persecution, and oppression rarely receive detailed attention in the social science literature on deviance. This is partly a function of the moral and political biases built into the deviance paradigm.

Recent research has begun to raise serious questions about these biases, especially the assumption that societal definitions of what constitutes good or bad forms of deviance is an adequate guideline for scientific study. For example, in a study of the attitudes of American GI's in Vietnam, Charles Moskos found that the battlefield hero was often as disliked as the coward and the home-front superpatriot was as disrespected as the peace demonstrator.[30] Cowards were disliked because they represented threats to the lives of men in a fire fight. If one could not count on the support of his buddy, he was more vulnerable to being wounded or killed by the enemy. At the same time, the hero was seen as one who often took unnecessary and dangerous risks, engaged in acts that called attention to him despite the needs of his buddies, or led dangerous missions to achieve honor and glory, thus endangering the lives of all for no military purpose. In a similar manner, state-side doves were viewed as people who gave aid and comfort to the enemy and denied support to their own fighting men, while state-side hawks were looked upon as hypocrites. Hawks asked others to do their dying for them, and when they visited the war zone to entertain or view the boys in action, they stayed out of the fire zones and lived in a privileged fashion. In other words, positive deviance was interpreted to be as much of a threat as negative deviance to the survival of the GI.

The deviance paradigm, then, has had difficulty in answering the crucial question: What form of deviance under what conditions is considered good or bad, and for whom and by whom? The research of Erving Goffman demonstrates how forms of deviance may become crucial to the sociopsychological survival of individuals in specific contexts. In an analysis of mental patients in a public hospital of over 7000 inmates and staff, Goffman found that patients adapted to the impersonal, bureaucratic, and pathological institutional context by engaging in what he called "secondary adjustments." *Primary adjustments* are adaptations that occur in the form of strict adherence to formal rules and regulations, in other words conventional behavior. In contrast, *secondary adjustments* occur in the form of using unauthorized means to obtain unauthorized ends; they are a means by which inmates can strike out against the rigid impersonality of the institution's formal organization.

Inmates generally selected secondary forms of adaptation, as did many on the staff. For example, radiators were used for drying clothes (unintended use of artifacts); therapy sessions were used for dating girl friends (exploitation of official routines); a back porch was used for associating with the staff as equals (rejection of the public character of the institution); a patient with canteen privileges filled shopping lists for those in restricted wards (underground transportation system); and surreptitious sexual relations were engaged in to gain favors from attendants or other patients (private coercion by making use of other persons).[31] In addition, absenteeism was used to combat the official requirement for attendance at functions, pretended illness to combat the requirement for cure and good health, and apathy to combat the requirement for involvement. Goffman points out that these acts aimed at beating the system were more than simple rebellion. These forms of deviance became the only way in which many inmates and staff members could express dissociation from the formal environment, while also expressing the potential they possessed as creative, unique, and independent individuals. Deviance, therefore, not only became a natural part of the mental hospital system, it also became necessary for the survival of many within that system. In this sense, deviant behavior became an expression of normality, and conventionality became aberrant.

Who Is Aberrant?—The Example of "The Good People" and "The Dirty Workers."   Goffman's study of the deviant context of the mental hospital relates to the continuing work of Everett Hughes, who has asked, "Who really deviates?" This, essentially, is the second major criticism of the deviance paradigm, which raises fundamental questions about using accepted norms as a basis for judging conforming citizens to be normal and conventional and deviants to be the ones who are *uniquely* aberrant. Hughes suggests that many deviants do what they do because conventional society wants them to perform these tasks. Thus, conventional society only appears to be conformist as a kind of respectable veneer of civilization, while at root most citizens may be latently as deviant as those they label deviants. This view is closely related to the new pathology perspective. In an essay written after he had viewed the remains of the Nazi *Endloesung* (final solution) of "the Jewish problem" in Germany in 1948, Hughes dealt with the question of how such an unbelievable program of mass murder, torture, and sadism could take place in the name of racial superiority and purity in a seemingly civilized and modern society.

In raising this question, Hughes suggests that two issues are involved.[32] One concerns the "good people," who did not themselves do the "dirty work," but who obviously let it happen. The other concerns the people who actually did the "dirty work." Hughes found in conversations with ordinary Germans after World War II that a specific relationship emerged between good people and dirty work. Characteristically, the good people of Germany disclaimed any knowledge of what was actually happening in the death camps. Hughes points out, however, that while those in command of the program (the Black Shirts or

S.S.) kept the more gory details a secret, the common people of Germany knew the camps existed. Some people had disappeared into them, and some could be seen in rags being transported to them or working in forced labor in factories or fields nearby. Furthermore, Hitler's *Mein Kampf* clearly stated that no fate was too horrible for the Jews and other inferior people. Though the good people of Germany disclaimed any knowledge of what was happening (some type of knowledge was available despite secrecy enforced by fear and terror), they also expressed the anti-Semitic feelings that something had to be done about the Jews, who were generally considered inferior and threatening to the prevailing social system.

Hughes concludes that the pariahs who do the dirty work of society are really acting as agents for the good and conventional people. In this manner, the good people can have it both ways: they can dissociate themselves from dirty acts, claim ignorance of the most extreme manifestations, and express shame when the extremes are made evident. Yet, at the same time, they can let someone else handle the problem that they themselves do not want to deal with or even know about. Hughes indicates that the obvious analogy to contemporary society is the manner in which the conventional permit and encourage special handling for criminals, the mentally ill, the aged, youthful demonstrators, narcotic users, and frustrated residents of black urban ghettos. As long as the dirty workers do not beat, oppress, or kill members of these groups in public, good people are content to know that "something is being done about the problem" of crime, dangerous psychotics, useless aged citizens, ill-mannered youth, deviants who use narcotics, or inferior races.

As Hughes points out, the problem is compounded by the fact that every society contains a supply of candidates for the job of dirty workers. Often these individuals are men or women who have a history of failure, of poor adaptation to the conventional demands of work and leisure, and of inadequate commitment to the humanitarian norms of larger society. Indeed, dirty workers very often come from the same socioeconomic and environmental backgrounds of those whom they are asked to control or handle. If they were not dirty workers, they might be the objects of someone else's dirty work. In addition, most societies seem to contain a sufficient reservoir of psychopathic personalities to do any amount of dirty work the good people will countenance. It is not surprising, then, that modern prisons are often inhumane, that police sometimes employ brutality, that homes for the aged frequently resemble "snakepits," or that mental institutions tend to be real nightmares.

Who Is Aberrant—The Case of the Police, Soldiers, and Ghetto Agency Workers.   Other social scientists have pointed to recent additional aspects of the problem of good people and dirty workers. William Westley's investigation of the uses of violence by the police, done long before the popular concern for police brutality, raised the question of whether there was something inherent in the role that encouraged the extralegal or illegal use of physical force.[33] Such research has specific relevance to the continuing legal debate over the rights of individuals versus the need to control crime in the apprehension, arrest, and processing of suspects. Westley found that the police most often perform as dirty workers, and, as a result, they may be hated and feared equally by the objects of their dirty work and by the good people for whom they do the dirty work. During a participant-observation study of the police force of a Midwestern city, Westley asked police under what conditions they thought they were justified in roughing up a man. Over one-third mentioned disrespect for police; about one-quarter mentioned situations in which violence was impossible to avoid, and almost 20 percent designated contexts where information had to be obtained. Eight percent or less justified the use of violence when it was necessary to make an arrest, in the treatment of hardened criminals, when a policeman knew a man was guilty, and when dealing with sex criminals. In other words, only about one-third of the police made reference to *legal* uses of violence (when it is impossible to avoid and in order to make an arrest). The remaining reasons given were based upon *illegal* uses.

Observation of the police in their daily roles led Westley to conclude that the propensity toward illegal use of violence was a function of several characteristics of the police role, all related to the issue of good people and dirty work. First, living in the public eye, the policeman is constantly criticized, particularly if crime rates increase; therefore, he must continually prove himself. At the same time, while criticizing overt brutality, good people demand efficient arrests. The good pinch, then, becomes important to the cop on the beat and if evidence or a confession can be obtained by beating a suspect up in an alley, then these means will most likely be employed. The good people demand especially fast police work in the case of crimes involving sexual deviance, particularly child molestation. Where police beat up suspected sex offenders, they merely see themselves as carrying out the wishes of conventional society for a quick arrest and to "teach the guy a lesson."

For the policeman, the single most important use of violence is seen as the necessity to coerce respect. The frustrations of being a dirty worker boil over when a suspect acts as a "wise guy," a situation that policemen in Westley's sample felt justified the use of violence. At the same time, though there are individual variations among police in terms of attitudes about the use of violence, policemen do not condemn each other privately or publicly. Thus, violence, including its illegal use, becomes collectively sanctioned as a natural aspect of the aggressive and tough-guy nature of the role. It also becomes a relatively easy matter for policemen to cover up violence by claiming that a suspect resisted arrest or was accidentally injured in the confusion of the arrest procedure. Again, public attitudes demanding a militaristic, aggressive, and tough police force simply reinforce these propensities. Westley's research explains much of the reaction of the police in the late 1960's to youthful demonstrators, particularly at the time of the 1968 Democratic Convention in Chicago.

Westley's research also raises questions about other agencies of social control, such as the military. The commission of atrocities, where they occur as a matter of frequency and policy, are not isolated accidents of war. On the contrary, they may be military responses to the frustration of having to do the dirty work of good people with little or no reward. Or they can be the results of dirty workers doing what they believe the good people wish them to do. The tacit approval of the good people is often manifested by attitudes such as the majority public sentiment which favored leniency for Lt. William Calley when he was tried for killing defenseless civilians in a Vietnamese village. In 1972, Everett Hughes updated his original thesis by referring to the massive bombing of North Vietnam being conducted under the Nixon administration:

Every day several hundred young Americans, of the finest types, fly in their aircraft over North Vietnam and even over parts of South Vietnam, and perhaps over the borders into neighboring countries, and throw down bombs. The intent of these bombs is to destroy the country. . . . We have great ships firing from off shore at the mainland. . . . One can only say that the open aim of this bombing is to destroy the country and whatever people happen to get in the way. The people who don't happen to get in the way of the bombs still have to live in the desolated land. . . . This is a campaign of dirty work of a greater magnitude, I should think, than any other in history except what the Nazis did in their time. . . . It is obvious, certainly, from anyone who remembers the last World War, that there are great numbers of casualties of all kinds, women, children, men, soldiers—people of all kinds. . . . All we kill are, I suppose, communists by definition and, therefore, I suppose, not specially worth considering. The Jews were not considered human by the Nazis. . . . Do we make a great outcry against this destruction? We make hardly any outcry at all. We read the paper, lay it down, and turn on the weather.[34]

The concept of dirty work, then, questions the validity of the assumption that deviance is distinct from or unrelated to conventional behavior and citizens. That it is not may even be apparent to contemporary American dirty workers themselves. Lee Rainwater has pointed out that the job of controlling and confining the black ghetto-nation within America has been consigned to a number of dirty-work agencies by the majority of good white people:

As the urban ghettos have grown, so has the cohort of functionaries who receive the covert assignment to "keep the coloured out of our way." In the process, many institutions officially designed to further well-being and opportunity have become perverted into institutions of custody and constraint. Social-welfare workers find that their profession, designed to help, has been perverted into one designed to spy and to punish. More dramatically, the schools have become custodial institutions in which less and less learning takes place. . . . The proliferation of policemen in schools, of special schools for "incorrigible" children, and the like, testify to the prisonlike functions that undergird the educational rhetoric.[35]

Rainwater points out that, at the same time, the good people have generally been indifferent to the welfare of the dirty workers. Therefore, people recruited for those jobs have tended not to be the main breadwinners of their families, have been temporary workers, or have been motivated by desires for job security and tenure rather than by conventional American goals (such as money and social mobility). Furthermore, if teachers, welfare workers, and police were ever to spell out in precise detail what their duties really are, the delicate balance and dependence between the dirty workers and the good people would be seriously upset.

Yet this is exactly what has started to happen. Dirty workers are striking not just for increased pay but also for demands related to the dangers of the dirty work and for the respect denied them by the good people. In other words, prison guards, welfare workers, teachers in urban schools, and policemen have all begun to strike for "combat pay." The response of the good people has been bewilderment, denial of complicity, or shame, similar to the response of the good people of Germany after World War II. At the same time, the objects of the dirty work have also begun to strike. Prison inmates, black ghetto residents, ghetto schoolchildren, welfare recipients, and others are increasingly and vocally demanding that they be freed from the good-people–dirty-work syndrome. Rainwater concludes that:

It is encouraging that those expected to do the dirty work are rebelling. But it is really too much to expect that they will admit their own individual culpability, at least as long as the rest of us won't. [Any more than the S.S. or the good people of Germany have ever voluntarily admitted their participation in the extermination of the Jews.] Even so, the more the teachers, the police, and the welfare workers insist on the impossibility of their tasks, the more that society at large, and its political leaders, will have to confront the fact that our tacit understandings about the dirty work that is to be done are no longer adequate.[36]

In summary, the research and theory construction of Moskos on the military, Goffman on mental institutions, Hughes on dirty work, Westley on the police, and Rainwater on the revolt of the dirty workers raises basic questions about the inherent assumptions that only deviants are deviant. This type of work also introduces the fundamental question of who defines and who *should* define an act as deviant, which leads to the final major criticism of the paradigm.

Problems in Defining and Recognizing Deviance. Use of the paradigm implies the additional assumption that most people overtly agree upon the nature of social problems as exemplified in deviant behavior, that deviance is easy to define and study because it is so obvious and evident. Recent experience suggests the opposite. In an increasingly heterogeneous and rebellious social context, most people do not agree on normative limits for behavior, and deviant behavior becomes extremely difficult to recognize and categorize. The contemporary debate over appropriate limits to drug usage is an obvious example. Is marijuana to be treated in the same fashion as hard narcotics? Should the laws exempt drug use for religious or medical purposes? In addition, classic sociological distinctions between traditional and white-collar crime suggest that criminal behavior is not always readily recognizable and that, as Hughes has suggested, conventional people frequently have a close relationship with deviants and with deviant behavior.

Edwin Sutherland was the first social scientist to define white-collar crime as a violation of criminal law by a person of upper socioeconomic status in the course of his or her occupational activities.[37] Whereas *traditional crime* includes acts against property or persons committed by underprivileged and marginal citizens, *white-collar crime* includes acts such as fraud, stock manipulation, embezzlement, income tax cheating, misrepresentation in advertising, the buying of public favor and political influence, and the like. The problem is that such acts may not normally be considered deviant in a criminal sense (indeed, some argue that they are simply good or smart business), and the influence of the white-collar criminal makes arrest and prosecution highly unlikely. The concept today has also been used to refer to many of the activities of syndicated crime (prostitution, gambling, illegal narcotics and alcohol), which depend upon the support of the good people as clients for their maintenance and the support of legal authority for their continuance. The concept can also be applied to the kinds of actions disclosed in the hearings and trials following the 1972 U.S. presidential election. These included investigation of alleged political spying and espionage (the Watergate incident) conducted for members of the White House staff, illegal submission of FBI evidence to White House personnel, attempted interference by International Telephone and Telegraph in a presidential election in Chile, and illegal methods of obtaining campaign contributions by the National Committee to Reelect President Nixon. Here, too, many citizens dismissed evidence of these deviant acts as "just politics." The concept of white-collar crime, therefore, illustrates the difficulty in precisely defining exactly what constitutes a deviant act, since what seems to be deviance to some appears to be normal or expected behavior to others, even if the act involves some violation of laws and practices.

Deviance is not only difficult to define, but it is also difficult to identify and describe in precise terms because of inadequacies in the existing paradigm. One difficulty is that the deviance paradigm may not distinguish between the *motives* of individuals and the resulting deviant behavior. Judith Blake and Kingsley Davis argue that there are four possible relationships between motives and behavior (see Table 4–2).[38] The deviance paradigm typically deals with consistent conformists and consistent deviants, those whose motives relate directly to their actual behavior. Most social programs based upon reeducation to alter deviant acts assume this type of relationship. However, unintentional deviance is also possible, where individuals (because of error, misunderstanding of the rules, or inability to

Table 4–2
The relationship between motives and actual behavior for different types of conforming or deviating persons*

Type of Person	Motives	Behavior
Consistent conformist	+	+
Unintentional deviant	+	−
Intended but unsuccessful deviant	−	+
Consistent deviant	−	−

* After Judith Blake and Kingsley Davis, "Norms, Values, and Sanctions," *Handbook of Modern Sociology*, Robert E. L. Faris, ed. (Chicago: Rand McNally, 1964), p. 468.

conform) wish to conform but actually deviate. In addition, there are those who might intend to deviate but do not do so either because they are motivated by the rewards and punishments for approved behavior or because they lack the opportunity structure for deviation. The latter situation could be the reason why Sutherland and others have found that white-collar crime is relatively low among lower socioeconomic racial and class groupings.

Therefore, it follows that some deviance can be unrecognized and that some deviants may be falsely accused in terms of their motives. Table 4–3 depicts the relationship between actual behavior and perceptions of that behavior by others, for conforming and deviating behavior, as delineated by Howard Becker.[39] Again, the classic deviance paradigm tends to assume that most cases will involve either true conformists or true deviants, that is, those who conform or deviate and are clearly identified as such by themselves and others in society. Becker, however, argues that there are two other categories of possibilities, which might be more relevant to contemporary society. Secret deviants are successful in keeping their behavior from observable public view. For example, the special condemnations of homosexuality in many contemporary societies make it necessary for most engaging in this form of behavior to keep their acts a private matter. As a consequence, they become

Table 4–3

The relationship between actual behavior and perceptions of that behavior by others for conforming and deviating behavior*

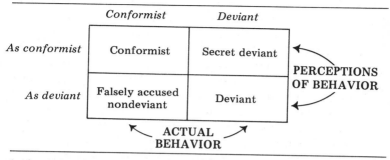

* After Howard S. Becker, *Outsiders: Studies in the Sociology of Deviance* (New York: The Free Press, 1963), p. 20.

susceptible to blackmail and other unique social pressures. For this reason, the Gay Liberation Movement has demanded the right to open, public acceptance of homosexuality, for those adults who voluntarily choose this type of behavior, and reports like that of the English Wolfenden Commission have attempted to respond legally to this need.

Becker's identification of falsely accused nondeviants is particularly important and has become the basis for the most persistent and successful recent criticism of the deviance paradigm, labeling theory, which is discussed in detail in the next section. What this typology suggests is that forms of behavior per se may not differentiate deviants from nondeviants. On the contrary, the responses of conventional and conforming people to suspected deviance may be more important in understanding the social processes that transform individuals into deviants. As John Kitsuse and Kai Erikson have indicated, the essential characteristics of a deviant or a deviant act may be external to the actor or the act.[40] In other words, the public, utilizing the myth of evil equals evil, frequently associates "unusual" or different behavior with all forms of deviance. Thus, those who dress, speak, or work and play in bizarre ways are seen as individuals who also engage in illicit sex, experiment with narcotics, steal, or commit atrocities and obscenities. None of these assessments may be correct. However, the more such views are expressed and the more they become a basis for programs of action to "correct the deviance," the more likely it is that accused individuals will come to conceive of themselves in these terms. Therefore, resulting true deviance may have become a function of public definitions that were not necessarily appropriate at the outset. Critics of deviance using this argument maintain that social scientists who adhere to the traditional deviance paradigm merely encourage and sustain this process.

Thomas Szasz has employed this perspective in denouncing public views of mental illness and resulting psychoanalytic and institutional care. He argues that "mental disease" is an imposed social definition placed upon individuals judged by others to be a threat to the community (therefore, deviant), to be disturbing or frightening (for example, someone who claims to hear voices), or to be burdensome (the aged).[41] By calling them mentally ill, the good people permit the removal of these people from the social order by dirty workers. This is a moral and political act, under the guise of a medical and scientific act. Szasz feels that the resulting treatment, which involves techniques such as involuntary group therapy, is inquisitorial oppression of the worst kind—it is society's attempt to enforce codes of conduct without regard for the personal needs of the individual. Furthermore, a normal person becomes defined as one whose behavior and beliefs coincide with those of the examining psychiatrist.

In cases of extreme deviance (for example, a man who killed his mother, cut off her head, and cooked it), the concept of mental illness or sickness merely becomes a seemingly scientific way of explaining an act that no one, including scientists, can understand. Szasz suggests that an explanation based upon witchcraft would be as helpful. Furthermore, compulsory treatment or incarceration in a mental institution merely substitutes psychiatric punishment for legal punishment. Acquittal for a crime by reason of insanity may result in an individual's being locked away in a madhouse for the remainder of his life. *The ironic fact of contemporary society is its willingness to confine people who are scientifically determined to be dangerous and insane, but not people who are dangerous but sane.* For example, statistics clearly indicate that mental patients are less dangerous than other groups in society. To be consistent, society should first confine all former convicts, all ghetto residents, right- and left-wing political extremists, all youth (especially males), and a significant number of businessmen and politicians. Actually, as Szasz suggests, the argument about danger is simply a cover. Most people confined for mental illness are not dangerous, but merely troublesome; and it is easier to blame the victim than to address the real problem. For example, the aged man who wanders through the community laughing and talking with young children may be forced into involuntary confinement or therapy because he is suffering from "senile psychosis." He is judged to be sick and potentially dangerous because his behavior does not conform to expectations. The actual reasons for the behavior may be neglect by his own family or children, but society, rather than treating these causes, chooses to punish the individual. This type of criticism of the use of the traditional perspectives of deviancy has given rise to an influential new school of thought in the last several decades: that of *labeling theory.*

Labeling Theory: A Paradigm Revolution?

As indicated in the previous discussion, the school of labeling theory is a partial attempt to respond to the evil-equals-evil notion inherent in the classical deviance paradigm. In addition, where the deviance paradigm assumes that problems are explicitly a result of deviant behavior, labeling theory questions the very existence of some forms of deviance, at least as it is defined by society. Labeling adherents criticize the traditional definition of social problems as *objective* conditions, identifiable by a significant number of people and subject to resolution through elaborate private and public programs of action. In contrast, they suggest that the *subjective definition* of a social problem as deviant behavior by individuals and groups within society is more important and may be unrelated to objective facts.[42] Labeling theory has become attractive to many new pathologists, since it concentrates on deviance in society rather than on deviance within individuals.

Labeling theorists are indebted to the early work of

Charles Cooley and George Mead who pointed to the important role of society in the creation of the *personal self* within individuals.[43] They argued that man is not born human but is made human through processes of socialization. He must learn values, norms, attitudes, styles of behavior—indeed, the newborn infant must learn everything about a society and culture in order to develop into a functioning adult member of that context. Cooley utilized the concept of the *looking-glass self*, which theorized that we come to see ourselves as we think other people see us. Just as we look into glass mirrors to obtain a concept of our physical nature, we look at the actions of others toward us, a kind of social mirror, to obtain a concept of our personal nature. Thus, it is not surprising that when teachers continually respond to underprivileged children as deviant or less capable than others, the underprivileged eventually come to see themselves in these terms.

In a similar manner, Mead argued that the *social self* consists of two distinct, but related, parts: the "I" and the "me." The "I" constitutes a reservoir of spontaneous, creative energy, is subjective in character, and enables humans to initiate behavior as independent actors. The "me" constitutes the individual's perceptions of himself as a result of behavior of others toward him, is objective in character, and enables humans to conform to the expectations of others. In the young child, Mead felt that the "me" developed initially, since the infant was so dependent for all of his physical and social needs. In the formative years, he is consistently treated as *an object* of the actions of others. In the balanced adult personality, however, a delicate relationship between the daring "I" and the conforming "me" will exist, but since the "me" emerges first, the propensity to see ourselves largely as others see us is predominant. As a consequence, if someone is continually treated as inferior, dangerous, and deviant, the chances are great that he will come to see himself in this way and act accordingly. In other words, the "me" will predominate over the "I" (which might be expected to resist and strike out against these social definitions), and an individual will conform to expectations, even if the expectations of him are unconventional. This process can often be observed in child rearing where a sibling considered exceptional begins to act in exceptional ways; a child labeled as active, in aggressive ways; or a child seen as "the quiet one in the family," in reticent ways.

The quick success and scientific popularity of labeling theory, as evidenced by the fact that it has already attained the status of a school of thought, is a function of a number of things. First, it is clearly rooted in basic and fundamental theories within the discipline of sociology, such as the theories of Cooley and Mead. That is, it is soundly sociological in nature. At the same time, however, it is raising serious questions about many classic sociological assumptions and perspectives, specifically the organic analogy, which sees social problems and deviance as unnatural. Second, like all successful contending paradigms, it leaves room for much theory formulation, puzzle solving, and empirical elaboration of basic perspectives, as well as provocative application of these views to contemporary issues.

Contributions of the Labeling Perspective—The Symbolic Importance of Deviant Acts. For example, Joseph Gusfield has suggested that the symbolic importance of deviant acts with regard to given norms, rather than the acts themselves, determines the societal response to a problem.[44] Therefore, if we wish to understand historical changes in the treatment of various forms of deviance, we must look at public responses, not at the deviance itself. Gusfield begins by distinguishing between instrumental and symbolic purposes of law. Most citizens view laws as having instrumental intent—that is, laws supposedly deter criminal offenses by making examples of those who break the law or by frightening those who contemplate law breaking. Many laws, however, have little instrumental value but do perform symbolic functions. These are frequently the laws that seem to be instrumentally unenforceable (those dealing, for example, with gambling, prostitution, abortion, narcotics, and alcohol use). The existence of such laws may comfort those, even a minority in society, who feel a commitment to the norms and values they represent. Symbolic laws also reflect a public affirmation of one set of norms or one type of behavior over another; that is, they express which subcultures are legitimate and which are not and, thereby, enhance the social status of groups committed to the norm and degrade those who are not by defining them as deviant. Such a symbolic function can, in many cases, be as effective a control as an instrumental function. For example, though there is widespread "patterned evasion" [45] of abortion laws, these laws do serve to label some individuals as deviants, with the result that abortions are difficult to obtain and must be sought through an underground subculture.

Gusfield points out that, particularly in the case of symbolic laws, the public will respond differently to deviant acts depending upon the degree to which the acts seem to threaten the symbolic importance of the law. Using this perspective, he identifies four different types of deviants. The *repentant deviant* is one who does not question or threaten the norm that has been violated. For example, a reckless motorist may willingly admit the legitimacy of traffic laws, or an alcoholic may agree that both he and society would be better if he could stay sober. Repentant deviants, therefore, are not considered a major problem; on the contrary, repentance and ultimate redemption are often considered, by the public-at-large and by courts, to be naturally related. Therefore, many juvenile delinquents use repentance as a technique for seeking lighter sentences, and the favorable differential treatment of middle-class delinquents over lower-class delinquents may be a result of the former's readiness and ability to play this game. Thus, deviant acts that attack a norm can be neutralized by repentance.

In contrast, deviant acts judged to be the result of sickness or illness neither attack nor sustain a norm. The *sick deviant* is given a social label by society in order to justify differential treatment in the form of cures or rehabilitation, rather than punishment, though as Szasz pointed out a more insidious form of punishment may result. Important to Gusfield's theory, however, is the fact that designating one as a sick deviant makes overtly hostile public response toward him inappropriate.

Gusfield calls those who commit professional crimes *cynical deviants*. Although acts such as kidnapping, burglary, murder, or theft call for control, they do not substantially threaten the legitimacy of the social order. Such conventional crimes are usually committed by individuals for self-serving purposes (for money, for personal revenge, in anger) and do not represent attempts to question prevailing convention. Even where criminals utilize appeals to repentance or sickness, their attempts to gain leniency are interpreted by the public as self-seeking, as an understandable attempt to get around the rules. Thus, Gusfield argues that traditionally accepted forms of deviance, such as crime, do not severely threaten the social system.

In contrast, the most severe threats come from the fourth type of deviance: *the enemy deviant.* In contemporary society, what is deviance in one context is seen as acceptable, even laudatory, behavior in another. Antitrust violations considered criminal by the middle class are interpreted as smart business tactics by the upper classes. Physical aggressiveness and prowess at stealing considered criminal by the middle classes are marks of leadership to some juvenile gangs. In other words, the deviant in these cases becomes an upholder of an opposite norm; within a certain group or context his behavior is therefore accepted as proper, and the public or some other definition of it as deviant is designated illegitimate. When such a situation arises, Gusfield argues that the ultimate definition of an act as deviant becomes a matter of power and status. The more powerful will prevail in terms of whether the law is upheld or modified. If formerly designated deviants achieve power through time, they may shift their efforts from violations of the norm to attempts at changing the designation. The history of the civil rights movement can be understood in these terms. What was once considered obviously deviant in a clearly segregationalist society is now open to political compromise. One of the reasons for these kinds of changes is that, in the case of enemy deviance, the powerful, or designators of deviance, may have power but they do not have legitimacy. Gusfield also suggests that the history of the temperance movement and prohibitions against the use of alcohol can best be understood in these terms, rather than in terms of some form of absolute deviance (drinking) being generally disapproved by fewer and fewer people:

My analysis of the American Temperance movement has shown how the issue of drinking and abstinence became a politically significant focus for the conflicts between Protestant and Catholic, rural and urban, native and immigrant, middle class and lower class in American society. The political conflict lay in the efforts of an abstinent

Protestant middle class to control the public affirmation of morality in drinking. Victory or defeat were consequently symbolic of the status and power of the cultures opposing each other.[46]

As the power and status of the Protestant middle class waned and the influence of the Catholic lower class became less threatening, alcoholism became defined less as enemy deviance and more as sick deviance. The popular definitions changed, rather than the nature of the act itself. The reactions to this form of deviance, therefore, are to be undertsood in terms of power and social conflict, not in terms of the inherent qualities of the act.

Societal Versus Self-Labels—The Source of Labeling Theory's Strength and Weakness.   In attempting to correct for the biases inherent in the deviance paradigm, labeling theory runs the risk of its own particular exaggeration. There is a tendency in the labeling perspective to assume in many cases of social problems that society's definitions are inappropriate or unrelated to the deviant's definitions and behavior. In reality, most cases of deviance do not seem to involve unintentional deviation or completely false accusations of deviance. On the contrary, much problem behavior involves a process of complex interaction between self-definitions and behavior by deviants *and* society's definitions and behavioral responses (as Mead's concept of the interaction between the "I" and the "me" indicated). The unique strength of labeling theory is to be found in its attempts to construct a theoretical bridge between the deviance paradigm, which concentrates only upon individual deviants as sources of problems, and a perspective which concentrates only upon the inappropriateness of many social responses to deviance.

Edwin Lemert has contributed a refinement of labeling theory that moves toward an integration with the traditional deviance paradigm. He distinguishes between primary and secondary forms of deviance. *Primary deviations* refer to daily norm violations committed by individuals who are clearly seen as being deviant relative to acceptable norms by themselves and others. *Secondary deviance* occurs when an individual assumes the role of a deviant as a means of defense, attack, or adjustment to societal reactions to him.[47] Lemert argues that classic deviance theory tended to deal only with primary types, whereas secondary forms are more important. Though, as we shall see at the end of this section, labeling theory is difficult to apply to covert deviant behavior, this distinction between primary and secondary deviance can be used to understand problems such as pre-marital sexual intercourse, normally a secret act. Ira Reiss has suggested that the process of labeling may begin when boys or others in a school or community categorize a girl as an easy sexual mark. A girl so labeled may decide to continue or increase her sexual activities in response to this group definition. Secondary deviance will, therefore, result when the girl develops an ideology to defend her behavior. She may come to define herself as sexually "mature and honest" and counterlabel her opponents as hypocritical prudes.[48]

To study the extent to which deviants play an active or deliberate role in the labeling process, two other researchers, Williams and Weinberg, analyzed responses to questions by members of the Mattachine Society of New York and the Society for Individual Rights in San Francisco, both homophile organizations. Respondents were asked if they had served in the military, what type of discharge had been received; whether a less than honorable discharge had been associated with homosexuality; and what experience they had with homosexuality prior to and in military service.[49]

Those respondents who had been discovered as homosexuals while in the military were recognized in three major ways. First, and most common, was discovery through another person as a result of jealousy, a lover's quarrel, or blackmail. In some cases, servicemen were discovered and persuaded by authorities to reveal previous sexual partners through threats, promises, or a search of personal effects (such as a diary). The second major means of discovery was found to be voluntary admissions, which is a means for obtaining release from military service. Since the military requires proof of homosexuality in order to grant a release from service, supplying names of partners becomes necessary. The most common reason given to Williams and Weinberg for the desire for release from military service was dissatisfaction with military life not, as might be expected, the unique pressures associated with homosexuality (fear of disclosure or ridicule, inability to control impulses). The final though relatively unimportant manner of discovery was through the homosexual's own indiscretion.

Williams and Weinberg found that most of the men they questioned who had received a less-than-honorable discharge had a high frequency of homosexual sex before induction into the military. In contrast, only about a third of the men questioned who had received an honorable discharge had frequent premilitary homosexual contacts. Similarly, a majority of those who had received a less-than-honorable discharge had a high frequency of sexual activity while in the service, compared to about 40 percent of those who received honorable discharges. In other words, there was a *correlation between the behavior of the men designated as homosexuals*, both in and out of the service, *and the perceptions and actions of military officials*. In addition, most of those men with less-than-honorable discharges usually had a military man as a sexual partner, compared to less than 20 percent of those with honorable discharges. In addition, it was found that those homosexuals who had high sexual frequency before induction were more likely to come to the attention of authorities by their own wish, that those whose in-service sexual activity was high were likely to be discovered through another person, and that those whose partners were predominantly other servicemen were more likely to be discovered through indiscretion. Williams and Weinberg conclude, therefore, that deviants do often play an important role in the labeling process. The relationship between type of military discharge and homosexuality, can only be fully understood in terms of the manner of discovery, or, in other words, in terms of the perceptions of deviants themselves, which in turn lead to the creation of official perceptions and definitions. Self and social labels, therefore, can be intimately related in problem behavior.

The primary importance of official definitions and perceptions of deviance, even in the face of contrary evidence, was dramatized in a recent experiment by D. L. Rosenhan of Stanford University.[50] Professor Rosenhan and seven associates shammed mild symptoms of mental disorder in order to gain admittance to public and private institutions. The participants lied only about their names and occupations (besides Rosenhan, there were two psychologists, a pediatrician, a psychiatrist, a painter, a housewife, and a graduate student) and the assertion that they heard unclear voices saying "empty," "hollow," or "thud" to them. They told the truth about normal emotions, actual relationships with others, and life histories and experiences. In seven cases, the diagnosis was schizophrenia; in one, manic-depression. Once admitted to an institution, each participant ceased simulating *any* symptoms of deviance and acted only in a cooperative manner, being instructed by Rosenhan to stay only as long as they could stand it. None were detected as frauds by the staff either before or after admittance, although one-third of the *inmates* during the first three hospitalizations recognized the absence of real mental problems. Some of these inmates commented to the participants that they believed them to be social scientists or journalists sent to spy upon conditions in the hospital. Even those participants who openly took lengthy field notes on observations were not discovered. The daily nursing comment on one participant read: "Patient engages in writing behavior."

Rosenhan concludes that psychiatrists, because of the fallability of conventional diagnosis, cannot distinguish between people who are mentally disturbed and those who are sane. The experiment also supports the theories of radical psychologists, such as R. D. Laing, who argue that mental disease has become a convenient social label designed to make life easier for doctors and relatives of bothersome patients. Finally, the context and environment of mental hospitals distorts judgment, through depersonalization and bureaucratization, and leads to the assumption that all inmates are deviant, regardless of the actual substance of their behaviors. In the case of Rosenhan's experiment, what had begun as a result of an interaction between self and social labels of deviance ended with *social labels predominating*, even though the allegedly deviant behavior had vanished. Having once been labeled as schizophrenic, manic-depressive, or insane, there was nothing a participant could do to overcome this definition. Even upon discharge, participants received the designation "in remission," which signified that in the hospital's view he or she was never sane and remained insane, albeit in latent form.

The Relationship Between Social and Self-Labels—Implications for Problems of Health and Alcoholism. Judith Lorber has contributed a typology, shown in Table 4-4, that attempts to relate different processes of social labeling and self-labeling to one another.[51] In addition, she uses this typology to study the concept of physical illness in an attempt to deal with the difficulty that labeling theory has in studying secret, undetected, or accidental deviance. In the first column of Table 4-4, it is shown that if an individual feels in good health and seems and acts to

Table 4-4
Social labels versus self-labels, and the results of their interaction in terms of social adjustment, for different types of conforming and deviating behavior*

	Conformity	Accidental deviance	Deliberate deviance
Conformity	Health	Minor illness	Concealed illness
Accidental deviance	Illness discovered by doctor	Treated illness	Conversion hysteria
Deliberate deviance	Refusal of treatment	"Parlayed" compensation case	Malingering

SOCIAL LABEL (right side)
SELF-LABEL (bottom)

* After Judith Lorber, "Deviance as Performance: The Case of Illness," *Social Problems, 14* (Winter 1967), p. 304.

others as though he is in good health, he conforms to expectations. If, however, he should go to a doctor who discovers he is ill, he becomes an accidental deviant. Two results are then possible. Either the individual accepts the doctor's definition and treatment, or he refuses treatment and may become categorized as a deliberate deviant, since he is permitting himself to get worse.

In the second column, workers who stay home from the job because of a fever or cold, define themselves as accidentally deviant, though they do not feel sick enough to visit a doctor or to obtain other social validations for the deviance. If the individual feels sick enough, he may visit a doctor to receive validation for his self-definition and thereby move to the "treated illness" category. Some workers may attempt to utilize self-defined illness for financial or personal gain but be refused validation by social authorities. Studies suggests that this latter form of deviance often occurs when one can no longer manage the demands of a job (for example, hard labor because of advanced age) or some socially imposed personal problem (from which retreat is necessary). In other words, disability is faked because it is a valid reason for escaping from the obligations of life, when publically accepted as true deviance. In addition, proven disability may bring financial recompense.

In the third column, individuals may want to avoid the label of illness, though knowing they are sick, in order to live as normal a life as possible. By trying to convey the impression that they are healthy to others, they become secret deviants. In the case of what Lorber calls "conversion reactions," individuals attempt to obtain a social label of accidental deviance rather than deliberate deviance. Hysterical symptoms are utilized to communicate an impression of physical disability, and a role of sickness is acted out. For example, women may use conversion reactions to reinforce dependence upon men, or men in veterans' hospitals may play this role to gain compensation for illnesses. If the social definition of accidental deviance cannot be obtained for the individual's symptoms, the label of malingerer may be given by doctors, psychiatrists, or one's family and work associates. Sometimes a psychiatric label of illness, instead of a medical label, can resolve the problem of distinguishing between accidental and deliberate deviance from the doctor's point of view. If the malingerer experiences no special disadvantages from such a label, it may also adequately serve his purposes and needs. In summary, Lorber points out that some deviants can attempt to manipulate social labels deliberately for special purposes, while others are the victims of arbitrarily imposed definitions.

One final example of the challenging use of labeling theory and research is to be found in the work of Harrison Trice and Paul Roman on Alcoholics Anonymous.[52] A.A. has constantly fascinated social scientists and citizens alike, because of the possibility of applying its method to other problems, a method that seems to deal successfully with a social problem for which there appears to be no other permanent solution. Trice and Roman argue that the processes of *delabeling* and *relabeling* are as important as initial labeling, and A.A. seems to be a unique agency for carrying out these processes. This is especially important since many forms of deviance, particularly alcoholism and mental illness, seem irreversible once the deviance has become secondary in nature. Trice and Roman suggest that there are three ways in which delabeling can take place. First, organizations of deviants may attempt to change the definitions of larger society (as in the case of Gay Liberation societies or those advocating the social use of marijuana). Second, professionals who play a key role in the labeling process may initiate delabeling ceremonies after treatment of the deviant has taken place. Delabeling consists of legitimate public pronouncements that the deviant is now ready for reentry into conventional society. To those who see this view as a possibility, the system of perfunctorily turning men out of prison (with a suit of clothes and a few dollars) after their term has ended is deplorable. When the criminal is processed, a fairly elaborate procedure labels him publicly deviant (arrest, processing, trial, incarceration). When he is released, no process delabels or relabels him.

Third, self-help organizations may be developed that encourage strict conformity to conventional norms and provide role models that are acceptable alternatives for the deviant. Alcoholics Anonymous uses this third method of resolving the problem of alcoholism. The organization accomplishes delabeling and relabeling in several ways.

First, it combats the general popular stereotype of alcoholism as a chronic problem that reflects inherent weakness or immorality by promulgating the *allergy concept*:

> *The substance of the allergy concept is that those who become alcoholics possess a physiological allergy to alcohol such that their addiction is predetermined even before they take their first drink. Stemming from the allergy concept is the label of "arrested alcoholic" which A.A. members place on themselves. The significance of this concept is that it serves to diminish, both in the perceptions of the A.A. members and their [family and friends], the alcoholic's responsibility for developing the behavior disorder. Furthermore, it serves to diminish the impression that a form of mental illness underlies alcohol abuse [a stigmatizing label]. . . . Associated with this is a very visible attempt on the part of A.A. to associate itself with the medical profession.*[53]

The allergy concept does aid the alcoholic in his reacceptance into conventional society, and it also provides him with a clear way of showing others and himself that he is rehabilitated—by giving up alcohol altogether. With the cessation of drinking, it can be assumed that the deviance will disappear and the problem has been solved. Trice and Roman point out that this type of delabeling process may not be applicable in all cases of deviance. For example, in the case of psychiatric disorders the question of what is wrong is rarely clear, and there are seldom any evident signs of cure, as Rosenhan's experiment indicated. Narcotics use seems to constitute a situation that falls somewhere between alcoholism and mental illness.

Second, A.A. stresses a *repentant role*, one, which as we have seen, is admired and accepted in many societies. This role provides the former deviant, the arrested alcoholic, with a vehicle whereby he can enter a new behavioral pattern acceptable to society. The role is vividly portrayed through public expressions of remorse and visibly reformed behavior.

A final means by which A.A. delabels and relabels, one that is closely related to repentance, is A.A.'s stress upon the skid row image and *upward mobility*, despite the fact that research indicates most members come from the middle or lower middle class. A.A. stories about "hitting the bottom" and total degradation maximize the distance traveled by arrested alcoholics in the process of their rehabilitation. Stress upon continued upward mobility fits the American ideology of the Horatio Alger myth. Thus, a new label, one acceptable to both the former deviant and society at large, is substituted once the old label has been removed.

Criticisms of Labeling Theory. This discussion has already implied several of the prevailing criticisms of labeling theory. Though Ira Reiss felt that the theory had some applicability to understanding illicit sexual behavior, he indicated that the utility of the perspective was partial and incomplete. He suggests that labeling theory is better suited to explanations of deviant behavior with high visibility and minimal subgroup support. Only when significant numbers of people in the larger population can clearly identify deviance, and when the labeled persons are a cohesive group capable of deliberate response, do social definitions of deviance seem to play a key role. For example, research on premarital sexual behavior shows that the majority of females who are promiscuous have relationships with very few partners. They also constitute a minority of the population. Though some may have accepted promiscuity because of social labels, *most* report an intimate love relationship with the male partner, accept their behavior as proper, and express little evidence that they have been driven to this form of deviance.[54]

Other scientists, such as Ronald Akers, have argued that labeling theory unjustifiably exaggerates the influence of social definitions. Akers agrees that labeling can create deviance and often operates to increase the probability that certain stigmatized persons will commit future deviant acts. He maintains, however, that the label per se does not create the behavior in the first place. People do commit deviant acts because of special social circumstances in their lives quite apart from the labels applied to them. Nor is the labeling process completely arbitrary and unrelated to the behavior of those detected and labeled.[55] To some extent, however, Akers' criticism is based upon an exaggeration of the most extreme adherents of labeling theory. For, as we have seen, theorists have utilized labeling theory, in combination with other views, to conceptualize and explain instances of falsely accused nondeviance (which do occur), deliberate secret deviance, and accidental deviance. All these instances can involve little relationship between self-conceptions or behavior and public social definitions.

Jack Gibbs has made a more telling criticism by pointing out that labeling theory cannot adequately explain why the incidence of a particular act varies from one subgroup to another; why some persons commit deviant acts and others do not; and why an act may be considered deviant in some societies and not in others—all important sociological questions.[56] In other words, *new labeling theory is not a total substitute for the old deviance paradigm; rather the two should be incorporated and combined.* The paradigm can supply answers to the kinds of questions raised by Gibbs, whereas labeling theory introduces the importance of other variables. For example, Leroy Gould studied the relationship between official delinquency statistics (public perceptions) and self-reported delinquency measures (self-labels) in three racial groupings: black, white, and oriental.[57] He found that the traditional and official association between race and delinquency (high for blacks, low for whites, lowest for orientals) did not hold for his samples when self-reported measures were used. Furthermore, officially reported and self-reported acts of delinquent behavior seemed to be related only among whites. Gould concludes that the process of taking on a social label as one's own perspective (being arrested a number of times and defined by authorities as delinquent) seemed to work only for white youth, not for black or oriental boys. In the case of oriental boys, official delinquency is so rare that it seems to play no role in self-definitions. In the case of black youth, officially designated delinquency is prevalent, to the extent that authorities continually label blacks as troublemakers, and, therefore, self-appraisals have become irrelevant. Gould argues that this is an example of the need for sociologists to study three types of deviance simultaneously: the nature of the acts themselves, official definitions and perceptions of the acts, and self-perceived conceptions of the acts—and the relationship among these three types. Similarly, Akers suggests that the new labeling theory leaves unanswered the question of whether the ultimate aim of scientific investigation is to explain deviant behavior or explain the reactions to deviant behavior. He indicates that both must be analyzed.[58]

Finally, some adamant critics of labeling theory, often fierce defenders of the deviance paradigm, have claimed that the perspective is fundamentally wrong for some types of deviance. In answer to Szasz and others, Walter Gove examines the research on mental illness and concludes that the theory of labeling is incorrect.[59] He finds that evidence shows that a majority of persons hospitalized have serious psychiatric disorders whether or not processes of secondary deviance have taken place. In addition, persons in the community rather than readily labeling all bizarre behavior as sick, tend to deny mental illness until a personal situation becomes intolerable. The designation of sickness, particularly in the case of mental disorders, is a derogatory classification that tends to be avoided at all costs, often in the face of contrary evidence. Finally, Gove points to the substantial screening process that takes place before a person is hospitalized, a process that he feels fairly successfully sorts out those who are being railroaded and those who are less ill.

Labeling Theory's Response to Criticisms. It is possible for labeling theorists to respond to these charges in three ways. First, the more cautious adherents of the new school have admitted that labeling theory cannot be universally applied to all deviant behavior and that, in the case of problems such as traditional crimes, other perspectives may need to be employed. Second, and more importantly, the new theory is in the form of an emergent preparadigm school of thought, which requires empirical validation and conceptual sophistication. The lack of evidence to justify the primary importance of labeling in criminal deviance, for example, may simply mean that this aspect of the problem has not been investigated thoroughly and needs to be looked at more intensively. Third, and most critically, past definitions, based upon the deviance paradigm, may be biased by unproven assumptions. For example, Gove's conclusions about mental illness and the existing research he utilizes (especially, for example, the judgment that individuals actually suffer psychiatric disorders) is itself already predetermined by prevailing views of what constitutes mental illness as a form of deviance, as Rosenhan illustrated. What labeling theorists are doing is raising basic questions about these potential biases, since present research may simply prove the bias rather than investigate or discover other more important factors.

In summary, labeling theory contributes two critical things to contemporary perspectives of social problems. First, it scientifically points to aspects of problem behavior that the deviance paradigm cannot explain. Second, it raises fundamental moral and political questions of importance when programs of action are considered, for, as Kuhn pointed out, all scientific paradigms have moral and political implications. As Howard Becker has put it, "whose side are we really on" as social scientists and concerned citizens? [60] Are we on the side of an oppressive social system that often wants to control at any price, or are we on the side of the deviant who may be the unjustified victim of this oppression? There are risks in raising this type of question, to be sure, since such questions seem to imply the substitution of partisanship and activism for the traditional notion that scientists should remain disengaged and value free.[61] Nevertheless, the question cannot be avoided, since scientists are not as detached as they like to believe. The concept of victimization of those who are formally designated as social problems in contemporary society has been one of labeling theory's major moral contributions. It is a direct response to the popular myth of blaming the victim. Labeling theory also has disclosed the bias of older views, no matter how latent, which assumed that evil equals evil and which resulted in programs of action that frequently punished the victim for his deviance regardless of personal accountability for that behavior.

Whether adherents of the deviance paradigm can incorporate these fundamental criticisms into their perspective and retain their theory in revised form remains to be seen. If not, however, we may be witnessing a paradigm revolution that could culminate in a new perspective, one that combines elements of both the deviance and labeling theories. At the same time, adherents of another influential paradigm will be playing an important role in this debate and process: a paradigm that views social problems as a result of social and cultural disorganization.

Notes to Chapter 4

1. See the discussion of social pathology in Earl Rubington and Martin S. Weinberg, *The Study of Social Problems: Five Perspectives* (New York: Oxford University Press, 1971), especially pp. 15–22.

2. For example, see Charles R. Hendersen, *Introduction to the Study of the Dependent, Defective, and Delinquent Classes and of Their Social Treatment* (Boston: D. C. Heath, 1909).

3. David M. Austin, "Social Services and Dependency: The Critical Dilemma for Social Work," *The Urban and Social Change Review*, 5 (Spring 1972), pp. 50–54.

4. Daniel P. Monihan, *The Politics of a Guaranteed Income: The Nixon Administration and the Family Assistance Plan* (New York: Random House, Inc., 1972). See also the excellent review of this book by Michael Harrington, "Failures of Money, Confusions of Mouth," *Saturday Review of The Society*, 1 (January 20, 1973), pp. 59–60.

5. David M. Austin, "Social Services and Dependency: The Critical Dilemma for Social Work," *The Urban and Social Change Review*, 5 (Spring 1972), p. 51.

6. Leonard Goodwin, "How Suburban Families View the Work Orientations of the Welfare Poor: Problems in Social Stratification and Social Policy," *Social Problems*, 19 (Winter 1972), pp. 337–348.

7. *Ibid.*, pp. 345–346. In 1973 a joint U.S. House-Senate Subcommittee on Fiscal Policy, chaired by Representative Martha W. Griffiths (Democrat, Michigan), reported an analysis of how welfare policies can be counterproductive, since they tend to be based upon incorrect assumptions about both poverty and the poor. See George Lardner, Jr., "U.S. Study of Poverty Areas Shows Inequities in Benefits," *International Herald Tribune* (March 27, 1973), p. 3.

8. Marc Pilisuk and Tom Hayden, "Is there a Military-Industrial Complex Which Prevents Peace?" *The Journal of Social Issues*, 21 (July 1965), pp. 67–117.

9. Jeffrey M. Schevitz, "The Militarized Society and the Weapons-Maker," *Sociological Inquiry*, 40 (Winter 1970), pp. 49–58.

10. *Ibid.*, p. 50.

11. Irwin Sperber, "The Sociological Dimensions of Military Co-optation in the United States," *Sociological Inquiry*, 40 (Winter 1970), pp. 49–58.

12. *Ibid.*, pp. 61–62.

13. *Ibid.*, p. 65.

14. *Ibid.*, p. 70.

15. Jack P. Gibbs, "Conceptions of Deviant Behavior: The Old and the New," *Pacific Sociological Review*, 9 (Spring 1966), p. 10.

16. Earl Rubington and Martin S. Weinberg, *The Study of Social Problems: Five Perspectives* (New York: Oxford University Press, 1971), pp. 126–127.

17. See Ritchie P. Lowry, "Toward a Sociology of Secrecy and Security Systems," *Social Problems*, 19 (Spring 1972), 437–450.

18. Emile Durkheim, *Suicide*, G. Simpson, ed.; J. A. Spaulding and G. Simpson, trans. (New York: The Free Press, 1951).

19. Ruth S. Cavan, "The Concepts of Tolerance and Contraculture as Applied to Delinquency," *The Sociological Quarterly*, 2 (October 1961), pp. 243–258.

20. For examples of studies dealing with youth gangs, see Walter B. Miller, "Lower-Class Culture as a Generating Millieu of Gang Delinquency," *Journal of Social Issues*, 14 (1958), pp. 5–19; James F. Short, Jr., and Fred L. Strodtbeck, *Group Process and Gang Delinquency* (Chicago: University of Chicago Press, 1965); Frederick M. Trasher, *The Gang* (Chicago: University of Chicago Press, 1927); William Foote Whyte, *Street-Corner Society* (Chicago: University of Chicago Press, 1943; 2nd ed., 1955); and Lewis Yablonsky, *The Violent Gang* (New York: Macmillan, 1962). For examples of studies dealing with the new left groups, from bohemians to beatniks and hippies, see Thomas Albright, "San Francisco's Rolling Renaissance," and Francis Rigney, "Creativity in Bohemia," *Rolling Renaissance: San Francisco Underground Art in Celebration, 1945–1968* (San Francisco: Intersection and the Glide Urban Center, 1968); Bennett M. Berger, "Hippie Morality: More Old than New," Fred Davis, "Why All of Us May Be Hippies Someday," and Geoffry Siman and Grafton Trout, "Hippies in College: From Teeny-Boppers to Drug Freaks," *Transaction*, 5 (December 1967); Pam Miller, "Shift to Speed: Bad Break for the Haight," *Mental Health Communicator*, 5 (Spring 1969), pp. 12–13; Francis J. Rigney and L. Douglas Smith, *The Real Bohemia* (New York: Basic Books, 1961); and Lewis Yablonsky, *The Hippie Trip* (New York: Pegasus, 1968).
21. Robert K. Merton, "Social Structure and Anomie," *American Sociological Review*, 3 (October 1938), pp. 672–682; and *Social Theory and Social Structure*, rev. ed. (New York: The Free Press, 1956).
22. Edwin H. Sutherland, *Principles of Criminology* (Philadelphia: J. B. Lippincott, 1955); 5th ed. rev. by D. R. Cressey.
23. *Ibid.*, pp. 74–81.
24. See, for example, the studies of youth gangs cited above, and Marshall B. Clinard, *Anomie and Deviant Behavior* (New York: The Free Press, 1964); Richard A. Cloward and Lloyd E. Ohlin, *Delinquency and Opportunity* (New York: The Free Press, 1960); Albert K. Cohen, *Delinquent Boys* (New York: The Free Press, 1955); and Donald R. Cressey, "Epidemiology and Individual Conduct: A Case from Criminology," *The Pacific Sociological Review*, 3 (Fall 1960), pp. 47–54.
25. For example, see Donald Clemmer, *The Prison Community* (New York: Rinehart and Company, 1958); Edwin H. Sutherland, *The Professional Thief* (Chicago: University of Chicago Press, 1937); and Paul W. Tappan, *Crime, Justice and Correction* (New York: McGraw-Hill, 1960).
26. This discussion is based upon an unpublished paper available through the Graduate School of Public Health, University of Pittsburg, Pittsburg, Pa.—Edward A. Suchman, "Accidents and Deviance" (1969)—based on research conducted under a grant from the National Center for Urban and Industrial Health, Injury Control Program.
27. See also the following references: J. Bauer, "The Teen-age Rebel and His Weapon: The Automobile," *Traffic Safety, 518* (November, 1955), pp. 10–13; J. J. Conger *et al.*, "Psychological and Psychophysiological Factors in Motor Vehicle Accidents," *Journal of the American Medical Association, 169* (April 4, 1959), pp. 1581–1587; H. Hacker and E. Suchman, "A Sociological Approach to Accident Research," *Social Problems, 10* (Spring 1963), 383–389; W. Haddon, E. Suchman, and D. Klein, *Accident Research: Methods and Approaches* (New York:

Harper & Row, 1964); V. Krall, "Personality Characteristics of Accident-Repeating Children," *Journal of Abnormal and Social Psychology, 48* (January 1953), pp. 99–107; and E. A. Suchman, "A Conceptual Analysis of the Accident Phenomenon," *Social Problems, 8* (Winter 1960–1961), pp. 241–253.

28. Stan Cohen, "Criminology and the Sociology of Deviance in Britain: A Recent History and a Current Report" (University of Essex), a paper delivered at the British Sociological Association Conference (14–16 April 1971).

29. Alexander Liazos, "The Poverty of the Sociology of Deviance: Nuts, Sluts, and Perverts," *Social Problems, 20* (Summer 1972), pp. 103–120.

30. Charles C. Moskos, Jr., *The American Enlisted Man: The Rank and File in Today's Military* (New York: Russell Sage Foundation and Basic Books, 1970).

31. Erving Goffman, *Asylums: Essays on the Social Situation of Mental Patients and Other Inmates* (Chicago: Aldine Publishing Company, 1959).

32. Everett C. Hughes, "Good People and Dirty Work," *Social Problems, 10* (Summer 1962), pp. 3–11.

33. William A. Westley, "Violence and the Police," *The American Journal of Sociology, 59* (July 1953), pp. 34–41.

34. Everett C. Hughes, "Good People and Dirty Work—1972," informal paper presented at Boston College (1972) (unpublished).

35. Lee Rainwater, "The Revolt of the Dirty-Workers," *Transaction, 5* (November 1967), pp. 2, 64.

36. *Ibid.,* p .64.

37. Edwin H. Sutherland, "Crime and Business," *The Annals of the American Academy of Political and Social Science, 217* (September 1941), pp. 112–118. For a report on white-collar crime in contemporary West Germany and the lenient official and public attitudes toward it, see John M. Pearce, "White-Collar Crime: Germany's Lenient Attitude," *International Herald Tribune* (March 27, 1973), p. 23.

38. See Judith Blake and Kingsley Davis, "Norms, Values, and Sanctions," *Handbook of Modern Sociology,* Robert E. L. Faris, ed. (Chicago: Rand McNally, 1964), p. 468.

39. Howard S. Becker, *Outsiders: Studies in the Sociology of Deviance* (New York: The Free Press, 1963), p. 20.

40. See John I. Kitsuse, "Societal Relation to Deviant Behavior: Problems of Theory and Method," *Social Problems, 9* (Winter 1962), p. 253; and Kai T. Erikson, "Notes on the Sociology of Deviance," *The Other Side: Perspective on Deviance,* Howard Becker, ed. (New York: The Free Press, 1964), pp. 9–21, and in *Social Problems, 9* (Spring 1962), 307–313.

41. Maggie Scarf, "Normality Is a Square Circle or a Four-Sided Triangle," *The New York Times Magazine* (October 3, 1971), pp. 16–17, 40–45, and 48–50. See also Bruce Ennis, *Prisoners of Psychiatry: Mental Patients, Psychiatrists and the Law* (New York: Harcourt Brace Jovanovich, 1972).

42. See Earl Rubington and Martin S. Weinberg, *The Study of Social Problems: Five Perspectives* (New York: Oxford University Press, 1971), p. 163.

43. Charles H. Cooley, *Social Organization*, Elsie Jones Cooley, ed. (New York: Charles Scribner's Sons, 1937); and George H. Mead, *Mind Self and Society* (Chicago: University of Chicago Press, 1934).

44. Joseph R. Gusfield, "Moral Passage: The Symbolic Process in Public Designations of Deviancy," *Social Problems*, 15 (Fall 1967), pp. 175–188.

45. Robin Williams, *American Society* (New York: Alfred A. Knopf, 1960), pp. 372–396.

46. Joseph R. Gusfield, "Moral Passage: The Symbolic Process in Public Designations of Deviancy," *Social Problems*, 15 (Fall 1967), p. 178.

47. Edwin M. Lemert, *Social Pathology* (New York: McGraw-Hill, 1951), pp. 75–76.

48. Ira L. Reiss, "Premarital Sex as Deviant Behavior: An Application of Current Approaches to Deviance," *American Sociological Review*, 35 (February 1970), pp. 80–82.

49. Colin J. Williams and Martin S. Weinberg, "Being Discovered: A Study of Homosexuals in the Military," *Social Problems*, 18 (Fall 1970), pp. 217–227.

50. D. L. Rosenhan, "On Being Sane in Insane Places," *Science*, 179 (January 19, 1973), pp. 250–258; and Nigel Hawks, "Fake Patients Fooled the Psychiatrists," *The Observer* (January 21, 1973), p. 3.

51. Judith Lorber, "Deviance as Performance: The Case of Illness," *Social Problems*, 14 (Winter 1967), pp. 300–310. Also see Stephen Cole and Robert Lejeune, "Illness and the Legitimation of Failure," *American Sociological Review*, 37 (June 1972), pp. 347–356.

52. Harrison M. Trice and Paul Michael Roman, "Delabeling, Relabeling, and Alcoholics Anonymous," *Social Problems*, 17 (Spring 1970), pp. 538–546.

53. *Ibid.*, p. 540.

54. Ira Reiss, "Premarital Sex as Deviant Behavior: An Application of Current Approaches to Deviance," *American Sociological Review*, 35 (February 1970), pp. 81–82.

55. Ronald L. Akers, "Problems in the Sociology of Deviance: Social Definitions and Behavior," *Social Forces*, 46 (June 1968), pp. 455–465.

56. Jack Gibbs, "Conceptions of Deviant Behavior: The Old and the New," *Pacific Sociological Review*, 9 (Spring 1966), p.12.

57. Leroy C. Gould, "Who Defines Delinquency: A Comparison of Self-Reported and Officially-Reported Indices of Delinquency for Three Racial Groups," *Social Problems*, 16 (Winter 1969), pp. 325–336.

58. Ronald L. Akers, "Problems in the Sociology of Deviance: Social Definitions and Behavior," *Social Forces*, 46 (June 1968), p. 456.

59. Walter R. Gove, "Societal Reactions as an Explanation of Mental Illness: An Evaluation," *American Sociological Review*, 35 (October 1970), pp. 873–884.

60. Howard S. Becker, "Whose Side Are We On?," *Social Problems*, 14 (Winter 1967), pp. 239–249.

61. For example, see David Bordua's criticism of partisanship in "Deviant Behavior and Social Control," *The Annals*, 369 (January 1967), pp. 149–163; and Alvin W. Gouldner's defense in "The Sociologist as Partisan," *The American Sociologist*, 3 (May 1968), pp. 103–116.

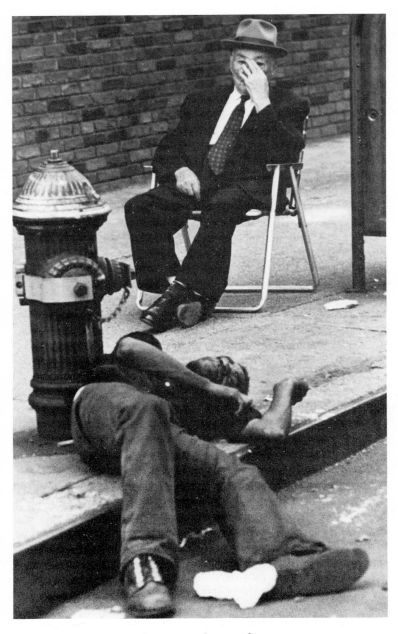

Disorganized men or a disorganized society?
(Kenneth Karp, Black Star)

5. Problems as Social and Cultural Disorganization

As in the case of the deviance paradigm, the disorganization paradigm appeared in its earliest form as a theory of pathology using an organic, medical analogy. From the inception of the discipline, sociologists have been puzzled and concerned by forms of behavior that seem to symbolize the disintegration of normal society. Divorce, crime, delinquency, war, narcotics use, suicide, personal violence, alcoholism, and other social problems have been seen as resulting from the fragmentation of the usual bonds between people that society depends upon for its persistence and stability. The most appropriate medical analogy is the view of problems as a kind of cancer for which the adequate cure seems to be removal of the disorganizing and disrupting events from the system. Use of surgery, chemicals, or X-ray treatment to remove cancerous calls from the human body allows normal cells to return to their orderly and intended growth and functioning. In a similar manner, removal of cancerous behavior from societies or individuals is a means of assisting individuals and societies to return to normal states and activities.

Social Disintegration: Old and New Views

In addition, as in the case of deviance theory, the older views that see disorganization as pathological attribute the cause of disorganization to individuals and their immediate environments, while the newer view tends to blame a disorganized society within which victimized and helpless individuals are forced to live. The older view, therefore, is latently conservative, while the newer is often openly radical.

The Older View—The Zonal Theory of Urban Disorganization. The older view developed as a consequence of two major kinds of social scientific studies early in the history of sociology. The first type was conducted in the 1920's and 1930's at the University of Chicago and became identified with "the Chicago School of Sociology." During that period of time, dozens of professors and graduate students at Chicago concentrated their attentions upon urban environments and identified the fact that forms of behavior varied according to different zones or regions in which city populations lived. Using the city of Chicago as a type of "ideal" model, Ernest Burgess developed the *concentric zone theory* of urban growth and development.[1] He suggested that cities begin at some key point, usually at the intersection of main communication and transportation lines. Around this central point, grows Zone I, a region of financial and commercial activity with administrative institutions for city government. The few residents in Zone I tend to be transients in hotels, while daytime populations consist of commuters who live in distant regions. Surrounding this central core in the shape of a doughnut is Zone II, a region in rapid transition. Located here are light manufacturing, residents of slums and blighted areas, and some "bright light" activities to appeal to the more affluent in Zone I and distant zones (activities such as prostitution, night clubs, gambling facilities, and so on).

Zone III contains the homes of workingmen, some owned but many rented. Commercial activity consists of small, street-corner businesses. Burgess found that within Zone IV apartments and middle-class homes are mixed together, and that Zone V is characterized by upper-class residential areas, outlying business districts, heavy industry (in some cities), and distant suburbs. Subsequent scholars criticized and modified Burgess' theory by pointing out that some cities did not look like a series of uniform concentric circles (zones more nearly represented cells in a grid pattern, slices of pie, or crazy-quilt patterns). Furthermore, the developments of suburbanization in the late 1940's and the subsequent migration of middle-class residents, most whites, much small business, and some white-collar and light industry to more distant zones modified many of the social and commercial characteristics of the regions described by Burgess.

Nevertheless, Burgess' theory still essentially remains a classic depiction of what cities tend to look like ecologically, or in terms of social geography. The theory spawned dozens of studies showing that crime, violence, and other forms of deviance and problem behavior tended to vary greatly from one zone to another. This theory was extremely popular for two reasons. First, it had strong roots in the antiurban biases and reformism of early social science. Second, it could be subjected to extensive and rigorous scientific analysis. In other words, much scientific effort could be expended in "proving" the theory by using new statistical techniques. For example, Robert Faris and H. Warren Dunham found that mental disorders varied by city zones, and Clifford Shaw and Henry McKay found that juvenile delinquency rates varied by zones.[2] The theory left room for various types of puzzle solving within the context of the disorganization paradigm.

In general, problems were found to be more prevalent in zones characterized by disorganization (I, II, and III) because of the transience, mobility, or lower-class status of the residents (see Diagram 5–1). Thus, sociologists began to talk about urban areas where behavior became disorganized because of the unique and unusual pressures of daily life upon individual residents. In contrast, residents of other zones (IV and V) seemed more adjusted to the strains of urban life and less disorganization in the form of problem behavior was observable. As Kuhn pointed out, popular paradigms also leave room, ironically, for much criticism in terms of contradictory puzzles. The urban zone theory of disorganization provided this potential, when later studies disclosed that seemingly integrated residents of other zones also exhibited forms of deviant behavior. For example, suburbanites could have high divorce rates, suggesting familial disorganization.[3] White, upper-middle class children

Diagram 5–1

An idealized schematic representation of the zonal theory of urban regions*

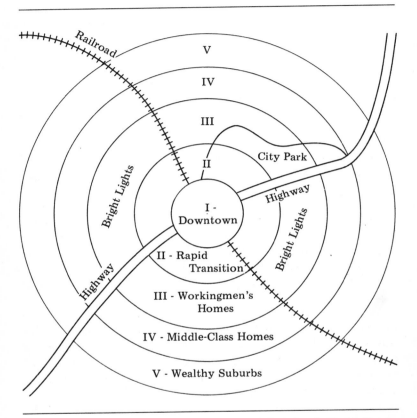

* After Robert E. Park, Ernest W. Burgess, and Roderick D. McKenzie, *The City* (Chicago: University of Chicago Press, 1925).

could use narcotics and commit delinquent acts as readily as residents of other zones. These acts were harder to observe because of the ability of middle-class children to avoid prosecution or the tendency of society to define what was considered deviant for one segment of society as nondeviant, even desirable, for another. In other words, other paradigms such as the concept of deviance could be employed to criticize the disorganization paradigm. At the same time, the zonal theory could also be adapted to incorporate some of these criticisms, since it could be argued that suburbanites experience disorganization because of rapid mobility and social change.[4]

The Older View—Disorganization as a Disintegration of Norms. The second major kind of study that influenced the older view of disorganization as pathological was typified by the work of W. I. Thomas and Florian Znaniecki.[5] They defined disorganization as a disintegration of the values and rules that govern everyday behavior. Evidence of this kind of disorganization was found by Thomas and Znaniecki in letters written by Polish emigrants to the United States to relatives and friends back home in Poland. Thomas and Znaniecki suggested that the conflict experienced between the new culture in America and the old Polish culture, and between the young and old generations in emigrant families, led to a number of different social problems, including crime, delinquency, alcoholism, and mental illness. These problems occurred because the emigrant family could no longer control and channel the behavior of its members into normal, expected patterns of behavior. From such research came other studies that dealt with the time necessary for emigrants to become integrated into the new American culture (often seen as three generations, among the children of the children of the emigrants), that is, the time it took to dissociate themselves totally from the former culture, and, thereby, deal with the problems stemming from the initial disorganization brought about by migration and cultural shock. These theories also supported the American ideal of ultimate integration for all ethnic groups. Thus, ecological studies of urban life and the analyses of the experiences of migrants led many sociologists to conclude that sudden change and conflict created conditions within which individuals were more likely to exhibit disorganized behavior. Both change and conflict came to be seen as undesirable in extreme or predominant forms, and solutions were thought to lie in reeducating or retraining individuals to accept and conform to prevailing norms and standards in the larger society. In short, divorce, delinquency, alcohol use, and aberrent behavior were "bad," while adaptation to normal expectations were "good."

Nowhere has this older view been more prevalent than in the recent conservative criticisms of the new-left movement in its various forms, especially the more violent protests of the 1960's. Robert Nisbet, one of the most thoughtful of these conservative critics, for example, has suggested that the most striking fact of the present period of revolutionary change is the erosion or disintegration of traditional institutional authorities: the church, the family, the legal system, the local community, and the school and university.[6] What is particularly alarming to Nisbet is the fact that these institutions have been the principle sources of order and liberty for Western man for over 1000 years. If the old sources of authority are destroyed without substituting viable new ones, anarchy, violence, and resulting repression will occur from several sources (the antiestablishmentarians and the representatives of the establishment). Nisbet saw the turmoil in the streets of Chicago during the 1968 Democratic Party convention as evidence of the beginnings of this process.

Nisbet uses as a basis for his theory the distinction between power and authority. *Power* is related to force, either overtly or covertly, while *authority* has to do with legitimacy. That is, individuals respond to power because they are fearful of force, whereas they respond to authority because they believe it is inherently legitimate. Nisbet argues that this distinction is vital, since freedom depends upon authority, not force. People are free when most in a society voluntarily accept authority and, thereby, live in relatively harmonious and ordered ways with one another. When authority is challenged, the specter of social anarchy and chaos appears, and threatened authorities are likely to turn to naked power and force, with the approval of most citizens, to maintain order. Nisbet points to the fact that most citizens approved of the extreme use of force by police in Chicago, while disapproving of any of the actions of the demonstrators (including simple protest against the Vietnam War).

He concludes that while most human beings will tolerate almost anything except the loss of authority in contemporary society, the new left continually challenges old authorities in every social and cultural context.

Criticisms of the Old View.   Although Nisbet's theory is valuable analytically, especially his distinction between authority and power, it is based, at least implicitly, upon the older view of disorganization as pathological and as related to deviant subgroups. Radicals and protestors represent people who have theoretically become disorganized by being estranged or cut off from older sources of authority. Their actions threaten the entire social system with chaos, a pathological state; therefore, citizens approve any actions, including repression and the loss of freedom, necessary to restore order. The disorganization and pathology is seen as residing within deviating individuals and groups.

Other scholars have questioned this perspective, particularly the view of protest as disorganized behavior, and in so doing have suggested that what may be disorganized is larger society, not the individual behavior of subgroups. For example, Kenneth Keniston has pointed out that student unrest and turmoil in underdeveloped countries has become expected, but that the spread of this activity to more industrialized, and, therefore, presumably "stable" modern nations (America, France, Germany, Italy, Czechoslovakia, Poland) alarms many.[7] He implies that this alarm is based upon the unwarranted assumption that individuals are more likely to be disorganized in undeveloped social contexts where living conditions are miserable, unemployment is predominant, and poverty is evident. This conservative bias tends to lead to a "war against the young" in various forms: Governor George Wallace's and Vice President Spiro Agnew's attacks upon "radiclibs" or "anarchists"; George Kennan's moral condemnation of "revolting students"; Lewis Feuer's theory that youth are in Oedipal rebellion against the older generation; or Daniel Bell's thesis that student rebellion is really a counterrevolution by a group of romantics who feel social change has left their basic values behind (in other words, youth are unrealistically rejecting science, rationality, industrialization, and urban life in an attempt to return to some small community utopia of an idealized past).

Keniston criticizes and rejects all of these explanations as politically biased and as dangerous, since they can be used to justify almost any actions taken against demonstrating youth. More importantly, he points to the relationship between youth (defined as those under 30 years of age) and the established authority and institutions, in terms of the opportunities for continuing intellectual, ethical, economic, and social growth and development in developed societies. In previous societies, childhood ended at around 10 to 12 years of age, at which time a youth could take his or her full place in the adult world. In contrast, modern society has a prolonged period of adolescence (often lasting through 30 years of age), during which time a youth cannot take a place in the adult world and is subjected to many repressive institutions, as well (such as school, university, undemocratic family, the military). Added to this intolerable situation is the fact that many democratic ideals go relatively unexpressed in social reality, and youthful members of subjugated minorities must experience further indignities (women, blacks and other nonwhites, the poor). At the same time, a prolonged period of adolescence, which cuts youth off from meaningful involvement in contemporary institutions, also frees him or her to engage in acts of rebellion and protest. A modern youth is not tied to the responsibilities of a job, a family, or a conforming role in the local community. Keniston's criticism of Nisbet's theory of youthful rebellion reflects the newer view of social pathology.

The New View—Disorganization in Society. What Keniston has suggested is that the seemingly disorganized behavior among the young in contemporary society is really a result of *conditions in society* per se, not a consequence of pathology unique to the young. Indeed, larger society may be pathological and disorganized to the extent that it encourages exclusion for so many subgroups in the society, including the young. Actually, then, the protest actions of youth are sane rebellions against a sick society. Philip Hauser has also argued that disorganization is endemic to society as a whole through the use of a more scientific approach. He maintains that contemporary society, domestically and internationally, can best be categorized as "the chaotic society" or "the anachronistic society." [8] Therefore, idiosyncratic acts of disorganization (youth revolution, women's lib, crime, narcotics use, and so on) merely reflect a more pervasive societal condition.

Hauser suggests that a certain degree of chaos or disorganization is obviously characteristic of all societies throughout history. However, contemporary chaos differs in kind in several ways. First, modern society contains more cultural layers and, therefore, possesses a greater potential for conflict and disorder. Second, these cultural layers often involve significant variations, which provide a basis for great dissonance between elements of a population. Third, modern society contains the means for its self-induced total destruction, the explosion of nuclear devices. Finally, the knowledge necessary to meet this situation is available, even social scientific knowledge, but it is doubtful whether modern society contains the will to use this knowledge. In other words, for many citizens in contemporary society, collective suicide appears to be a distinct possibility. All of these conditions are a function of what Hauser calls *the social morphological revolution.*[9]

This concept refers to changes in the size, density, and heterogeneity of a population and the resulting impact upon human behavior. The revolution has been related to four developments in the last several hundred years: the population explosion, the population implosion, population diversification, and increased technological and social change. Not only has there been a population explosion, but there has been a concentrated growth, which continues unabated, within a relatively short time span. Hauser points out that it took 2–2½ million years for man, and his distant relatives, to generate a world population of 1 billion persons (achieved about 1825), only 105 years to reach 2 billion persons (1930), and only thirty years to reach over 3½ billion (present). Despite the wishes of family planners, statistics indicate a continuation of this trend, especially in developing nations of the world. The only thing that seems capable of ending this trend is catastrophe; present fertility and mortality rates predict a world population of around 7½ billion by the year 2000.

The process of population implosion refers to the increasing concentration of world population on small portions of the earth's surface, the process of urbanization and metropolitanization.[10] This process, too, is of relatively recent origin:

Clumpings of population large enough to be called towns or cities did not emerge until after about 3500 B.C., and mankind did not achieve the technological and social organizational development to permit cities of 100,000 or more until as recently as Greco–Roman civilization. . . . With the emergence of Europe from the Dark Ages and the series of "revolutions"—the Agricultural Revolution, the Commercial Revolution, the Industrial Revolution, the Scientific Revolution, and the Technological Revolution—man achieved levels both of technological and social organizational development that permitted ever larger agglomerations of people and economic activities. In consequence, the proliferation of cities of 1,000,000 or more inhabitants became possible during the 19th century, and the emergence of metropolitan areas and megalopolis, the coalescence of metropolitan areas, during the second half of the 20th century. . . . The trend towards increased urban and metropolitan concentration of population is likely to continue. The reasons for this are to be found in the advantages of clumpings of population and economic activities.[11]

At the same time, population diversification has occurred with increasing heterogeneity of peoples occupying the same geographic areas and life space. This process is evident by the contemporary diversity in culture, language, religion, values, behavior, ethnicity, and race, found in major communities throughout the world. Diversification when coupled with population concentration leads to the multiplication of conflicts over communication, interests, and interaction. Finally, these three processes of population development have been influenced by more rapid technological change, leading to rapid social change, and, in turn, exacerbating cultural strains and dissonance.

This trend has been particularly evident in the modern nations of the world, including the United States. Hauser suggests, therefore, that the host of contemporary social problems (involving physical, personal, social, institutional, and governmental issues) can only be adequately understood in this context. Housing, pollution, crime, mental disorder, violence, protest, war, and ethnic conflict are all related to the social morphological revolution that is leading us toward a chaotic society. Disorganization and disorder in contemporary society have resulted from a transition, still under way, from a smaller, more intimate community life of the past to a masslike society. Hauser argues that observable social problems are merely a manifestation of cultural lag, the inability of prevailing institutions and authority to adapt to new demands and conditions. This inability is a function of conservatism (an attempt to hang on to old ways and values despite the need for new ones), inadequate understanding of the problem (blaming the victim for his behavior, rather than questioning the social order), and the ready acceptance of simple political slogans that result only in worsening the problem ("law and order" instead of "law, justice, and order"). In other words, modern institutions, as anachronisms of older social orders that no longer exist, are the truly pathological and disorganized components of modern society. Where Nisbet's theory leads one to conclude that attacks upon traditional authority are often pathological, Hauser's theory leads one to conclude that the persistence of traditional authority in unchanged forms is anachronistic and pathological.

An Example of Social Problem Solving Using the New View of Disorganization. The new view of disorganization has led many to propose different resolutions for contemporary social problems. For example, experts like Dr. John Knowles, who has served as head of Massachusetts General Hospital and The Rockefeller Foundation, have criticized older views of the medical problem in the United States for assuming that individual pathological behavior was its cause. In other words, the fee basis of medical pay (presumably making medical care a profit-making business), badly run hospitals, costs that are too high, and cheating by individual doctors have been pointed to traditionally as the reasons why America cannot provide adequate or sufficient medical care. These older criticisms argue for tighter controls on fees, medical standards, and medical practice as a way of controlling individual deviance or individual cases of disorganized behavior. In contrast, Dr. Knowles and others argue that the entire system is disorganized and chaotic. We do not have sufficient emphasis upon preventive medicine compared to other societies (Britain, Russia, Scandinavia) because of pathological fears of socialism. We have no medical halfway houses (institutions that provide medical care for those not seriously or critically ill) placed in local communities, where the less ill can recuperate close to home. Halfway houses could relieve the extensive burdens placed upon our hospitals, which are actually intensive care oriented. Knowles also has pointed out that the almost total absence of adequate and reasonably priced nursing homes for the aged, a portion of the population that needs continuous preventive and less-than-intensive care, exemplifies our anachronistic medical system. Actually, elements of the population other than the aged also need nursing and home types of institutions. However, a new type of medical system will call for major changes in traditional values and beliefs, particularly the notion that community and governmental support and assistance constitutes socialism or the view that a few chiselers and crooks in the medical profession or in the society at large, who take unnecessary advantage of medical services, really cause the problem.

The conflict between old and new views of social disintegration, its nature and causes, suggests the possibility of a paradigm revolution. We will return to this question in the consideration of the criticisms of the disorganization paradigm and the newly emerging interest in conflict theory, at the end of this chapter. However, both the old and new views are based upon the use of the concept of disorganization as a way of analyzing social problems in all contexts and forms. In addition, where the deviance paradigm was related to the naturalistic popular myth of social problems, the disorganization paradigm is most closely related to the popular concept of evil equals evil and can result in blaming the victim. Nevertheless, the paradigm has been popular and successful in social science because it has encouraged ingenious and provocative work on special problems and it has been fundamentally grounded in a sociological perspective of human society.

The Disorganization Paradigm

The concept of problems as a consequence of disorganization obviously implies the importance of social organization. Specifically, adherents of the disorganization paradigm see social problems as resulting from either a set of behaviors that conflict with or contradict expected patterns of conformity or from a confusion about or absence of norms and values covering these behaviors. In general, the first approach can be called a *theory of social disorganization* and the second approach, a *theory of cultural disorganization*. These views are related to the popular notion of problems arising from a breakdown in moral values, a disintegration of personal behavior, or a permissive society.

Social disorganization theorists argue that, while no social system is in an absolutely perfect state of routine equilibrium, all societies must stress conformity to accepted roles in order to survive. Social change and conflict frequently occur when some individuals refuse or are unable to act as expected. This upsets social equilibrium, and steps must be taken to rectify the problems that result. If the steps are ineffective, either the system will change or it will die out.

Cultural disorganization theorists accept the same general premises and merely sharpen the focus. They argue that social problems occur when specific conditions and events are incompatible with generally accepted values in a society. *Value conflict*, then, is the essential cause of problems, and it may result in either competition or contract. Competition can lead to the success or failure of either prevailing social values or the values of the deviant subgroup, depending upon the distribution of power. Contract can lead to compromise and orderly change in major values.[12]

Both theories see conflict and change as the motivating factors in creating problem behavior and, therefore, tacitly assume the generally undesirable nature of these processes, especially in the extreme forms that produce traumas in society. Value conflict theorists, however, have developed the foundation for the emergence of conflict theory, which tends to argue that conflict and change are as natural and necessary a part of any social system as order and stability. This perspective will be considered at the end of the chapter as a major criticism of the disorganization paradigm, and as a possible foundation for a paradigm revolution. Both theories also lend themselves well to either old or new interpretations of disorganization in terms of possible remedies to social problems. Social disorganization can be combated by either punishing, retraining, reeducating, or rehabilitating disorganized individuals, or by locating the systematic sources for disorganized behavior and reforming or revolutionizing that part of society. Cultural disorganization can be combated by either forcing or training those with different values to conform, or by locating the anachronistic and pathological values of larger society that create the conflict and changing or revolutionizing them.

Contributions of the Paradigm: Alienation and Cultural Lag. In Kuhn's terms the disorganization paradigm has been popular throughout the history of social science because it provides opportunities for all types of puzzle solving and for all kinds of political and moral perspectives. Furthermore, it is rooted in traditional sociological views of the nature of man, yet, at the same time, permits much work in refinements of theories and the unique uses of new theories and concepts. For example, fundamental to the disorganization paradigm are the classic concepts of social alienation and anomie. In the last chapter, we considered the way in which Emile Durkheim utilized the notion of *anomie*, a dissociation from the normal bonds of society, to explain a type of suicidal behavior. We also considered the work of Charles Cooley, which argued that our ability to come to see ourselves as we thought others saw us, and then to act in accordance with these societal expectations, determined whether we were defined by others as conformist or deviant. The concept of *cultural lag*, as developed by William Ogburn and employed by scholars like Philip Hauser, is also involved.[13]

Alienation refers to the condition that results from withdrawal, as a consequence of the lack of commitment to any norms or roles.[14] It can result from feelings of powerlessness, normlessness, or marginality in terms of status and social influence. In other words, the individual has little or no feeling of place and location in accepted society, and, as a consequence, he feels estranged from that society and ultimately alien to even himself. This feeling may result when rapid change makes it difficult for individuals to adapt old beliefs to new conditions. The recent popular concepts of "turning off" or "copping out" characterize an alienation response. Though the concept has been used in an attempt to explain almost all kinds of problem behavior, Robert Nisbet suggests that it is frequently employed incorrectly. What looks to larger society like the behavior of alienated individuals (for example, extreme social protest, including bombing, street violence, arson, and so on) may in reality be the response of *committed* individuals:

Failure to make the clear distinction between alienation and social protest does much disservice to each. Social protest, resulting in social reform and revolution, forms one of the richest and most creative chapters in the history of civilization. It reflects a mobilization and channeling of energies toward specific ideas and goals, in the process of which acts destructive of the existing order are frequently required. "Alienated" is hardly the word to describe the leaders of the English, American and French Revolutions in the seventeenth and eighteenth centuries, or the Bolsheviks who took over the Russian government in 1917, or for any of the long line of reformers to be found in Western history from Solon to Franklin D. Roosevelt. Social protest, revolt, activism, or revolution is conspicuously committed behavior, as committed in its way as the behavior of those who choose to defend rather than attack a social order.[15]

In reality, it may be appropriate to talk of some problem behavior as *both alienated and committed*, that is, alienated from existing values and order and/or committed to new values and order, depending upon the unique circumstances.

For example, assassination of public figures in America (such as Martin Luther King, Robert Kennedy, or Jack Kennedy) or attempted assassinations (Harry Truman, George Wallace, Theodore Roosevelt) seem to be the work of two types of individuals: either those who are alienated and lonely, and, therefore, looking for some kind of place in society or history, no matter how deviant the role (for example, the would-be assassin of George Wallace, who apparently was nonpolitical), or those who are deeply committed to norms and values that seem to be threatened by their victim (for example, the pro-Arab assassin of Robert Kennedy). In contrast, political assassinations in developing countries in Latin America and Africa often reflect a deep tradition of political instability, nonlegitimacy for formal leaders, and violence during political transitions. In the absence of routinized methods for bringing about governmental change, assassination or *coup d'état* may be employed by committed power groups who also feel alienated from the prevailing regime. Violence in politics in such a context can become routine and expected rather than exceptional and idiosyncratic.

In a similar manner, drug use can be analyzed using the concepts of alienation and commitment. Some narcotics addiction is an alienated flight from reality or a psychic and physiological numbing that results in alienation. Other forms of narcotics use, however, actually symbolize a strong commitment to deviant subgroup norms and values, which are simply different from accepted standards. For example, Howard Becker has described the elaborate peer group process of socialization necessary to teach marijuana novices how to use the drug and how to interpret the induced feelings as pleasurable. Smoking grass requires a different technique than smoking ordinary cigarettes. In addition, resulting feelings could be alarming or frightening to the novice without group support for new definitions of what it is to be "high." [16]

The concepts of anomie and alienation are the more sophisticated contemporary by-products of the disorganization perspective. Modern studies of suicide have enlarged upon Durkheim's classic concepts, largely elaborating on his basic typologies, to include the entire range from anomie-induced suicide to group-commitment-induced suicide. Herbert Hendin has distinguished between suicide in Scandinavian countries and black suicide in the United States.[17] Suicides in Denmark seem to be attempts to inflict guilt feelings upon others or to join loved ones who have died. Suicides in Sweden reflect an independence of personal action, rather than a strong dependency upon others that has somehow been shattered. In contrast to these two different types, Hendin has found that suicide in American black ghettos is one outcome of pent-up rage and hostility, induced by a lifetime of degradation that leads to low self-esteem. At a recent meeting of the American Association of Suicidology,[18] participants attributed a sharp increase in suicide rates for people under 30 years of age to the fact that young people are breaking away much earlier from old sources of social and cultural support, primarily the family. They also noted a rapid rise in the rate for women, possibly a consequence of conflict over woman's role in modern society. Thus, the notion of disorganization, and the related concepts of anomie and alienation, play a continuing important role in the analysis of problems like suicide.

Application of the Disorganization Paradigm to Unusual Problems—Studies of Dying, Child Abuse, and the Unresponsive Bystander. In addition to these examples of provocative research, the assumptions of the disorganization paradigm have been latently employed to look at unusual types of problems in new ways. Studies of dying and of child abuse illustrate this usage. In an analysis of elderly patients admitted to New York State Fairview Mental Hospital in 1967, Elizabeth Markson suggests that modern society constructs hiding places for dying under the guise of other purposes.[19] Man has always feared death, much as small children fear the dark, since it seems to be an unknown and unknowable process representing the most ultimate form of alienation (possible total cessation of personality and being). Markson indicates that a general fear of death is certainly valuable for survival but that a romanticization or denial of death leads to major problems. Her analysis of a sample of patients at Fairview led her to conclude that dying can be viewed as a process of successive anomie and alienation and that the good people of society permit the staff of mental institutions to do some of the dirty work in this process. In short, state hospitals seem to function as geriatric houses of death to which the elderly are relegated because of the despair by their families (over unusual, senile, or bizarre behavior) or the shortage of general hospital beds (for those aged affected by physical afflictions). In other words, because we do not know what to do with old people who are sick or "queer," we assign them to mental institutions, whose purpose it is to administer the process of dying, not to cure the old person of his "problem."

Markson indicates that her research suggests that this pattern is especially true for lower socioeconomic groups, who are unable to afford special care or private institutions. Three social and cultural factors seem to be involved in abandoning the aged to a state mental hospital. First, the elderly appear to be socially dying already because they are forced to relinquish roles and relationships in everyday society (children grow up and start their own families, forced retirement from work, non-involvement in local community affairs). Second, there is in the elderly a high probability of dying, and this may appear to be a justification for institutionalization. Third, the elderly possess low social status and are almost powerless. Furthermore:

A combination of great age, powerlessness and *terminal illness makes one despised by medical and lay people alike and, unless death comes on schedule, suggests transfer to a state mental hospital. Here the old are hidden away, or taken away, from all that is familiar to them and left to await death. Death here, as Rilke observed, is "factory-like, of course. Where production is so enormous, an individual death is not so nicely carried out, but then that doesn't matter. It is quantity that counts."* [20]

In contrast, many among the rich die at home or in comfortable surroundings in expensive private institutions, which attempt to provide some attachment to daily life until the very moment of death. Markson also found that younger patients at Fairview who had terminal illnesses were treated differently; they were more likely to be sent home for short periods of time only to return near the moment of physical death.

Research on child abuse has also employed the perspectives of the disorganization paradigm. The "battered child" syndrome has been a consistent problem in modern society. How extensive the problem is no one knows; however, there were some 60,000 cases reported in the United States in 1972, plus countless unreported cases. Abused children are often hard to detect, since parents and other adults who have caused the injuries may hide them by claiming accidents (a 13-month-old baby with broken bones allegedly fell from her crib or a five-year-old boy with blackened eyes and broken teeth allegedly fell off the porch). In an analysis of what is known about battered children, Serapie Zalba has pointed out that physical abuse of a child does not usually occur only once but represents acts that have been going on for a period of one to three years.[21] Abusive parents tend to come from the complete range of socio-economic classes, many having well-kept homes, but all seem to be characterized as impulsive, socially isolated, and in serious difficulties with regard to their marriage, money, and the like. Furthermore, the parents themselves had been neglected or abused as children. Zalba points out that some research suggests that battered children also have a severely impaired relationship with the abusive parent, and not just as a consequence of the abuse. The children tend to overreact to hostility and are depressed, hyperactive, fearful, and destructive. Another study characterized abused children as bed-wetting, truant, fire setters, and withdrawn. In summary, the research on child abuse suggests a cycle or self-sustaining process involving both parents and children in situations that can be characterized as alienated, anomic, and disorganized. Propensities toward such contexts may be passed on from one generation to the next, where an abused child later becomes an abusive parent, and so on.

Zalba's research and analysis raises a fundamental question about many social problems, one that is also related to the disorganization perspective: Why do many extreme acts of violence in contemporary society go unanswered after recognition? For example, Zalba suggests that it is not only difficult to recognize the truly battered child, but that once a physician or neighbor does detect that abusive parents are the cause of a child's injury, they rarely go to the aid of the child because of a desire not to get involved in the affairs of others. Some scholars have suggested that this lack of response is a function of widespread alienation and apathy in modern society. In a study of why people often refuse to come to the aid of victims, Bibb Latané and John Darley reject these concepts as inadequate explanations.[22] They argue that a bystander confronted with an emergency is faced with a series of decisions that he must make under threat, urgency, and stress:

The overall decision of whether to intervene or not depends on his choices all along the line—that is, whether he notices an event or not, perceives it as an emergency or not, feels personal responsibility or not, is able to think of the kinds of interventions necessary or not, and has sufficient skill to intervene or not.[23]

The really important question is why some people select alienation, avoidance, or withdrawal when faced with crisis.

Latané and Darley hypothesize that the most important variable in the decision-to-intervene process is possible social influence; that is, whether or not other people have noticed the same event, perceived it as an emergency, and are present to observe (and, therefore, judge) the behavior of the potential intervener. If other people are present, a bystander is less likely to intervene. Latané and Darley suggest several reasons why this is so. The presence of other people may simply inhibit actions that could be interpreted as bizarre, unnecessary, or peculiar. If a bystander is not sure whether an event constitutes an emergency (is this child really battered, or is it merely an accident victim), he will look to others for cues. If the cues are not forthcoming to indicate that the event is critical, a response by the observer is unlikely. In addition, it is well-known that many victims of abuse and violence often resent intervention. Police characteristically encounter resentment when they attempt to intervene in domestic quarrels by trying to save a wife from being beaten by her husband. Not infrequently, the wife will turn upon the police with hostility. For this reason, some police forces are now using patrolwomen and specially trained personnel for domestic crises duties.

Latané and Darley also found, through a series of laboratory experiments involving various types of alleged emergencies, that not reporting the actions of someone committing a crime can be a mode of showing consideration for that individual as a person. No matter how reprehensible an act, people tend to hesitate for fear that the accusations might be inappropriate and intervention "might get someone into trouble." Furthermore, when only one bystander is present during an emergency, he carries all the blame for the ultimate consequences of nonintervention. In contrast, when others are present, responsibility for nonintervention can be psychologically shared with others. This type of finding has particular consequences for assessing the desirability of fail-safe systems involving nuclear devices and the single responsibility of the President of the United States to determine the necessity for military response to a threat involving nuclear warfare. The research by Latané and Darley, together with other studies, indicates that group decisions are often more undesirable because of the sharing of responsibility. Specifically, if the President in conjunction with the Joint Chiefs of Staff and Cabinet Heads were to decide collectively upon a military response during an international crisis, research shows a greater likelihood for them to select harsh, extreme alternatives, since each member of the decision-making group can share with others in an impersonal manner some of the responsibility for the outcome. In the same way, groups of people observing a mugger killing a young girl in an alley are less likely to intervene because they can share and, thereby, shift to others part of the responsibility for what happens ("I wasn't the only one who didn't do anything; why didn't the others respond?").

The study by Latané and Darley does not prove that disorganization in the form of alienation or apathy is unimportant. In fact, it presents a more sophisticated approach to understanding just how individuals come to dissociate or alienate themselves from particular events, that is; why they engage in responses that can be characterized as forms of disorganization. Ironically, the informal group bonds, by placing restraints upon behavior, can operate to create a larger social situation that seems marked by apathy and noninvolvement.

Strengths of the Paradigm—Its Implications for Policy in Race and International Relations. Another unusual use of disorganization theory to analyze problems and generate policy implications is Gunnar Myrdal's classic study of black–white relationships in the United States, which constructs a *model of cultural conflict* in which certain actualities of a society are seen to be in conflict with that society's ideals.[24] This study, completed in 1944, had an impact upon the Supreme Court ruling of 1954 on school desegregation and the passage of the 1960 Civil Rights Act. Myrdal argued that the American race problem constituted a severe dilemma, since the actual treatment of black citizens was in such obvious conflict with many basic American ideals (and was, therefore, a situation of *cultural conflict and disorganization*). However, unknown to most citizens, the immediate desires and aspirations of most blacks and whites, though seemingly in conflict, might be both met through compromise in appropriate legislation and social action. Myrdal referred to an inverse rank order of discrimination, which contrasted black goals with white goals. When whites were asked what they most opposed in terms of integration, they mentioned intermarriage and other intimate forms of personal contact (dancing, eating, and living together) as the most important to prevent, and steps such as integration in jobs, politics, or the legal system as the least important to oppose. Blacks, on the other hand, designated integration of educational and public facilities as their greatest desire to achieve, and intermarriage and other forms of personal contact to be of the lowest importance or priority.[25] Myrdal suggested, therefore, that although black and white goals were seemingly in conflict, they might in actuality be joined. To a very large extent, both the Supreme Court decision of 1954 and the shifting emphasis of Martin Luther King's movement in the 1960's achieved this merger. At the same time, many blacks still call for a kind of isolation or independence in personal affairs through appeals to black power, black identity, and black ethnicity. Most probably the passionate response of many white citizens to busing is not a manifestation of disagreement over integration of education, but rather an expression of opposition to intimate contact in neighborhood contexts and the fear that this may lead to the disintegration of white, ethnic urban zones.

A similar type of cultural conflict model can be used to explain some problems America has faced in international relations, specifically the seeming tendency to identify with and give support to many nondemocratic governments while, at the same time, theoretically espousing democratic goals for the peoples of these governments. It has been argued that the process of national development in the modern world tends to follow four sequential steps: (1) national independence and identity, (2) effective centralized government; (3) responsible government; and, lastly, (4) democratic government.[26] In other words, democracy is a distant goal for many leaders of newly emerging nations, since it seems at the moment not yet viable or possible. Of primary importance is thought to be the establishment of a strong, legitimate, and effective government, separated from previous colonial or other exogenous powers. Such a requirement can often best be met through the use of undemocratic and militaristic institutions and appeals. Not until this separation has been accomplished, and processes of economic and social development have brought about stability, can these governments institute truly democratic reforms. Yet the United States, using an idealized stereotype of the American Revolution, often seems to insist that the process be reversed, that new nations become democratic immediately. The attempts to encourage electoral processes resembling the American pattern during the war in South Vietnam are an illustration. This dilemma usually succeeds only in creating great conflict between American goals and the actions of other nations, thereby leading to a situation of international disorganization.

Strengths of the Paradigm—Its Application to Other Paradigms. An additional unique use of the disorganization paradigm was employed by Gloria Count Van Manen to criticize the deviance paradigm. She analyzed deviance in the Southeast Asian city of Singapore and found a number of dilemmas in terms of prior theory—what she called "a deviant case of deviance." [27] The incongruities were represented by high rates of immigration (therefore, supposedly marked mobility and disorganization), yet low rates of delinquency; three distinct ethnic groups (supposedly a propensity toward cultural conflict), yet low rates of crime; increasing industrialization in the urban area, yet minimal increases in delinquency and crime; cultural adaptation of Western traits, yet no significant use of marijuana or alcohol; and low socioeconomic status of the Malay, yet low rates of psychoses. Van Manen explains the low prevalence of deviance, where a high rate might be expected, by arguing that a high degree of social organization, not disorganization, actually characterizes Singapore society.

Isolation and segregation of subcultures seems to play

a role. Higher rates of deviance are observable among Singapore Indian–Pakistani populations than among Chinese and Malaysians—the former do not have separate geographic communities whereas the latter do. Van Manen hypothesizes that a lack of gradual assimilation of varied cultures can give rise to social maladjustment. Where migrant groups are not permitted to create ghettolike neighborhoods, disorganization may occur. However, not all ghetto communities minimize deviance. In the Chinese community of Singapore, low rates of deviance could be associated with strong and stable family settings, a strong sense of familial responsibility, and a commitment to tradition. Furthermore, observers have emphasized the increase in public services offered by a socialist state to its citizens as a factor in minimizing propensities toward deviance. Schools, community centers, and public housing provide some residents with the means for maintaining communal solidarity. In addition, the goals and values among the Malay (the more deviant) tend to be at variance with the goals and values of the predominant population, the Chinese. Finally, the distribution of deviance in Singapore seems to condemn serious offenses (severe crime and alcohol use) but condone minor deviance (hedonistic drug use and gambling). In summary, an unusual combination of several factors may explain the seemingly high degree of organization in Singapore, where high rates of deviance might be expected on other grounds.

This type of approach is obviously rooted solidly in the perspectives of early disorganization theorists, such as Thomas and Znaniecki, and has been utilized by others in an attempt to explain differences between American ethnic subgroups. For example, it has often been observed that America's Chinatowns seem uniquely free from the street-violence and juvenile delinquency that mars other ghetto communities. Richard T. Sollenberger has argued that special child-rearing practices seem to account for this paradox.[28] Ironically, Sollenberger found that a sample of 69 mothers from New York City's Chinatown were more permissive than a comparable group of women in Cambridge, Massachusetts. Many Chinese mothers waited until children were two years old before weaning them. The majority of Chinese mothers did not begin toilet training until

15 months of age, while only one-fifth of the Cambridge mothers waited that long. Almost all Chinese mothers reported childrens' bedtimes as 8:30 P.M. or later, while almost three-quarters of the Cambridge mothers had their children in bed before 7:30. Sollenberger found that none of the Chinese parents in his study had been divorced or separated, that mother attitudes toward husbands were positive, that family authority was shared by both parents, and that mothers had high aspirations for their children. He suggests that the solidarity of Chinese family life leads to harmonious and secure relationships for all members.

Sollenberger found that in only one respect did Chinese parents demonstrate more strictness than American parents: in prohibitions against aggressiveness. Almost half of the Chinese mothers did not permit family fighting at all (even between brothers and sisters), and the remainder were only moderately permissive. In contrast, only 6 percent of the Cambridge mothers did not permit sibling fights, 74 percent were moderately permissive, and 20 percent let the children fight as much as they wanted to. Over one-third of the Cambridge mothers actually taught their children to fight back or defend themselves, while three-quarters of the Chinese mothers made no demands that their children be aggressive. Whereas no Chinese mother would punish her children for running home for help, 15 percent of the Cambridge mothers indicated they would. Sollenberger concludes that the unique permissiveness in some child-rearing practices helps create a stable and congenial context within which family members develop trust and security. At the same time, aggressiveness and violence are condemned as adequate ways of resolving problems and crises.

If, then, aggression, particularly in the form of street violence, is identified as an example of deviant or disorganized behavior, one can argue that some forms can be taught either overtly or latently. In other words, not all deviance and disorganization is pathological—that is, foreign to a particular social system. On the contrary, some deviance and disorganization may be a natural, expected part of the system. This type of view, suggested by research like Sollenberger's, is the essential perspective of the functionalist paradigm, which will be discussed in the next chapter. Therefore, just as we saw a strength of the deviance paradigm to be its applicability to other perspectives, the disorganization paradigm leaves room for additional views as well. At the same time, the work of Sollenberg and Van Manen begins to raise questions about possible biases inherent in the disorganization paradigm, in contrast to the essentially paradigm-proving and supporting studies of Myrdal, Latané and Darley, Zalba, Markson, and Nisbet.

Possible Biases of the Disorganization Paradigm—The Case of the Black Family. Questions concerning the possible biases of the disorganization paradigm became evident in the mid-1960's in a national debate over the character of the American Negro family. In June 1965, President Lyndon Johnson gave a speech at Howard University, which, at first, seemed to show remarkable sensitivity by a white leader for the nature and extent of the basic problem of black Americans.[29] Furthermore, the speech emphasized the necessity to provide blacks with the resources for obtaining civil rights, including adequate jobs, decent housing, education, and community and family life supports. The speech also seemed to reveal a departure for the federal government, as seen in the government's intent to use decades of social science research findings to implement massive programs of needed reform. In back of that speech, however, lay a report that was to be known later in 1965 as "The Moynihan Report," after Daniel Patrick Moynihan, the Assistant Secretary of Labor and White House adviser. This report (*The Negro Family: The Case for National Action*) created a continuing controversy and caused severe splits in government agencies, the civil rights movement, and the social scientific community.

The report argues that the deterioration, or disorganization, of the Negro family system lay at the root of contemporary racial problems. To be sure, this deterioration was created by one of the worst systems of slavery the world had ever seen, the pathologies that naturally accompany rapid urbanization (divorce, separation, desertion), and the massive unemployment and poverty arising from widespread discrimination. The fundamental problem, however, was reflected in the fact that black husband–wife roles were the reverse of white husband–wife roles, that most black criminal and delinquency offenses were committed against other blacks, and that a gulf was appearing between a few stable, middle-class black families and the majority of unstable, lower-class black families. The report, therefore, suggested that immediate integration was almost impossible, since blacks lacked the means and resources to attain the level of achievement necessary for successful integration into the dominant culture. Governmental programs should therefore be designed to enhance the stability and resources of the black family by direct means.

Certainly, the major thrust of President Johnson's speech and The Moynihan Report appeared to be humane and compassionate. However, when the contents of the report became fully known in late 1965, they came under increasing criticism, most of which was related to the assumptions behind a disorganization perspective. Critics charged that the designation of the father-absent matriarchical family system as pathological was a moral and social judgment, not a social scientific fact. This family system, characteristic of some black families, seemed to be pathological only because it did not fit the white stereotype of father-dominant patriarchy. Critics claimed that this use of the disorganization paradigm actually could give rise to a more virulent form of racism, where weaknesses inherent within black society and blacks themselves, rather than within systems of white discrimination, are interpreted to be the major problem (thereby blaming the victim). In actual fact, the unique black family was a workable adaptation to a larger society that was disorganized as a consequence of slavery and discrimination. Under slavery, the male was most likely to be sold. Therefore, stability, tradition, and continuity in the black family had to be built around stable and permanent roles—usually that of an older black female (mother or grandmother), who was least likely to be sent off to other work. When black families migrated from rural contexts to urban centers, they brought with them this tradition of matriarchy. The tradition has been difficult to change largely because of continuing pathological behavior in the society as a whole—that is, white racism makes it almost impossible for black males to obtain adequate employment, become fully functioning members of normal community life, and establish stable roles for themselves. This type of criticism did not totally disavow the disorganization perspective so much as it argued that there were other sources of disorganization. The critics believed that individual behavior was not disorganized, but that larger society itself was.

Other critics pointed out that the assumption of black family disorganization was biased and distorted, since it focused only upon deviant and exceptional cases. Some research indicated that the majority of both blacks and whites in America live in contexts of high family stability.[30] Even where a greater propensity for black family instability (than for white family instability) can be detected, significant correlations between measures of disorganization (for example, male delinquency) and the matriarchal form of a black family cannot be found. Where such associations do exist in very weak form, the correlation is probably a function of other, far more important factors (white racism).[31] In other words, by choosing to concentrate upon deviant and unusual cases (those minority of black families that are different than most white families and other black families) and by unjustifiably assuming that these cases typify most black families, the social researcher and policy maker runs the risk of a self-fulfilling prophecy. Since the case was defined as deviant to begin with (a matriarchy), other forms of deviance and disorganization within the context (crime, delinquency, divorce and separation, and so on) are assumed to be related to the initial deviance, and most other classes of events in the same category (all black families) are assumed to be something like the deviant case. This is not social science—rather it is prejudgment and stereotyping of the worst kind. Therefore, the second major type of criticism did not reject the idea that the disorganization paradigm can be used to analyze some problems. It did argue, however, that the disorganization perspective did not apply to all or most cases and that it was essentially a moral and political view rather than a purely scientific one.

A third type of criticism, however, rejected the disorganization paradigm and its tacit assumptions, which were exemplified by the view that the black family is somehow deprived or disadvantaged, as contrasted to prevailing white, middle-class values and standards. This kind of argument becomes the basis for understanding increasing attacks in recent years upon the disorganization paradigm.

Critiques of Disorganization

As Kuhn pointed out, scientific paradigms dictate appropriate methods and techniques for research. The disorganization perspective lent itself particularly well to statistical analysis, and was, therefore, extremely popular during the decades when sociology was striving for scientific status. However, the methods employed frequently resulted in unwarranted conclusions.

The Need to Look Scientific—Problems with Statistical Correlations. W. S. Robinson was one of the earliest critics of the tendency to obtain and/or justify inaccurate findings through certain uses of statistical analysis.[32] He distinguishes between *ecological* and *individual* correlations. An ecological correlation uses statistics that characterize a group of people, whereas individual correlations use statistical measures related to some individual, indivisable social phenomenon. For example, if one finds that there is a high correlation between the percentage of a population that is Negro and the percentage of that same population that is illiterate, he has found an ecological correlation. Indeed, early disorganization studies showed this relationship for the 48 American states in the 1930's. Problems occurred, however, when it was then assumed that this finding disclosed a relationship between race and illiteracy. Actually, what the finding described was a population (all people living in the 48 states), which had a certain percentage black and and a certain percentage illiterate. The finding disclosed nothing about individual phenomena, particularly black citizens in certain areas. Robinson found that when one measured the correlation between the percentage of Negroes who were illiterate and the percentage of whites who were illiterate in the total population (individual correlations), the statistical difference was extremely low; indeed, the correlation was statistically insignificant and could have occurred by mere chance. What little difference in illiteracy did exist between blacks and whites was easily accounted for in terms of discrimination. What Robinson did was to measure individual properties (black versus white) rather than ecological properties (all people living in the 48 states). Robinson's intent was essentially to criticize the propensity of the disorganization paradigm to lead to the use of meaningless and misleading statistics (*the need to look scientific*).

Definitions of Disorganization Are Culture Bound. Other theorists have argued that the disorganization paradigm is inherently *culture bound* in methodology. That is, because it must define disorganization according to what are considered to be significant deviations from accepted norms or practices, the disorganization paradigm may be appropriate in one specific context but totally inapplicable in another, since accepted practices vary from one culture to another. In addition, the inherent value bias of such a definition is rarely questioned by practitioners of the paradigm. Lois DeFleur found evidence of this difficulty when attempting to apply Albert Cohen's theory of delinquency, generated within an American context, to a Latin American city (Cordoba, Argentina).[33] Cohen argued that a deviant juvenile subculture develops as a means of coping with problems caused by society's imposing unachievable middle-class values and aspirations upon frustrated lower-class youngsters. Major institutions of socialization, particularly the school and family, are seen as playing a major role in encouraging lower-class youngsters to create a "reaction subculture," one that rejects larger societal values and strikes out against them.

DeFleur analyzed a sample of the acts of delinquency that had come to the attention of the juvenile court in Cordoba during a four-year period, and interviewed a number of hardcore offenders. A delinquent gang subculture did exist in Cordoba, and the types of gangs appeared to be small, stable, and cohesive, though loosely organized. Orientation was toward immediate hedonistic gratification, and stealing was seen as a way of funding these pleasures. Other activities included sports, fighting, drinking, and girls, but not widespread drug use. DeFleur called this an *instrumental-theft type of subculture*, in contrast to Cohen's hypothesized *reaction subculture* of American gangs (similar to Cavan's contraculture).

DeFleur theorizes that differences in the social structure

of Argentina, in contrast to the United States, account for the variation in delinquency patterns. The poor in Argentina are more distinct, distant, and isolated from the dominant society than they are in America. In short, they are deprived of meaningful contact with the major social institutions of the organized society, which could act as communication links for transmitting cultural norms and values to the child:

The family of the lower class in Cordoba . . . was almost uniformly characterized by concubinage, desertion, illegitimacy, and free unions. . . . [Furthermore] lower-class families . . . were more authoritarian in their role expectations, and less open as communication systems within which the individual was free to express his emotions or to air his personal problems. . . . The lower-class youth does not have an extensive school experience. . . . For the lower-class boy of Argentina, . . . school is a brief period, often only one or two years, which he soon leaves to begin in some ill-paid and unpleasant work, where he has many of the responsibilities expected of an adult but few of the privileges.[34]

DeFleur points out that marginal participation in educational institutions is also matched by marginal participation in economic institutions. The only employment available to both the young and the more mature lower-class worker is the odious work no one else wants to do: hauling garbage, lifting, digging, carrying things on his back, and menial hand work. For this individual, the concept of work as punishment (*trabajo es castigo*) is relevant, in constrast to the American Protestant work ethic (of work as an avenue to personal fulfillment). Even the church in Cordoba, with its traditional defense of the interests of the upper class and the concomitant alienation of large segments of the lower class, has ceased to be meaningful as a link between the poor and the rest of society. DeFleur concludes that if a useful general theory of delinquency, applicable to a variety of national contexts, is to be produced, new approaches will be required. Traditional deviance and disorganization paradigms are inherently biased and cannot, therefore, be generally applied to the same type of problem behavior in different kinds of cultures.

Latent Moral Biases of the Paradigm. The problem of *latent moral bias* has led other scholars, particularly Oscar Lewis, to question the notion that lower status subcultures are deviant or disorganized, and to suggest instead that a culture of poverty or the underprivileged can have positive as well as negative aspects.[35] The violence, aggression, deviance, and sexual promiscuity of the poor, seemingly problem behavior to middle-class society, are actually meaningful ways in which these groups can contend with their status as underprivileged people. Such behavior provides means whereby individuals can survive in a hostile and threatening environment (prostitution may be one of the few success avenues open to females). Furthermore, some forms of problem behavior actually contribute to strong familial or in-group ties and relationships, thereby providing a basis of stability for daily life (for example, the role of aggression in producing gang solidarity). Lewis and others have suggested, therefore, that the poor are not deprived in the sense that they have no stable social system or culture and are in a state of continuous disorganization. On the contrary, they often possess a rich society and culture, whose norms and values simply differ from the predominant society. In the same manner, some critics of the Moynihan view of the black family have suggested that the matriarchal family form represents a unique and potentially inventive experiment in contemporary society. While more and more white, middle-class wives and mothers are only now beginning to strive for independence, black wives and mothers have experimented successfully with such independence for years. Therefore, some critics argue that the idea of disorganization is a fiction and a pejorative term applied for political and moral reasons to others who do not conform to predominant expectations. What should be analyzed are different or alternative forms of social organization, not organization versus disorganization.

There is, however, a danger in this criticism of the disorganization paradigm as well as in the paradigm itself. The notion of social or cultural deprivation and the alternative view of a rich culture of the deprived can both be used to blame the victim, analytically and in terms of programs of social action.[36] The concept of environmental deprivation arose as a humanitarian reaction to early views that deviance was inherent within individuals. Ironically, however, though the new view seems to have shifted the emphasis from individual accountability to social causes, the explanation still blames the victim and avoids questioning the system. For example, William Ryan points out that the busing protest in neighboring black and white zones of Boston in the early 1970's was explained by many of the city's leaders (including, Louise Day Hicks, leader of the "anti-integrationist" forces) in the following ways: "The culturally deprived children of Roxbury need education, not transportation"; "Their parents have no backgrounds—they're just a pair of hands"; or "We do not have inferior schools—we have been getting an inferior type of student." [37] In other words, the perspective of innate inferiority was often officially denied, but it was replaced by a view of functional inferiority attributable to the stultifying effects of poverty. At the same time, the possible culpability of the schools and the consequences of racial bigotry were all but ignored. The older fatalism of biologically deterministic theories of problems had been replaced by a new fatalism of *environmental determinism*. Furthermore, leaders, teachers, and others adopting the view of inherent deprivation acted in these terms toward the children in ways that tended to initiate and sustain that perspective in the minds of the children themselves.

At the same time, the Oscar Lewis critique of this perspective, which argues that the culture of poverty is rich, rewarding, and meaningful, can also be used to escape responsibility, romanticize poverty and inferiority, and blame the victim. It implies a kind of middle-class idealism about the deprived, a view that looks upon the ability of the poor to get away with all types of deviance (aggressive behavior, sexual promiscuity, avoidance of responsibility) with a kind of jealous envy ("Aren't they unusual and different"; "Lucky them—wish I could get away with that"; or "They really have it pretty good"). This perspective, too, can be used to imply that the problems lie inevitably within the behavior of the individuals concerned, not as a consequence of a larger social system that is amenable to adjustment and change. Indeed, some radical criticisms of older, conservative social scientific theory run this risk of romanticizing problem behavior and the intolerable conditions of life. A kind of satisfied acceptance of deviance and disorganization, even in the most extreme and unacceptable forms, can result.

The Oversocialized Conception of Man—Is Disorganization Pathological?   Dennis Wrong has criticized the entire field of sociology for what he calls an *oversocialized conception of man,* a criticism that applies especially to the disorganization paradigm.[38] This conception assumes that almost all of what man does is learned, that such learning is essential in order to create social order and stability, and that, as a consequence, societies must stress conformity in all their socialization processes. Wrong distinguishes between two meanings of the term socialization: (1) as a process of the transmission of culture and (2) as a process whereby individuals become human. He points out that where emphasis is always given to both of these meanings, an oversocialized view of man develops. That is, all men are social, but not all are socialized. All men are made human by society, but not all accept the transmission of basic cultural norms and values. It follows, then, that events that interrupt either of these processes will be considered undesirable by those committed to an oversocialized view. The view also implies that deviance and disorganization must be corrected and discouraged, that they cannot simply be seen and dismissed as exceptions to the rule in normal societies. As Ruth Jacobs points out, such a conception presents to students of sociology a fundamentally pacific picture of society, a relatively smoothly functioning system, which once in a while becomes disrupted by too rapid social change or extreme social conflict.[39] She hypothesizes that this may be why so little has been done by sociologists on studies of war as a major social problem and why many students today often violently reject sociological perspectives.

To many consumers of contemporary social science, what is called disorganization is not only *not* pathological and aberrant, but to them it seems to have become normal and typical. War, for example, appears to be a continuing fact of international life; therefore, in what sense can it possibly be considered abnormal? Many students and laymen also do not see modern society as a smoothly functioning system and, therefore, reject the notion of inherent stability. Could not instability be as inherent? Jacobs concludes that the almost total lack of sociological interest in war is a result of the fact that prevailing paradigms cannot deal with the problem. It has, therefore, been largely set aside, in Kuhn's terms, for other generations of scholars. However, for those citizens who are worried about the problem today, this is not a satisfactory response. In addition, since traditional sociological perspectives are not adequate for the analysis of war, bizarre and nonsocial concepts are often employed (analogies with aggression in other animal species, notions of a violent instinct in man). These are not only unsatisfactory in terms of social action, but they are also morally distasteful and dehumanizing to many.

Azmy Ibrahim suggests that a primary difficulty with the disorganization paradigm is its reference to *social* disorganization rather than to disorganization *in society*. Actually, the concepts "social" and "disorganization" are antithetical.[40] By definition, something that is disorganized cannot be social, according to prior assumptions based on the oversocialized conception of man. Ibrahim examines commonly used definitions of "social" and finds that they include three characteristics: these are that (1) more than one individual is involved; (2) organization and interdependence is necessary; and (3) resulting group actions are purposeful or they do something positive for the social system. In contrast, common definitions of "disorganization" emphasize a loss of organization, imperfect organization, or incongruity and conflict within society. Ibrahim concludes that the latter definitions describe what disorganization is, but they do not relate this phenomenon to the concept of what "social" is. Furthermore, they actually describe some alternative form of organization, that is, a difference only in kind that conflicts with the arbitrary standards of larger society. Ibrahim implies that the prevailing paradigm needs major reassessment. A great deal of what has been studied as social disorganization is really only disorganization in some special aspect of society (an act of violence that threatens basic values or severs familial bonds for a short time), or social organization in a new, contending form (the deviant behavior of contra-culture youth gangs or hippie subcultures).

Ibrahim's criticism points to the final difficulty inherent in the disorganization paradigm. Those concepts developed within the paradigm to analyze and explain forms of disorgani-zation (particularly anomie and alienation) become antisocial or asocial by definition. For example, anomie and alienation are seen as states characterizing social disorganization and, there-fore, as phenomena that cannot fulfill meaningful purposes for the system. Only destructive conflict will result, and the system will falter and cease to work effectively. Nowhere is this per-spective more prevalent than in the popular and social scientific views of political democracy. Apathy and alienation are seen as bad, while political participation and involvement are seen as good. With predictable regularity, Americans are implored and cajoled to vote in every election ("It doesn't matter how you vote—just vote"), since the system would presumably not func-tion if voter apathy and alienation became widespread. The concept of the alienated voter has become a standard way of explaining contemporary discontent and protest, often seen as leading to totalitarian forms of political involvement.[41]

Such popular views have a solid basis in traditional social science research. Political theories appear in three general forms: the *pluralistic*, *elitist*, and *mass-society* theories. While all use somewhat different approaches, they tend to come to the same general conclusions. Pluralistics argue that the existence of many diverse pluralistic groups, competing within a stable system, guarantees the maintenance of democracy. Through the efforts of these groups, different views become represented, many individuals can participate in decision-making processes, and orderly processes of compromise and consensus can be developed. Alienation and apathy represent threats to this type of system. Elitists argue that political action is often the pro-vince of covert power elites, who acquire and then maintain the ability to make the most important decisions because of wide-spread apathy and alienation among the citizenry. This dis-sociation from politics on the part of most citizens is simply compounded by the continuing existence of elites, and undemocratic processes result. Mass-society theorists argue that the tendency toward this type of system encourages apathy and alienation and makes maintenance of democratic processes all but impossible.[42] Thus, while these theorists argue about whether contemporary society is pluralistic, elitist, or masslike, most agree that citizen participation and involvement is fundamental for maintaining democracy.

Other research, however, raises serious question about the assumed pathological and detrimental nature of apathy and alienation. For example, if apathy is defined as simple disinterest and noninvolvement, a significant diminution in citizen apathy could lead to quick polarization and immediate conflict within the political system. As disparate and diverse subgroups became more and more actively involved in political processes, dissensus and debate would grow and eventually prevail, and accordingly the possibility of satisfactory compromise would decrease. Studies of the rise of fascism have also indicated a correlation between increased voter turnout and interest and the consolidation of a majority behind authoritarian leaders and parties. This was true in the case of the rise to power of Adolf Hitler in Germany during the 1920's and 1930's.[43] In other words, don't believe the slogan and "Just vote" for it *does* make a difference *how* one votes. Evidence from recent years also indicates that previously apathetic voters often tend to become true believers in extreme movements when they enter the political arena (for example, many among youth, the aged, women, and so on). In addition, the presence of a large uncommitted and apathetic proportion in the electorate can provide a potential basis for competing leaders and parties to confront one another in terms of basic issues. No political party can really take apathy of the voters for granted because of the possibility that such apathy could be converted to interest in and commitment to the opposition. Again, studies of the rise of fascism show that with decreasing apathy and increasing involvement goes increasing majority commitment to fewer (or single) candidates and issues. To this extent, then, voter apathy could be a contributing factor in the maintenance of democratic processes.

In a similar manner, alienation may serve positive purposes in a political system. If alienation is defined as withdrawal from commitment to prevailing norms and values, it can lead to estrangement from the prevailing alternatives and the creation of new ones. As Nisbet indicated in the discussion earlier in this chapter, the seemingly alienated are often also among the most committed. Far from being always pathological, then, alienation can become a reservoir for new talents and ideas.[44] Evaluations of this sort employ the functionalist paradigm, discussed in the next chapter, to criticize the disorganization paradigm. Where the disorganization paradigm assumes that problem behavior is useless or threatening, functionalist critics suggest that under certain conditions the same problem behavior may be vitally important to the maintenance of the system. Such criticism does not necessarily mean that apathy and alienation are always desirable, but it does mean that they are not always undesirable. This newer perspective has given rise in recent years to a rediscovery of the importance of social change and conflict in society. The present school of *conflict theory* embodies this view and represents a possible paradigm revolution in its implied criticism of the disorganization perspectives. For, as Kuhn suggested, paradigm revolutions begin when prevailing paradigms can no longer provide adequate answers to increasing numbers of acts in nature that appear to violate preconceived perceptions.

Conflict Theory: A Paradigm Revolution?

Early social scientists recognized the importance of factors leading to change, as well as of those leading to stability, in understanding social processes. For example, Karl Marx appreciated the potential role of seemingly disorganized conditions like anomie and alienation in mobilizing political movements.[45] Together with Marx, many other scholars (including Durkheim, Weber, Ferdinand Tönnies, Georg Hegel, Cooley, and others) tried to propose theories of change, as well as constructing models of social stability.[46] In addition to the efforts of these early sociologists, an analysis of the importance of social conflict was undertaken by Georg Simmel.[47] Despite these initial interests, however, the middle years of sociological development were dominated by a focus upon order and the assumption that change, conflict, and related processes represented disorder. Not until the very recent work of Lewis Coser and the emerging radical criticisms of traditional theories has the positive role of conflict in human societies been rediscovered.[48] This rediscovery has important implications for many programs aimed at the resolution of social problems.

Essentially, Coser and other conflict theorists, while admitting the disruptive aspects of conflict, also suggest that this form of behavior is vital to the maintenance of societies. At the same time, alternative processes that have usually been viewed as desirable may be undesirable. For example, cooperation obviously contributes to social cohesion and integration between subgroups, maintains order and stability, and encourages consensus and compromise. However, cooperation also discourages many types of change and variation, especially radical change, makes it difficult for groups to respond to unanticipated and unexpected crises or challenges, and maximizes collective conformity. In the same way, conflict can obviously encourage extreme forms of deviance, make maintenance of order difficult, and lead people to stereotype issues and respond to one another in only emotional ways. However, conflict also *strengthens bonds* within conflicting groups, *clarifies* issues and *goals* within conflicting groups, *lessens* the tendency for *individual deviance* within groups, and *encourages creativity* and innovation. The history of the civil rights movement in America amply illustrates the positive aspects of conflict in contemporary society, while the failure to resolve fundamental racial issues through cooperation alone illustrates the disadvantages of that process in many contexts. The recent history of the civil rights movement has been marked by the creation of new norms, institutions, and modes of social action, providing both satisfaction for many of the needs of black citizens and a basis for wider acceptance of black equality on the part of white citizens.

Coser also points out that conflict may initiate an economic and technological stimulus within a society. In the history of the Western world, technological improvement has frequently resulted from the conflict activity of trade unions with management, leading to the raising of wages. Improved wages make possible a substitution of capital investment for labor and an increase in the volume of investment. For example, militant unionism played an important role in the mechanization of coal-mining in America. In contrast, the moderate unionism of Great Britain has been identified as a factor in a stagnant economy and low productivity.[49] Coser suggests that this type of analysis raises serious questions about the traditional "human-relations" approach in industrial and management practice. Through an emphasis upon the collective purposes of the entire organization, the human-relations approach attempts to reduce conflicts of interest and manage tensions before they can result in conflict. In a similar manner, one might raise questions about the tendency of other institutions to adopt similar procedures in recent years, including universities, the military, governmental organizations, and the initiation of group therapy and sensitivity sessions within community and institutional contexts. If conflict over basic differences in values and beliefs is avoided or quelled, a crucial source of change and renewal may be eliminated and an emphasis upon conformity to general group norms may be substituted. Traditional paradigms, such as the disorganization perspective, have also assumed that conflict (and other social contradictions, that is, deviations from the normal) represents the breakdown or absence of norms. This mistaken notion is prevalent in the current thinking about war.

Positive Effects of Conflict—The Example of Human Warfare and the Study of Nonviolent Resistance. The beliefs that warfare is a barbarity that frequently occurs because other means for resolving differences fail and that warfare cannot be fought by rules or regulations reflect the commitment to a disorganization paradigm. In reality, the few studies of warfare that are available suggest the opposite. Warfare is not conflict where other means have failed, primarily because other means do not presently exist (means such as world law, a world court, an effective international peace-keeping force). On the contrary, war itself has become the norm to be employed in international relationships. Furthermore, wars are fought by rules, which are often informal but which nevertheless govern appropriate and inappropriate behavior, even within such an extreme context.

In a classic analysis of warfare throughout human history Quincy Wright traces the close connection between warfare and cultural change.[50] He identifies three basic types: *primitive, historic,* and *modern* warfare. Primitive warfare was communal conflict directed against a common enemy, sanctioned by tribal mores, and sustained by total participation of all members in the activity (not merely a special elite or class of citizens). Primitive women often accompanied men into combat or witnessed and supported the fighting from the sidelines. Since strong in-group taboos existed against murder, primitive warfare became an acceptable outlet for pent-up aggressions. Personal drives, such as sex and hunger, were satisfied when conquered people and their material goods were taken as rightful booty. Warfare was highly ritualized in primitive societies, with great emphasis upon celebration before and after battle and minimum emphasis upon killing and destruction. As a consequence, the basic function of primitive warfare was the maintenance of tribal and clan solidarity, and conflict rarely led to cultural change.

In contrast, Wright indicates that historic warfare (from the Mesopotamian civilization to about the 15th century) promoted radical social change, resulting in the disintegration and disappearance of many civilizations. Personal drives toward war were replaced by private interests of ruling elites and cliques. Mercenary and colonial armies became commonplace. Total defeat or subjugation of an enemy became the ultimate goal, as conflicts were waged to gain access to valuables possessed by another, such as strategic frontiers, natural resources, markets, potential for religious conversion, wealth. Wright indicates that though no international rule of law existed to govern conduct, historic civilizations did possess two sets of doctrine controlling behavior. One set dealt with the appropriate behavior toward friends and enemies and was drawn from religion and ethics. The other set consisted of norms upholding the natural and divine right and prerogative of rulers to wage war.

Finally, Wright suggests that from the 15th century to the end of World War II a period of modern warfare emerged. The development of the ideas of humanism, liberalism, pragmatism, and relativism ironically made warfare more inclusive and, often, more destructive. Wars were waged less for economic, social, or political gain and more for ideological reasons ("to make the world safe for democracy," "to bring about a better civilization"). All combatants used the same types of appeals; thus, both Communists and anti-Communists saw their mission as salvation of the world, as did Nazis and anti-Nazis. In addition, since the new ethical values of the postmedieval world made men more interdependent, the likelihood that people could remain uninvolved or neutral during international conflict greatly decreased. Somewhat similar to primitive societies, total commitment to and participation in war-making was demanded of all citizens. As a consequence, the early distinction between combatants and noncombatants broke down, and widespread destruction of civilian facilities and populations was made more likely. The result of modern warfare was a unique combination of the results of primitive and historic warfare. Like historic warfare, modern war brought rapid social change leading to the collapse of many defeated civilizations (the Third Reich) or the radical transformation of others (the democratization of Japan after World War II). Even the victors were importantly influenced by contact with other societies and cultures. Yet, like primitive warfare, modern warfare also led to the consolidation of many alliances and nations and to a spreading of Western values committed to internationalism, thereby resulting in a kind of global stability. At present, the idea of world power blocs reflects this type of stability. The emergence of the League of Nations and later the United Nations symbolizes the general tendency towards an international community seeking means for the establishment of international law to govern and diminish violent conflict.

This type of conflict analysis does not assume that warfare is an example of disorganized behavior, resulting from a breakdown in norms and leading to only pathological results. On the contrary, scholars like Wright are arguing that even the

most violent and presumably morally abhorrent forms of conflict are related to fundamental human attitudes and values and
can serve, in some circumstances, to bring about needed change
or perform "positive" functions. What Wright has actually done
is to criticize traditional perspectives of warfare from a new
point of view that argues that conflict can be functional. Conflict theorists are not interested in how such forms of behavior
can be eliminated from society; rather they are concerned with
ways in which conflict behavior can be redirected into productive, not destructive, channels and directions. This notion of
conflict management differs markedly from the idea of human-
relations conflict management that arises from a deviancy or
disorganization paradigm.

An illustration of how new conflict theory leads scholars
to look for alternatives can be found in studies of nonmilitary,
nonviolent means of national defense, as a substitute for classic
aggressive defense. This perspective is commonly misunderstood by those who accuse the new theorists, often of radical
political persuasions, of pretending that war can be eliminated
despite threats from despotic rulers and of favoring a study of
surrender. "Better Red than dead" and "studies of surrender"
have been used as the slogans theoretically epitomizing the
emerging field of peace studies. This view, however, is totally
inappropriate and inaccurate. The more knowledgeable peace
researchers argue that in some cases national defense is understandably necessary (when a Hitler invades one's country).
They point out, though, that military resistance may be the least
effective mode of opposition and conflict and that it may be
self-destructive in the long run (causing great deprivation and
casualties to all combatants). The philosophy of nonviolent
resistance rests upon the assumption that withdrawal of support
or legitimacy for imposed authority is the most effective form of
conflict. This type of concept is related to Nisbet's contrast between power and authority. The new view of conflict argues that
nonviolent resistance has been commonplace throughout human
history (strikes, boycotts, refusals to work, sabotage, sick days,
refusals to vote or pay taxes) and has even been effectively
employed in the most extreme circumstances (resistance on the

part of some Jews in World War II, resistance activities in the Scandinavian countries during Nazi occupation). Therefore, it is argued that if national populations could be mobilized toward total, cohesive resistance, using nonviolent means (mass refusal to work, mass refusal to pay taxes or fines, disregard of official communication channels, and so on), any government attempting to coerce authority would rapidly fail.[51]

Alternatives to Rebellion and Revolution—The Institutionalization of Conflict. The new conflict theorists have also sought alternative forms for contemporary internal conflict by proposing adaptations in prevailing institutional structures. The obvious model from American history is the trade union movement. At first, labor–management conflict took place in the streets in the form of open warfare between the military representatives of prevailing institutions (the police, national guard and army, or hired "goons") and the workers and their violence-prone representatives. Through a series of significant changes in the institutional structure (unionism and organization of workers, the initiation of labor laws, and the like), the conflict moved from the streets into other social forms. Conflict was managed, therefore, to the extent that it was channeled into more productive routes. In a recent analysis of the continuing conflict in Northern Ireland, Anders Boserup suggests that some similar resolution may be possible within that context.[52]

Using the new conflict perspective, Boserup indicates that through history the antagonisms between Catholics and Protestants has become the primary way of maintaining the North Irish social system, not an example of social disorganization or disintegration. In other words, a fundamentally *antagonistic relationship* between two ethnic groups has become *the basis of the social order.* This is a function of several things. First, indigenous institutions are weak since Northern Ireland has been essentially a political and economic colony of Britain for decades. The fact that British troops, rather than local police, must be used to quell the contemporary disturbances is an example of this dependence and weakness. Second, Northern Ireland has lacked a traditionally strong ruling class. The old aristocracy was land based, an increasing anachronism in an industrializing context. Third, as a consequence, both major political parties (the Protestant Unionists and the Catholic Nationalists) must revive sectarian appeals to old religious prejudices and hatreds in order to mobilize support and continue the functioning of the political system.

Boserup suggests that the two parties stand in perfect relationship to one another. They are one another's opposite, and neither could continue to exist without the other as a kind of scapegoat. However, this type of conflict relationship is disadvantageous on two counts. First, it frequently erupts into violence, causing severe problems in the system. Second, it makes adequate recognition and resolution of the real problems of Northern Ireland all but impossible. These problems include the totally inadequate representation of many lower-class Catholics and some lower-class Protestants in the political system; the unavailability of adequate jobs, housing, and education for both Catholic and Protestant lower classes; the continuing economic and political colonialization of Northern Ireland by Britain (because of Northern Ireland's dependence upon Britain); and the continuing religious prejudices and hatreds. Boserup suggests that major institutional change, especially in the political arena, might rechannel the basic conflict into more meaningful forms. He concludes by indicating that Britain could use her power to set up a bicameral government: one branch Catholic, the other Protestant. Each branch of government would possess its own financial and political resources to decide upon basic needs in housing, education, and specific welfare problems. Both branches of government, however, would also control a larger budget used to address issues cutting across religious divisions (domestic order, sanitation, general welfare, industrial development, and so on). A majority of both branches would be required to initiate policy at either level. Finally, of course, Britain must withdraw its presence in North Ireland to permit internal adjustments free from outside influence. Thus, the basic divisions in the society would be recognized but channeled into institutional structures, while some degree of indigenous cooperation would be required for the functioning of the larger society.[53] In addition, this new form of government would create strength and independence for Northern Ireland. Such a model might also be used in certain communities in the United States where serious black-white differences impair or prevent the solution of community problems.

Criticism of New Conflict Theory. New conflict theory has been criticized on several grounds. Some scholars argue that, though it claims to be a better representation of contemporary reality than older paradigms, conflict theory does not work in many cases. For example, George Brager found in a study of Mobilization for Youth (a prototypical antipoverty program on New York's Lower East Side) that conflict with external enemies did not lead to internal solidarity and cohesion.[54] On the contrary, internal discord arose over the means that the organization employed to meet external threats. Thus, internal discord was a function of external conflict, not a function of internal malintegration. Other scholars have argued that, in its more radical forms, conflict theory runs the risk of romanticizing the conflict form of interaction and ignoring the fact that extreme conflict can cause extensive disorganization within social systems. Finally, some defenders of prevailing paradigms have maintained that conflict theory rests upon its own peculiar moral and political judgments. Cooperation, compromise, and consensus are viewed as pathological, to the extent they are seen to be used by the powerful to repress the majority, or by the majority to repress selected minorities. Thus, new conflict theory raises important questions about the disorganization paradigm, but in so doing, some of its adherents often commit many of the same kinds of errors of bias and exaggeration they accuse others of committing.

In conclusion, the battle between adherents of the disorganization paradigm and those seeking alternatives, such as conflict theory, tends to become, in Kuhn's terms, more than a scientific matter. The perspective that one adopts will depend upon the kind of ideal society one envisions for the future and upon one's personal judgments about what constitutes appropriate and inappropriate behavior. These judgments will in turn determine the type of problems that are selected for study, how they are studied, and what conclusions for social action are reached.

Furthermore, in this discussion of the criticisms of the disorganization paradigm, we have also seen evidence of the third and probably most popular paradigm in social science, which sees problems as *functions of the normal operation of the social system.* The success of functionalism has been a consequence of this paradigm's ability to handle many of the criticisms directed at others, particularly the charge that social problems must be viewed as bad or undesirable. At the same time, functionalism has been more vehemently attacked in recent years by those arguing for new perspectives. These attacks have arisen partly because of functionalism's moral and political biases, which tend to be more covert and subtle (and, therefore, allegedly more dangerous) and partly because of functionalism's status as the most influential paradigm, whose adherents constitute some of the most prestigious names in modern social science. Even in science, the major thrust of revolutionary movements tends to be directed against the elites of the system.

Notes to Chapter 5

1. Robert E. Park, Ernest W. Burgess, and Roderick D. McKenzie, *The City* (Chicago: University of Chicago Press, 1925).
2. See Robert E. L. Faris and H. Warren Dunham, *Mental Disorders in Urban Areas* (Chicago: University of Chicago Press, 1939); and Clifford Shaw, Henry McKay, *et al.*, *Delinquency Areas* (Chicago: University of Chicago Press, 1929).
3. A recent account of social disorganization in a seemingly ideal and planned housing community, outside of Paris, France, can be found in Mary Blume's "The Trouble with Paradise," *International Herald Tribune* (February 8, 1973), p. 14. Social isolation during the day and the absence of employment led wives to engage in exaggerated neurotic behavior, including repainting walls of an apartment a different color every six months, washing clean windows every other day, counting the infrequent cars that passed, or counting the curtains in people's windows. A local physician indicated that treatment was

difficult, since to mention a psychiatrist would imply madness, thus risking the possibility that a neurosis would become even more severe.

4. See, for example, Ritchie P. Lowry's critique of the myth that small, less urban communities are free from typical social problems, in "The Myths Behind Small-Town Conservatism," *Transaction, 3* (November/ December 1965), pp. 31–36; or a critique of the theory that small towns experience disorganizing pressures because they can be found within the larger context of a conflict-prone masslike society, in Arthur J. Vidich and Joseph Bensman, *Small Town in Mass Society* (Garden City, N.Y.: Doubleday, 1960).

5. William I. Thomas and Florian Znaniecki, *The Polish Peasant in Europe and America* (New York: Alfred A. Knopf, 1927).

6. Robert A. Nisbet, "The Twilight of Authority," *The Public Interest, 15* (Spring 1969), pp. 3–9.

7. Kenneth Keniston, "You Have To Grow Up in Scarsdale to Know How Bad Things Really Are," *The New York Times Magazine* (April 27, 1969), pp. 27–29, 122–130.

8. Philip M. Hauser, "The Chaotic Society: Product of the Social Morphological Revolution," *American Sociological Review, 34* (February 1969), pp. 1–19.

9. *Ibid.*, pp. 1–3.

10. *Ibid.* See Hauser's article for extensive references to other research related to this discussion of population problems.

11. *Ibid.*, p. 4.

12. See Earl Rubington and Martin S. Weinberg, *The Study of Social Problems: Five Perspectives* (New York: Oxford University Press, 1971), pp. 52–53 and 85–87, for an excellent summary of these two variations of the disorganization paradigm.

13. Philip M. Hauser, "The Chaotic Society: Product of the Social Morphological Revolution," *American Sociological Review, 34* (February 1969), pp. 1–19; and William F. Ogburn, *Social Change* (New York: B. W. Huebsch, 1922).

14. See Robert A. Nisbet, *The Social Bond* (New York: Alfred A. Knopf, 1970), pp. 246–280, for a thoughtful discussion of the uses and misuses of the concepts of alienation and anomie.

15. *Ibid.*, p. 264.

16. Howard S. Becker, "Becoming a Marihuana User," *The American Journal of Sociology, 59* (November 1953), pp. 235–242.

17. Herbert Hendin, *Suicide and Scandinavia* (New York: Grune & Stratton, 1964); and *Black Suicide* (New York: Basic Books, 1969).

18. "Roundup of Current Research—Young Suicide," *Society* (formerly *Transaction*), 9 (June 1972), p. 12.

19. Elizabeth Markson, "A Hiding Place to Die," *Transaction, 9* (November/December 1971), pp. 48–54.

20. *Ibid.*, p. 54.

21. Serapio R. Zalba, "Battered Children," *Transaction, 8* (July/August 1971), pp. 58–61.

22. Bibb Latané and John M. Darley, *The Unresponsive Bystander: Why Doesn't He Help?* (New York: Appleton-Century-Crofts, 1968).

23. *Ibid.*, p. 36.

24. Gunnar Myrdal, Richard Sterner, and Arnold Rose, *An American*

Dilemma: The Negro Problem and Modern Democracy (New York: Harper & Row, 1944).

25. See J. Allen Williams, Jr., and Paul L. Wienir, "A Reexamination of Myrdal's Rank Order of Discriminations," *Social Problems, 14* (Spring 1967), pp. 443–454.

26. See Ritchie P. Lowry, "Aspirations of New Nations, Developmental Processes, and the Role of the Military" in "To Arms: Changing Military Roles and the Military-Industrial Complex," *Social Problems, 18* (Summer 1970), pp. 8–11.

27. This discussion is adapted from a paper delivered at the Criminology Session of the Annual Meeting of the American Sociological Society in San Francisco, September 1969—Gloria Count Van Manen, "A Deviant Case of Deviance: Singapore."

28. "Why Chinatown's Children Are Not Delinquent," *Transaction, 5* (September 1968), p. 3.

29. For an excellent synopsis of important facts concerning this issue, see Lee Rainwater and William L. Yancey, "Black Families and the White House," *Transaction, 3* (July/August 1966), pp. 6–11, 48–53; and *The Moynihan Report and the Politics of Controversy* (Cambridge: MIT Press, 1967).

30. See, for example: Reynolds Farley and Albert I. Hermalin, "Family Stability: A Comparison of Trends Between Blacks and Whites," *American Sociological Review, 36* (February 1971), pp. 1–17.

31. Lawrence Rosen, "Matriarchy and Lower Class Negro Male Delinquency," *Social Problems, 17* (Fall 1969), pp. 175–189.

32. W. S. Robinson, "Ecological Correlations and the Behavior of Individuals," *American Sociological Review, 15* (June 1950), pp. 351–357.

33. Lois B. DeFleur, "Alternative Strategies for the Development of Delinquency Theories Applicable to Other Cultures," *Social Problems, 17* (Summer 1969), pp. 30–39.

34. *Ibid.*, pp. 35–37.

35. See, for example, Oscar Lewis, *La Vida* (New York: Random House, 1966).

36. For example, see the following references: M. Deutsch, "The Disadvantaged Child and the Learning Process," in *Education in Depressed Areas*, A. H. Passow, ed. (New York: Teachers College Bureau of Publications, 1963), pp. 163–179; Oscar Lewis, *Children of Sanchez* (New York: Random House, 1961); Frank Riessman, *The Culturally Deprived Child* (New York: Harper & Row, 1961); and William Ryan, "Blaming the Victim: The Folklore of Cultural Deprivation," *This Magazine Is About Schools, 5* (Spring 1971), pp. 97–117.

37. William Ryan, *ibid.*, p. 98.

38. Dennis H. Wrong, "The Oversocialized Conception of Man in Modern Sociology," *American Sociological Review, 26* (April 1961), pp. 183–193.

39. Ruth Harriet Jacobs, "American Sociology and the Ostrich Approach to War," informal paper presented at the Annual Meeting of Eastern Sociological Society (April 1972).

40. Azmy Ishak Ibrahim, "Disorganization in Society, But Not Social Disorganization," *The American Sociologist, 3* (February 1968), pp. 47–48.

41. For example, see Abraham Ribicoff, "The Alienation of the American Worker," *Saturday Review* (April 22, 1972), pp. 29–33.

42. For a summary and discussion of these types of theories, see Ritchie P. Lowry and Robert P. Rankin, *Sociology: Social Science and Social Concern* (New York: Charles Scribner's Sons, 1972), pp. 322–339; and Ritchie P. Lowry, *Who's Running This Town? Community Leadership and Social Change* (New York: Harper & Row Torchbook, 1968), pp. xvii–xxvii, 233–244. See also, Marvin E. Olsen, ed., *Power in Societies* (New York: Macmillan, 1970).

43. See Inge Breitner Powell, "The Non-Voters: Some Questions and Hypotheses," *Berkeley Publications in Society and Institutions* (now *Berkeley Journal of Sociology*), *1* (Spring 1955), pp. 25–35.

44. Ritchie P. Lowry, "The Functions of Alienation in Leadership," *Sociology and Social Research*, *46* (July 1962), pp. 426–435.

45. Ritchie P. Lowry, "Leadership Interaction, Group Consciousness, and Social Change," *Pacific Sociological Review*, *7* (Spring 1964), pp. 22–29.

46. For a summary of some of these theories, see Ritchie P. Lowry and Robert P. Rankin, *Sociology: Social Science and Social Concern* (New York: Charles Scribner's Sons, 1972), pp. 546–560.

47. Georg Simmel, *Conflict*, Kurt H. Wolff, trans. (New York: The Free Press, 1955).

48. Lewis Coser, *The Functions of Social Conflict* (New York: The Free Press, 1956); "Social Conflict and the Theory of Social Change," *The British Journal of Sociology*, *8* (September 1957); and *Continuities in the Study of Social Conflict* (New York: The Free Press, 1967).

49. Lewis Coser, *Continuities in the Study of Social Conflict, ibid.*, pp. 20–23.

50. Quincy Wright, *A Study of War* (Chicago: University of Chicago Press, 1942), 2 vols.

51. The developing literature on this new view of conflict and nonviolent resistance is extensive and cannot be meaningfully noted here. However, the following are examples of the types of theories and studies that are available: C. Delzell, *Mussolini's Enemies: The Italian Anti-Fascist Resistance* (Princeton, N.J.: Princeton University Press, 1961); G. Fisher, *Russian Opposition to Stalin: A Case Study in World War II* (Cambridge, Mass.: Harvard University Press, 1952); Johan Galtung, "Pacifism from a Sociological Point of View," *Journal of Conflict Resolution*, *3* (1959), pp. 48–67; William A. Nesbitt, *Teaching About War and War Prevention* (New York: Foreign Policy Association, 1971); *Peace Research Reviews*, *1–4*, Nos. 1–6 (1969–1972), available through Canadian Peace Research Institute, Oakville, Ont., Canada; Adam Roberts, ed., *Civilian Resistance as a National Defense* (London: Penguin Pelican Book, 1969); M. O. Sibley, ed., *The Quiet Battle: Writings on the Theory and Practice of Nonviolent Resistance* (Garden City, N.Y.: Doubleday, 1963); and J. W. Vander Zanden, "The Non-Violent Resistance Movement Against Segregation," *The American Journal of Sociology*, *68* (March 1963), pp. 544–550.

52. Anders Boserup, "The Politics of Protracted Conflict," *Transaction*, *7* (March 1970), pp. 22–31.

53. It is interesting to note that in early 1973 the British government issued a "White Paper" on the future of Northern Ireland, which suggested

restructuring of the political process similar to Boserup's model, with the important exception of the eventual withdrawal of British troops and influence. See Anthony Lewis, "The Irish Quagmire: After the White Paper," *International Herald Tribune* (March 24, 1973), p. 9. Another model for this type of political institutionalization of conflict, though a not completely successful one, can be found in Belgium, which has had to accommodate to the French-Flemish culture and language divisions within the country. For example, see Martin Vasey, "Politics: Coalition at the Crossroads," *The Bulletin* (of Brussels), 39 (October 20, 1972), p. 13; and "French Cultural Dominance Protested by 20,000 Flemish," *Brussels Times,* 377 (October 19, 1972), p. 9. Also see newspaper reports of the crisis threatening the coalition government of Belgium during November and December 1972.

54. George Brager, "Commitment and Conflict in a Normative Organization," *American Sociological Review, 34* (August 1969), pp. 482–491.

Threat to morality or a necessary safety valve?
(Hap Stewart, Black Star)

6. Problems as Functions of the Social System

No single paradigm in social science has experienced such widespread acceptance as functionalism has, particularly since the 1940's. As we have already seen in our discussion of popular myths, deviance, and disorganization, elements of this paradigm continually appear in other perspectives about social problems. Don Martindale has described the popularity of the functionalist view in the following way:

So popular did functionalism become in American sociology in the post-World War II period that it was fashionable in the 1950's to treat it as coextensive with sociology. In his presidential address to the American Sociological Association in 1959, for example, Kingsley Davis denied that there was some special method of functional analysis in sociology. Rather, he insisted that it was sociology.[1]

Martindale indicates that this view does a disservice to the variety of competing perspectives within modern sociology and makes it difficult to assess the special role of functional theory in the history of the discipline.

Old Versus New Views: Science Versus Humanism

According to Martindale, social science, especially sociology, has been marked by two major conflicts throughout its young history.[2] An understanding of these dialectical confrontations discloses the reasons for the unique success of functionalism. The most significant historical conflict has been between those in social science who espouse a predominantly *scientific orientation* (positivists) and those who argue for a maintenance of a *humanistic orientation* (antipositivists). Among the early founders of sociology, Comte was a positivist, who stated that the discipline should strictly model itself after the procedures, techniques, and framework of the natural sciences (especially biology). Max Weber tended more toward a humanistic interpretation of human experience, using the methods of history and empathic personal observation, though he did not deny the usefulness of some rigorous data collection and analysis. This debate still rages today. The Chicago School of Sociology and the period immediately after World War II were both marked by the ascendency of positivists, while recent criticisms of many prevailing paradigms have stressed the need for more humanistic views since the study of man has allegedly become dehumanized through overrationalization and overscientization.

The second historic conflict in social science has been between those who maintain that a *totalistic view of man* is most appropriate (holists), in contrast to those who argue for a more *individualistic view* (elementarists). According to Martindale, holists see society as an ultimate reality consisting of interrelated parts that transcend and are superior to the individual and his personal acts. Elementarists see society as simply the summation of individual acts, each act being fundamentally important in and of itself. Elementarists have accused holists of reifying and deifying the social system, while holists have accused elementarists of having a mechanistic view of human behavior. For example, an elementarist would argue that when a man holds up a store or smokes pot, the meaning of the act to him—and the immediate context of the act, which determines his interaction with others—are what is really important, not some artificial abstraction of larger society and its presumed influence upon him. Holists would argue that individual acts of deviance and disorganization can only be understood in terms of their relationship to larger social contexts—that they are not isolated, idiosyncratic events.

In other words, positivists and antipositivists argue about the appropriate methods for the study of man (science versus humanism), and elementarists and holists argue about appropriate views of the nature of social reality (Which is fundamentally more important? The individual and small groups of interacting individuals or the larger social system?). Martindale depicts the historical development of sociology in terms of the possible combinations of these two major conflicts (see Table 6-1).[3]

Table 6–1

Historical periods of development in the Western world, categorized according to types of major social-theory conflict*

Period of Development	Type of Theory by Major Conflicts
17th and 18th century philosophy of the Enlightenment	Positivistic Elementarism
Sociology's birth in the 19th century	Positivistic Holism
Mid-20th century criticisms of positivistic holism:	
New radical views of the social system	Antipositivistic Holism
A return to individualistic views of social reality	Antipositivistic Elementarism

* After Don D. Martindale, "Limits of and Alternatives to Functionalism in Sociology," in *Functionalism in the Social Sciences: The Strengths and Limits of Functionalism in Anthropology, Economics, Political Science, and Sociology,* Monograph No. 5, Don D. Martindale, ed. (Philadelphia: American Academy of Political and Social Science, 1965), p. 152.

The 17th and 18th century philosophers originated social scientific thought in their attempts to minimize distinctions between science and humanism. Indeed, they pushed for an extension of scientific thought into social and cultural problem areas. Although these men were reformist (they hoped to re-order society to meet individual needs more adequately), they were at the same time anti-revolutionary; therefore, they believed that the nature of social reality and of the ideal society resided in the potential of individuals, not in some super-imposed social system.

In the 19th century, when sociology was born, the world had experienced the dramatic revolutions (political, urban, industrial) leading to the development of the modern nation-state. An elementaristic view obviously seemed less applicable to prevailing reality, and the concept of society or humanity as an organic whole, transcending the individual, was developed. The new view was neither reformist nor revolutionary. In reality, Martindale indicates that sociology made its appearance as a conservative answer to radical socialism and had as its task the justification and consolidation of the newly emerged mass state in nonrepressive forms. The positivistic-holistic theory pre-dominated until the mid-20th century, a period again marked by upheaval and rapid change. This new turmoil suggested to many that positivistic holism was inadequate and dangerous on several grounds. It had become an overrationalized, overscientized handmaiden for the modern state and other repressive social organizations. Furthermore, positivistic holism was seen as having played a role in the growth of uncontrolled technology and rationalism, and the resulting increase in dehumanization. Antipositivistic holism rapidly developed under the influence of C. Wright Mills and other radical social scientists. This view retained the organic conception of society, rejected the overly scientific concern of earlier social science, and sought radically new forms of social organization that could provide individuals with better, more humane social contexts. At the same time, antipositivistic elementarism developed in new theories of ex-istentialism and phenomenology. Adherents of this view rejected both the scientism and holism of earlier theory and sought ways of returning to true human independence and individuality, free from any social constraints.

Many of the perspectives and criticisms of prevailing myths and paradigms considered in previous chapters reflect these four types of views in various ways. The popular myths of blaming the victim and evil equals evil are indebted to elementaristic views of social reality. In addition, they became incorporated into some positivistic (scientific) perspectives, such as the Jensen and Herrnstein conceptions of I.Q. as biologically determined. Early work that adopted the deviance and disorganization perspectives was based upon positivistic-holistic views, as exemplified by the work of Durkheim on suicide, Cavan and Cohen on delinquency, and Burgess on disorganized urban zones. In contrast, radical criticisms of prevailing paradigms, which argue that the social system, rather than the individual, is pathological or sick, and that deviance is a function of social labeling, typify antipositivistic-holism. Finally, current experiments based upon a return to individual experiences, life-styles, and awareness, experiments that involve nonrational and emotive interaction with others while rejecting dependence upon any social agency, illustrate the new forms of antipositivistic elementarism.

Using these four basic categories, Martindale classifies types of sociological theories and paradigms. It becomes apparent that, while functionalism is only one of many alternatives, it has played a special role in the evolution of social theory.[4] Table 6-2 delineates the relationships among the four basic categories, the major paradigms, and certain theorists. Categorization of this sort does some injustice to the paradigms, schools of thought, and theorists, since elements of all of the major conflicts in sociology continually appear in other contexts. For example, we have seen how functionalist theory can be incorporated into deviance and disorganization perspectives, how the disorganization paradigm can be adapted to deviant behavior views, and the like. In general, however, paradigms and theorists can be distinguished by viewing their major commitments in terms of scientific-humanistic methods and holistic-elementaristic philosophies of social reality.

The Popularity of Functionalism—A Humanistic and Innovative Perspective. Functionalism is important because it arose early in the discipline and experienced great popularity at a critical point in the development of social science. The reasons for this

Table 6–2

The relationship between types of social theories, paradigms or schools of thought, and specific theorists*

Type of Theory by Major Conflicts	Paradigm or School of Thought	Example of Theorist
Positivistic Elementarism	Behaviorism and Inter-action or Symbolic Interactionism	George Mead; Erving Goffman
Positivistic Holism	Marxism; much Devi-ance and Disorganiza-tion Theory; Non-Marxist Conflict Theory	Karl Marx; Emile Durkheim; Ruth Cavan; Ernest Bur-gess; Lewis Coser
Antipositivistic Holism	Functionalism; New Radical Sociology; View of a Pathological or Sick Society; Labeling Theory	Functionalists to be discussed in this chap-ter; C. Wright Mills; Howard Becker
Antipositivistic Elementarism	Phenomenology and Existentialism; Collec-tive Behavior and some new Behaviorist Theory	One form of anti-functionalist theory, discussed at the end of this chapter

* After Don D. Martindale, "Limits of and Alternatives to Functionalism in Sociology," in *Functionalism in the Social Sciences: The Strengths and Limits of Functionalism in Anthropology, Economics, Political Science, and Sociology,* Monograph No. 5, Don D. Martindale, ed. (Philadelphia: American Academy of Political and Social Science, 1965), p. 161.

early acceptance were several. First, the organic holistic view seemed to be a reasonable characterization of the nature of man's society. Not only was this conception borrowed from the natural sciences, the early model for social science, but the only alternative (a mechanistic view of man) appeared nonhuman and unacceptable. Man has a tendency to anthropomorphize, that is, to view all objects in his environment, including the nonhuman, as extensions of himself. Thus, man uses human names and terms when talking about cars, planes, and other technological devices. He attributes to these objects human personalities and nature. In a sense, organic theory did the same for social objects, such as human relationships, human groups, institutions, organizations, and society as a whole. Man reasoned that if these social objects were a result of human planning, they must possess humanoid characteristics, furthermore, since man was organic in nature, social objects must be organic—certainly they were not mechanical, inanimate things, or unrelated isolated parts of a larger system without design.

Second, with the birth of the discipline, initial emphasis was placed upon becoming totally scientific. As a consequence, functionalism became the only viable alternative for those who wanted to maintain an essentially humanistic commitment. Functionalism became the respectable refuge for antipositivists.

Third, the functionalism paradigm in Kuhn's terms, was general and broad enough to provide room for all kinds of puzzle solving and theory formulation. Indeed, its nonscientific bias meant that intellectual speculation, creativity, and imagination were encouraged. At the same time, functionalism was adaptable by positivistic adherents. Theories that developed within a functionalist framework could be subjected, although often with some degree of difficulty, to some kinds of scientific verification. For example, we saw that Robert Merton's goals–means concept of deviance, developed within an organic holistic perspective, is not easily testable; however, some scientists have utilized the basic ideas when analyzing various forms of deviant behavior. Cohen's studies of delinquent reaction subcultures, for example, are indebted to Merton's categories of rebellion and retreatism.

At the very start of social science, therefore, the functionalist paradigm became important because it seemed reasonable, workable, and a source of creative and critical work. By the mid-20th century, functionalism moved to predominance because of two new conditions, ironically a mixture of critical and conservative elements. The critical condition was the increased tendency for many scientists, students, and laymen to object to the work of scientians. Functionalism provided a traditional basis for launching such criticisms. Though this movement represented a marked attack upon the assumptions behind much social scientific work of recent years, it also had its basis in traditional appeals for a return to earlier humanism. The second new condition of the mid-20th century was the necessity for social scientists to disavow threatening radical and rebellious pretensions and ally themselves with the establishment. After World War II, social science, especially in America, was discovered by the establishment. As we saw in the first chapter, social scientists in large numbers were employed by all levels of government, industry, business, labor, churches, welfare agencies, and the like, to study problems and provide answers. This newly found status and acceptance could be easily lost if leaders and constituencies in these social contexts felt that social science represented a radical threat to the status quo. Functionalism provided a basis for criticism, but criticism that was reformist, not revolutionary. It also provided a way in which social scientists could disavow Marxism, at a time when many social scientists felt threatened by Cold War antipathies, Senator Joseph McCarthy's campaign against subversives, and the like. In other words, functionalism started as a humanistic criticism of scientism and evolved into a moderately reformist philosophy, congenial to the liberal and anti-Communist collectivism and statism of the Western world from 1940 to 1960.

Kingsley Davis' Analysis of Prostitution—An Example of the Strengths and Weaknesses of Functionalism.   An illustration of this dual character (criticism plus conservatism) can be found in Kingsley Davis' classic analysis of the functions of prostitution in contemporary society.[5] In the best myth-breaking tradition of sociological analysis, Davis begins by dismissing popular attitudes and previous explanations of this problem as inappropriate and misleading. He points out that the moralistic view of prostitution as an evil or sin that must be abolished cannot explain why this form of behavior has existed in so many social contexts throughout history. Furthermore, he indicates the emptiness of the argument that prostitution arises "naturally" because of the inherent nature of man. He also attacks purely scientific studies that collect statistics to "prove" that prostitution is bad because it spreads venereal disease. Davis points out that sexual promiscuity and carelessness in sexual relationships, not prostitution, create venereal disease problems; in addition, prostitution can, if desired, be medically monitored and controlled.

Essentially, Davis maintains, as a functionalist, that prostitution is bound to other social institutions in a self-sustaining fashion. By examining prostitution throughout history and in different cultures, he finds that the common characteristic is always some disapprobation of the prostitute because she indulges in sex promiscuously and apart from the institution of the family; this disapprobation is less severe, however, when prostitution becomes related to seemingly worthy purposes. For example, the *hetairae* of ancient Greece were distinguished from the lowest ranking prostitutes in brothels because they were educated in the arts, were available to the wealthy and powerful, and provided entertainment and intellectual companionship, as well as sexual gratification. In a similar manner, the *geisha* of Japan were trained in dancing, singing, samisen playing, and other forms of entertainment for guests in tea houses. Some were available as prostitutes, others were available as concubines, and still others sought marriage relationships with customers. In other words, prostitution can take on a variety of forms, the particular form being related to other social needs and requirements.[6]

In modern society, several interrelated factors explain the persistence of this form of behavior, despite continuing, though usually ineffective, attempts at eradication or control. First, the basic ingredient of prostitution is the use of sex for ulterior purposes—the gaining of money, special favor, personal gratification, or prestige and status. This characteristic, however, is not at all unique to prostitution. Sex is frequently traded for advantage in marriage, engagement, concubinage, advertising, beauty contests, and the like. Thus, the fundamental principle of prostitution differs from normal behavior in other social activities only in degree. In contrast to milder forms of sexual commercialization, prostitution maximizes promiscuity while minimizing affectional and social relationships. This process of making sex nonintimate is the reason why prostitution is generally condemned. At the same time, however, it explains the persistence of prostitution. The act becomes an acceptable outlet precisely because it involves *impersonal* contact; neither the prostitute nor the client has to become involved in affectional ties, that is, in a relationship that might severely threaten other institutions and social activities (for example, the family).

Second, the attempt to control sexual behavior in society as a whole, coupled with the impersonality of prostitution, creates an environment favorable to the continuance of prostitution. When prostitution is made illegal, it becomes particularly hard to control, since one of the participating partners is an ordinary law-abiding citizen. Although the activity is considered illegitimate, the ordinary citizen cannot be effectively punished, since the impersonal nature of the act makes apprehension and prosecution all but impossible. Furthermore, the resulting disruption caused by throwing the customer into jail (and thereby removing him from family, job, community, and civic involvement) is not worth the effort. In addition, the impersonality of prostitution serves other important social functions. As Davis puts it, when all other sources of sexual gratification fail, as a consequence of personal defects or unusual social circumstances, prostitution furnishes a release and outlet. Precisely because the monogamous family system attempts to harness the sex drive in conventional ways for purposes of enduring social relationships, prostitution becomes functionally advantageous to many—the social isolate, the man far distant from his home and family (a soldier), the man deprived of intimate ties because of physical or mental affliction, the individual seeking experimentation in the so-called perversions. In short:

The attempt of society to control sexual expression, to tie it to social requirements, especially the attempt to tie it to the durable relation of marriage and the rearing of children, or to attach men to a celibate order, or to base sexual expression on love, creates the opportunity for prostitution. It is analogous to the black market, which is the illegal but inevitable response to an attempt fully to control the economy. The craving for sexual variety, for perverse gratification, for novel and provocative surroundings, for ready and cheap release, for intercourse free from entangling cares and civilized pretense— all can be demanded from the woman whose interest lies solely in the price. The sole limitation on the man's satisfactions is in this instance not morality or convention, but his ability to pay.[7]

Third, Davis attacks the traditional argument that girls become prostitutes because of financial need. He refers to this as a variation of the Communist charge that prostitution is a function of capitalism. Both have essentially the same view—that women, particularly members of minorities, are deprived of adequate income, and, therefore, turn to prostitution as the only available compensation. Davis indicates that this myth is based upon the assumption that prostitution is easy work that is even enjoyed by many prostitutes. Not only does this argument contradict recent research suggesting that prostitution is a difficult and unpleasant occupation, but it also fails to appreciate the functional reason for economic rewards to the prostitute. She is not being compensated for labor, skill, or capital investment (as in the case of typical occupations); rather she is being differentially paid for a severe loss of social status. Therefore, women choose to enter prostitution not because the pay is good (which it may be) and the work easy (which it is not), but because they feel that the resulting loss of status is more than compensated for by the potential financial return. Davis concludes that it will take a great deal more than Communism or a socialized state that guarantees adequate employment (and income) to all to eliminate prostitution.

Fourth, in substantiation of this argument, Davis points to the frequent attempts (including legislation against pimps, bookers, hotel owners, and prostitutes themselves) to eliminate prostitution in both socialist and capitalist countries. Despite these efforts, prostitution has become an intimate part of large-scale syndicated crime and has been linked to labor union racketeering, bootlegging, pornography distribution, political influence, gambling, and the like. This is a consequence of the fact that prostitution is a form of behavior to which a large portion of the public is addicted, but which has become officially banned and formally illicit, and therefore, potentially profitable. Furthermore, legitimate institutions in many societies continue to support illicit, organized prostitution; business companies supply prostitutes to clients and government agencies supply sexual entertainment to important dignitaries. A definite interdependence exists between straight society and the deviant subculture.

Finally, the functional connection between prostitution and other conventional institutions, particularly the family, is supported by recent research on sexual behavior, which indicates that the sexual irregularities of respectable women can influence the functional need for prostitution. From the early Kinsey studies of sexual behavior to contemporary studies of "swinging," [8] research seems to suggest that increased sexual freedom among women of all classes reduces the role of prostitution. Premarital promiscuity among the young, extramarital promiscuity among older portions of the population, and the availability of group sex experiences provide the same impersonal, noninvolved outlet formerly available only through prostitution. As Davis indicates, this view is a paradox to popular mythology, which cannot conceive of an evil in one social arena as contributing to a good or virtue in another. Yet it is a view that epitomizes the functionalist perspective and contrasts that paradigm to others (such as early deviance and disorganization perspectives), which looked upon evil behavior as pathological and idiosyncratic.

Davis concludes that, since the causes and nature of prostitution are functions of the institutional control of sexual, social, and economic needs of both men and women, that are not met in other ways, this problem is not likely to disappear from contemporary society. A social system devoid of prostitution would require almost absolute sexual freedom, marriage without exclusiveness and jealousy, and totally equal sexual relationships (socially and psychologically) between men and women. The form of prostitution, however, may be in the process of change as modern society selects greater sexual freedom rather than an enlightened and compassionate view of prostitution. But this is a change in degree only, as Davis points out:

Not only will there always be a system of social dominance that gives a motive for selling sexual favors, and a scale of attractiveness that creates the need for buying them, but [prostitution in its modern form] is, in the last analysis, economical. Enabling a small number of women to take care of the needs of a large number of men, it is the most convenient sexual outlet for armies and for the legions of strangers, perverts, and physically repulsive in our midst. It performs a role which apparently no other institution fully performs.[9]

In such a conclusion can be seen both the critical, even radical, and the conservative, status quo orientation of functional theory. Davis' attack upon conventional moral myths and traditional approaches to the problem of prostitution represents a radical departure from the expected. At the same time, however, a conservative conventionality runs throughout his analysis. Not only does he specifically dissociate his analysis from Marxian views, but he also leaves one with the feeling that the present state of affairs can be modified only in minor ways. Given the contemporary American family system, prevailing status relationships between men and women, and an assumed inherent (though different) sexuality in both men and women, the theory argues that prostitution in some form or degree is inevitable. The theory also implies that these givens in the social system are not all that undesirable. These types of implications are questionable on both ethical and social scientific grounds. A number of social movements in recent years, particularly Women's Liberation, have raised important questions about the sexist and status assumptions in Davis' approach. Furthermore, some Communist and socialist societies (notably Cuba and China) seem to have had great success in all but eliminating prostitution in its older, traditional forms. Obviously, not everyone would politically choose the same institutional alterations that these countries have found necessary, but the mere fact that this problem has been effectively met does question the notion that prostitution is always and everywhere necessary to perform unavoidable kinds of functions. We will return to these types of criticisms of functionalism later in the chapter. For the moment, Davis' analysis stands as an excellent example of why the functional paradigm became so popular in the middle years of sociology's development, and why today it is under increasing challenge for its alleged biases.

The Functionalist Paradigm

The theory of prostitution proposed by Kingsley Davis also serves as an illustration of the basic elements of the functionalist paradigm. The concept of a function has a variety of different meanings in popular and scientific usage: a public gathering, an occupation, the activities of an incumbent of a social role, a mathematical relationship, and an organic process in biology that contributes to the maintenance of a total organism. In reality, the social scientific usage involves elements of all of these meanings, particularly the last. A function refers to the work done by one part of a social system for other parts, the relationship of one part to others, and the process whereby a smaller part of a system helps sustain the whole system. That is, functionalists argue that human society has a structure and organization as reflected in roles, statuses, relationships, behavior, norms, values, groups, institutions, and the like. These parts of the larger system are organic in nature, as is the larger system. Each part functions to accomplish its own special purposes and to contribute to the maintenance of the larger system, as well. No part, therefore, is really indispensable. The ultimate purpose of these organic social processes is to ensure a kind of social equilibrium —that is the orderly, predictable, and routine continuance of daily social activities.[10]

Manifest Versus Latent Functions.   Robert Merton and Robert Nisbet apply this concept to the study of social problems in the following way.[11] They begin by pointing out that the same social structure and culture that generates conforming and organized behavior also creates tendencies toward deviance and disorganization. Therefore, they reject the popular myth that evil equals evil. Social problems occur largely as the result of unwilled, unanticipated, or unforseen consequences of normal patterns of institutionalized behavior. As a consequence, deviance cannot be understood apart from conformity, and disorganization cannot be understood apart from organized behavior. All parts of a system, then, whether designated as good or evil, are interrelated. As a consequence, attempts to do away with one social problem very often create or encourage the emergence of others. Part of the reason for this apparent quagmire is that problems tend to have their recognized origin in discrepancies between accepted standards of behavior and actual life conditions. In other words, the public tends to identify and define problems by their consequences, their subjective aspects. At the same time, though, problems also have an objective aspect; which is their true but usually unrecognized cause and nature.

This distinction is what Merton and Nisbet call the difference between the *manifest* (overt, recognizable, and stated) aspects of a social problem and the *latent* (covert, unrecognized, unstated) aspects. The job of the social scientist is to play the role of detective, to seek out the latent processes hidden within the social system and make them manifest to others. The hope is that, when man really understands the true nature of social problems, he will be able to take more rational, intelligent actions to resolve them. For example, Davis pointed out that one of the allegedly manifest functions of prostitution was economic reward for females who could not find alternative employment because of inequities in the social system. Therefore, some theorists argued (notably socialist thinkers) that if the inequalities could be eliminated, prostitution would disappear. In reality, the most important latent function of prostitution, according to Davis, was support for the monogamous family system, which institutionalized sex for familial purposes. Therefore, if one wanted to do something about prostitution, either an enlightened view of the problem was necessary or major changes in basic institutions, especially the family, were required. In other words, social problems can never be assessed only by public views, since the public cannot detect the latent nature of the problems.

This distinction between manifest and latent functions has played a major role in the popularity of the functionalist paradigm. First, the distinction permits the social scientist to be sharply critical of things as they seem and, thereby, conform to the classic role of the intellectual. At the same time, it also enables analysis to be nonthreatening and, in this sense, to be a satisfactory alternative to disturbing radical philosophies. The idea of manifest versus latent functions does not challenge the existence of the prevailing social order. It merely raises questions about the way in which people think the prevailing social order functions, in the hopes that such knowledge will lead to modest reforms and a more enlightened view of problems. Second, the manifest–latent distinction allows social scientists to see several sides or aspects of a social problem, without being committed in a value sense to any particular view. For example, describing the inadequacies of manifest views of prostitution and the actual latent functions performed does not lead one to conclude that prostitution is either always bad or always good. Therefore, the functionalist paradigm is an answer to biases inherent in some deviance and disorganization theory and also appears to be an effective means for maintaining the classic value-free ideal of the social scientist.

Unusual Uses of the Functionalist Paradigm—The Study of the Incest Taboo.   As a result of its appealing characteristics, the functionalist paradigm has been applied to a variety of problems in provocative ways. Harry Johnson has raised the interesting question of why the incest taboo seems to be universal to all societies, though the definition of what constitutes close or blood relatives may vary.[12] Simply stated, all societies seem to have strong prohibitions against sexual intercourse between closely related family members, except husband and wife. This universality suggests that the incest taboo is functionally significant. The manifest explanation, reflected in popular ideology, argues that the taboo exists because incest is disgusting and instinctually perverted, and that free sexual contact within the same familial context would result in biological degeneration. Johnson dismisses these explanations as totally inadequate. Primitive societies, which also possess strong incest taboos, do not understand the principles of genetics. Furthermore, man actually practices a kind of incest when he breeds blood-related animals to obtained desired genetic results. In other words, the act of sexual intercourse between closely related beings does not necessarily lead to biologically undesirable consequences. Incest tends to be disgusting because of social definitions, not because of instinct. Indeed, if man possessed an instinct prohibiting incestuous contact, there would be less of a need for severe social sanctions or cultural prohibitions.

Johnson argues that the incest taboo actually performs

important latent functions for both the family and larger society. Within the family, prohibitions against promiscuous sexual activity maximizes cooperation between family members by minimizing possible conflict (Oedipal in nature) between father and son, mother and daughter, sister and brother, and the like. For society as a whole, the incest taboo binds the larger system together by assuring that family members will have to look outside intimate surroundings for partners and mates. This contributes to processes of cultural diffusion and change. The exclusivity of sexual contact between the parents solidifies their bond with one another, and they, therefore, can act as more effective socialization agents for society, particularly with regard to their children. In short, the incest taboo appears in all societies in some form, since it functions to maintain social equilibrium—that is, the orderly, predictable processes of social interaction. Incest, then, is a problem not because it is an extreme form of deviance or disorganized behavior, but rather because it threatens the equilibrium of the social system. In addition, no other social institution performs the needed functions of the incest taboo.

The Functionalist Paradigm and the Study of Crime. The functionalist paradigm can also be used to study typical problems in creative ways. Daniel Bell has utilized the functionalist perspective to argue that the persistence of crime, especially large-scale organized syndicates, in the United States, despite continuous attempts at control, is a consequence of the fact that crime functions to maintain the larger social system.[13] He argues that the recurrent cycle of crime on a large-scale in American society is a result of two things. First, American culture is marked by an extreme polarity: piety with regard to the enforcement of public norms versus widespread flaunting of many norms. This is a consequence of two cultural heritages: reformist Puritanism versus the rugged, individualistic, frontier ethic. Second, the American underworld is essentially a mirror of the overworld, and criminal activity has become a caricature of larger life. The criminal can use techniques similar to those employed by the businessman who prays on Sundays and preys on Monday;

the asphalt jungle gangster who buys his way to social status and prestige with a gun reflects the cowboy, hero, hunter, frontiersman model. This close relationship between the overworld and the underworld suggests that crime has a functional role in the social system.

Specifically, Bell suggests that much crime has historically performed three functions: it has served as a source of support and supply for a mass-consumption economy, a means of social mobility for many ethnic minorities, and an adjunct to urban political machines. The involvement of syndicates in gambling, prostitution, illegal alcohol and drugs, and the like indicates the manner in which criminal activity supports the unmet needs of a mass-consumption society. What Bell alludes to as "the myth of the Mafia" or the myth of the Cosa Nostra is actually a consequence of the fact that crime became an early route to social status for many members of deprived ethnic groups.[14] Bell suggests that the legend of the Mafia (as a single, all-powerful, criminal conspiracy) has been fostered by journalists and politicians seeking publicity. What actually seems to have happened is the rise to importance of members of the American-Italian community in politics from the late 1800's to the present, particularly in many large cities of America (Chicago, New York, Boston, Kansas City). Early big city politics frequently involved close connections with criminal activities. Furthermore, many American Italians living in the ethnic ghettos of big cities could get their start only in criminal activities (running numbers, bootlegging, and so on). As a matter of fact, one of the functional implications of Bell's analysis is that the existence of crime as a "socially acceptable" avenue to status in America may have acted as a check against more revolutionary processes (mass rebellion of immigrant minorities). In this sense, the systematic exclusion of American blacks from much of the organized underworld, as well as from the overworld, may explain why they have had to take more militant, violent paths to integration.

Bell, then, does not deny the existence of criminal organizations that resemble their counterparts in the accepted business world. Nor does he deny the fact that many American Italians took this route to success since other avenues were not available at the time. What he does deny, as a functionalist, is the view that a single criminal conspiracy predominates, that this conspiracy is a function of ethnicity per se, and that syndicated crime is a pathology existing within an otherwise normal social order. In addition, he stresses the fact that the close connection between big-city politics and crime in early America was a functional necessity. Before the advent of widespread taxation, political machines employed criminal activity as a method of funding. Furthermore, government by political machines, and corruption associated with machine politics, performed important functions for society when other institutional alternatives were not available. The urban political boss provided food, jobs, clothes, favors, and other benefits when large-scale welfare institutions did not exist. The early protection rackets functioned as a primitive form of business security before the days of effective urban police forces and easily available insurance. In this manner, the overworld and the underworld became dependent upon one another.[15] Bell's approach leads one to speculate that the rise of federal agencies, which offer alternative means for performing the necessary functions once performed by the underworld or the political machine accounts in part for the decline of political bossism and the present state of ineffectiveness and powerlessness of most big-city governments. It also may explain why syndicated crime has moved from involvement in local politics to relationships on the national level, and, why, therefore, such crime is so difficult to eliminate from the system.

Social-Action Implications of the Functionalist Paradigm. Because of its neutral, value-free emphasis, the functionalist paradigm is difficult to apply directly to recommendations for social action to resolve social problems. However, the functional perspective can be used to indicate cautions that must be observed when translating social scientific knowledge into public policy. For example, in an article published shortly after his death, Arnold Rose analyzed the popular assumption that law in its various forms (legislative statute, judicial decision, executive order, and so on) is always an effective means for social reform.[16] This is a belief that has been shared by many, including the Warren Supreme Court, advocates of legal representation for disenfranchised groups (consumers, women, blacks, the poor), and representatives of legal-action organizations (such as the American Civil Liberties Union). Rose pointed out that, in a number of ways, law can actually cause or contribute to the maintenance of social problems. For example, a social value can be enacted into statute or entered into common law but become inappropriate at a later time when values and behavior change (for example, the prohibition of soft-drug usage). Often the law supports one specific set of values in a conflict-of-values situation, thereby driving the opposing set underground or defining it as criminal. If the opposed set of values actually possesses widespread tolerance or acceptance, the legally defined deviant behavior can become profitable to illegitimate business (as is true for prostitution). At the same time, by making some types of deviance illegitimate, the law may drive compulsively or culturally deviant individuals to other illegal acts to maintain the behavior (robbery to support narcotics use).

The law can also create problems by defining special manifestations of ordinary "everyday" behavior as serious violations of norms. Rose points to those criminologists who argue that juvenile delinquency often arises through such a process:

Practically all children at some time or other engage in acts which violate the law, but either do not know they are lawbreakers, or excuse themselves as pranksters and do not define themselves as delinquent. It is when they are apprehended, accused in court, and dealt with by the court in some way that they are forced to re-examine their illegal behavior in relation to their conception of themselves.[17]

Furthermore, Rose points out that the same labeling process operates for adult offenses, when the judicial procedure "makes a criminal" by treating him more harshly than others who engage in similar or more serious acts. For example, we prosecute thieves but rarely businessmen who steal millions, or we condemn the individual use of violence in domestic society but often applaud the widespread use of institutionalized repression and violence (use of the National Guard to quell student demonstrations by death if necessary). To some extent, then, the law cannot only create crime, but it can also encourage problem behavior that might otherwise slowly wither away; or it can translate rather minor transgressions into acts of seemingly major importance. This can create fictitious manifest problems and make the recognition of major latent problems all but impossible (the emphasis upon the need for law and order rather than an emphasis upon the need for justice). Rose's analysis is also an example of the way in which the functionalist paradigm can incorporate elements of other paradigms (for example, labeling and deviant theory and the concept of a contraculture of deviance). The implication of Rose's approach is not that law is dangerous or useless as a means of addressing social problems, but rather that it should be used with care. In particular, any contemplated legal action should be analyzed for its potential functional implications in terms of the social system as a whole.

Stuart Palmer has utilized a similar approach in challenging the use of harsh methods of social control to minimize deviance.[18] His theory has radical implications for typical domestic and foreign policy techniques, and, therefore, is an interesting illustration of the way in which the functionalist paradigm, despite its value-free stance, can be employed for radical as well as conservative purposes. Palmer argues that methods of social control actually have the unintended, latent function of begetting the behavior they were designed to prevent. This view was initially suggested by some of the founders of the discipline (Durkheim's idea that deviance can be encouraged by straight society for special self-serving purposes) and has played a continually important role in recent theories (labeling perspectives, boundary-maintenance arguments of deviance theorists, and so on).

Palmer suggests that in some situational contexts the most effective form of control might be *to do nothing*, or at least to do nothing that is aggressive, violent, and definitive. He argues that all institutionalized social situations involve some degree of tension, and that the degree of tension depends upon the reciprocity of those interacting in that situation. The greater the reciprocity, the lower the tension, and vice versa. For example, petty bureaucrats interact with great reciprocity and relatively low tension, whereas a white sheriff and his men and a black leader and his followers interact with little reciprocity and high tension. Continued tension can lead to great frustration, since the participants of the interaction are blocked from acting out their roles in full, achieving their objectives, and meeting their needs. Therefore, sustained high tension can lead to outwardly directed aggression, which may have as its object those who are blocking performances or their available surrogates. In such contexts, social control is most frequently aimed at reducing aggression in a repressive fashion. This merely lessens reciprocity and increases the situational tension, and a vicious circle of self-fulfilling prophecy ensues. For example, police are called into a black ghetto to quell a disturbance; their appearance heightens tensions and reduces reciprocity; wholesale violence results, with the police and residents both using illegal force, which seems to prove the necessity for the presence of the police in the first place. A particular type of social control, then, has become the source of extreme problem behavior. The implications that Palmer's analysis has for many modern nations, which tend to use violent, repressive means both domestically and internationally in the name of "keeping the peace," are obvious.

Another example of functionalist theory with social action implications is exemplified by the work of Eliot Freidson on the professions.[19] He refers to recent and mounting criticism of the professions in all areas (medicine, education, law) that they are not living up to their professed ideals of ethical self-discipline and knowledge production for public benefit. Freidson indicates that the typical resolution to this problem has been seen as either assuming that the professions are nothing more than sanctimonious trade unions (therefore they should be simply treated as such) or that improved recruitment and training should be initiated to bring more capable people into these fields. Freidson rejects both views and argues, instead, that professions actually function to encourage unprofessional behavior. He sees their methods of self-regulation, a characteristic considered essential to professionalization, as a major weakness of the professions. Formal internal controls cannot be used since they would confine the work of professionals, which depends upon individuality, creativity, and independence. Informal controls often merely take the form of refusals to associate with a deviant member of the profession, a kind of colleague boycott. The difficulty then, is, that the nature of the work makes an effective form of control (the formal) impossible, while the alternative (informal ostracism) does not prevent a deviant professional from continuing his career in other circumstances. For example, the physician with a bad reputation in one town can always move to another; the unprofessional teacher can always move to another school. Such a process certainly cannot be said to be in the public interest and, therefore, represents a serious deficiency in ideal professional ethics.

A second type of functional deficiency within professions can be found in the stress placed upon a special personal commitment, a sense of calling, the idea that professionals serve mankind because of a unique feeling of responsibility. Such an altruistic motivation is certainly present within many professions, but it tends to be a sense of individual responsibility for one's *own* work and clients, rather than a general ethical commitment to *public* values or the profession as a whole. This, too, is a natural function of the professional requirement for independence and initiative. As a consequence, Freidson points out that professionals often develop insulated, narrow world views, divorced from (or sometimes opposed to) the vital affairs and interests of other men. For example, physicians may oppose government-supported medical programs because they see them as a threat to their client–patient relationships though on other ethical grounds the society has a major need for such programs. In other words, by the very nature of their specialized and personalized training and experience, professionals develop what some sociologists have called a *trained incapacity* to deal with some kinds of issues, primarily those that relate to major societal values and concerns. The exclusivity and imperialism characteristic of so many professions is sustained by this type of process.

Freidson points out that he is not claiming that these professional weaknesses are a consequence of venal or selfish intent, as much popular mythology maintains (the physician who charges too much simply because he wants to make money). On the contrary, in order to enter his calling, the professional must commit himself to a specific set of ideals embodied in the concept of professionalism. It is this process that transforms the ideal responsibility to serve public good into a limited responsibility to serve one's own personal needs and requirements, and the ideal responsibility to generate universalistically applicable knowledge into a particularistic sectarianism epitomized by occupational imperialism. As a consequence, Freidson concludes that since professional weaknesses stem from professionalization per se, professions can never correct internal problems by themselves. Though autonomy and independence from public control is an important ingredient in these types of occupations, professions cannot live up to their claims in spite of their good intentions. Therefore, to correct their internal problems, some degree of control and influence by external lay institutions is necessary.

It is obvious from these examples that the functionalist paradigm offers multiple opportunities for unusual, challenging, and provocative theory formulation and concept construction. However, just as obviously, the paradigm contains several weaknesses. These have become the basis of increasingly marked attacks upon functionalism in the last decade, criticisms that easily match in enthusiasm and vigor the justifications and commendations of the paradigm offered by its adherents.

Critiques of Functionalism

Criticisms of the functionalist paradigm tend to be of two general types: *methodological* and *substantive*. Methodological criticisms argue that the functionalist paradigm by its very nature makes precise, accurate, rational, and definitive research and analysis all but impossible, in contrast to alternative paradigms or theories. Substantive criticisms claim that functionalism is inherently biased ethically and politically, and that this bias seriously distorts the real nature of man and makes it possible for social science to be used by undesirable and repressive forces in society. As can be seen, then, substantive criticisms seem to constitute severe challenges to the functionalist paradigm, whereas methodological criticisms seem to involve relatively minor challenges.

Methodological Criticisms of Functionalism.   Though the methodological criticisms appear to be relatively minor, they actually raise types of questions that are the basis for the issues raised by the substantive criticisms. For example, C. Wright Mills has charged that functionalism is too abstract, vague, and non-empirical.[20] In the positivistic–antipositivistic battle that has raged throughout social science's history, functionalism represents too extreme a reaction to scientism. It is such an extreme, allegedly "humanistic," reaction, according to Mills, that it deifies some abstract, dissociated, almost nonhuman system that has repressive and deterministic impact upon individuals. As a consequence, it removes sociological analysis from the most important arena—life as it is really lived from day to day by average people—and, thereby, makes scientific verification impossible. For example, how does one really prove that the latent functions of prostitution are supportive for the monogamous family system? Certainly, such a conclusion cannot be reached by studying the interaction between or talking with prostitutes and their clients. Furthermore, what is an equilibrium-maintaining function, and, more importantly, whose or what equilibrium is being maintained by various forms of problem behavior, including war, crime, delinquency, overpopulation, poverty, racial discrimination, and the like? Even many functionalists (notably Robert Merton) have admitted that this type of methodological criticism is valid, that functionalism is more a general system for ordering observed data than a technique for working with that data in precise and empirical ways.

Other social scientists have charged that the functionalist paradigm is circular, tautological, and operates as a kind of self-fulfilling philosophy.[21] Its admitted teleology (the assumption that the nature and substance of daily life is always shaped by some ultimate goals or ends) forces adherents of the paradigm to argue in circular ways. I. C. Jarvie uses as an example the functionalist assertion that churchgoing reflects a functional need for social integration and solidarity. This assumption leads functionalists to test the solidarity of a social system by using measures of churchgoing. Not only is such reasoning hopelessly circular, but it may also lead functionalists to ignore more important aspects of social life (churchgoing as fulfilling other needs, nonchurchgoing as an expression of solidarity in certain contexts, churchgoing as anachronistic behavior that really serves no particular purposes at all and merely reflects habit or routine, and the like).[22] In other words, to say that people go to church because of a necessary function for social solidarity and that one measure of social solidarity is churchgoing is to say nothing important at all.

Melvin Tumin has pointed out that even those elements of more sophisticated functionalist theory that attempt to avoid this tautological problem (for example, the concepts of latent versus manifest functions) present difficulties.[23] Latent and unintended consequences of many events may constitute interesting side effects and passing observations, but they really do not explain the existence of the event. For example, some laws may function in unexpected ways to encourage deviance (drug laws that exacerbate the problem of marijuana use, or prohibition, which led to widespread alcohol abuse), but this observation does not tell us why those laws came into being in the first place, nor why people originally decided to engage in the deviant behavior.

Furthermore, functionalists make a fetish of social unity to the point where everything is assumed to have some kind of function, either manifest or latent. This leaves little room for the finding that some behaviors may be simply dysfunctional or nonfunctional; that is, some problems may simply be pure forms of deviant or disorganized behavior without any meaning or purpose for the larger system. As we saw in the discussion of labeling theory, adherents of that view contend that hidden, accidental, or mislabeled deviance are all possible alternatives. In other words, some deviants may break the law without knowing they are doing so (much juvenile delinquency), others may deliberately deviate but keep their behavior completely hidden from larger society (some homosexuality), and still others may be inappropriately labeled as deviant by larger society when they do not consider their behavior aberrant (aggression among the lower classes). In none of these cases, can traditional functional concepts contribute an adequate explanation.

The final methodological criticism of functionalism argues that the important, fundamental assumptions and elements of that paradigm are left almost unanswered by adherents. For example, functionalist Talcott Parsons has maintained that all social systems have four requirements: *pattern maintenance and tension management, goal attainment, adaptation, and integration.*[24] Every social system must transmit major social and cultural values to the next generation, must institute a system of social control to ensure this process; but, at the same time, it must provide ways of managing the tensions resulting from the fact that some individuals will violate norms and standards of behavior. Every system must also provide the means for obtaining major social goals, ways of adapting the resources of the system for this goal attainment, and, obviously, techniques for ensuring integration of the system as a whole. Therefore, Parsons suggests that social scientific analysis of human events must determine what particular function is being performed by those events in terms of these basic requirements.

In attacking these fundamental functional assumptions, Flanigan and Fogelman have asked the following kinds of questions.[25] Exactly when are social patterns being adequately maintained or tensions adequately managed? When are goals attained? What is considered functionally appropriate as a form of adaptation in order to attain goals (for example, is the robber adequately expressing the goals of rugged individualism and capitalist acquisition)? When does a function stop being latent and become manifest in terms of these four societal requirements? The functionalist paradigm's inability to provide precise answers to these types of questions has led some critics to propose that the perspective may not have much relationship to social reality. It may be merely an intriguing intellectual fiction, which does more to mislead than to offer needed explanations, particularly when it is applied to the analysis of social problems.

An example of the way in which functional assumptions can be misleading on the public policy level is to be found in contemporary Holland. The recent concern for ecological problems has led to the discovery that, in the race to modernize and industrialize, many countries often create greater problems—problems that would not have resulted if some of the old abandoned techniques and devices, assumed to be increasingly dysfunctional in a rapidly changing society, had been retained. Since World War II, the windmill has been fast disappearing as a part of The Netherlands' landscape. New forms of power, essentially natural gas and oil, have replaced the power of the wind in the operation of pumps that keep the sea water from inundating the Dutch reclaimed lands. But in order to pay for rapid industrialization, Holland has sold most of her gas to West Germany and faces the possibility of running out of that resource in a very few years. In addition, oil is expensive and it pollutes. Without adequate power in sufficient supply, however, Holland would face disaster; the North Sea would once again cover acres of presently fertile farms, industrial developments, and heavily populated communities. As a consequence, the Dutch government is considering returning to the windmill, which was deemed technologically dysfunctional after the war and only worth preserving in small numbers because of tourism. For example, special economic support is provided to those who wish to buy a windmill and rehabilitate it. Since the wind always blows in The Netherlands, and since it is free and nonpolluting, the Dutch government has decided that this natural resource, when harnessed by the windmill, may be as "functional" in a modern, industrial context as it previously was in a rural, undeveloped society. The fiction of inherent functionality in certain social contexts, and therefore of dysfunctionality in others, may have led the Dutch government to create an unanticipated problem.

Substantive Criticisms of Functionalism—Political and Ethical Bias. These types of methodological criticisms have become the basis for serious substantive challenges to functionalism. The substantive criticisms involve four major claims of inherent political and ethical bias. The first, and most recently persistent, claim is that *functionalism is inherently conservative* and stands in opposition to liberal, radical, or revolutionary philosophies. The second, and closely related, claim is that *functionalism tends to support maintenance of the status quo*, since it begins with the prevailing system as a given, almost inevitable, fact of life.[26] The charge of conservatism has often been exaggerated by critics and, just as often, misunderstood by functionalism's adherents. As we have seen, the functional paradigm can be used to raise challenging and potentially threatening questions about the status quo. It can and has been used to question prevailing popular mythology which is the basis for many accepted approaches to contemporary problems. Davis' analysis of prostitution, Rose's critique of law, and Freidson's condemnation of professionalism are all within the functionalist framework, and yet each represents liberal, humane, and challenging perspectives of things as they are usually considered to be. However, this kind of usage of functionalism historically tends to be an exception.

In fact, a good many functionalists tend to be conservative and status quo oriented in their outlook. The characteristics of the functionalist paradigm have been more congenial to this ethical and political philosophy, in contrast to the characteristics of other views that are more congenial to radical or revolutionary perspectives (for example, the notion of a pathological or sick society). One way of summarizing this inherent bias would be to suggest that most social scientific conservatives seem to be functionalists, though not all those utilizing functionalism are necessarily conservative. At the same time, the status quo and social system orientation of functionalism has enabled this theory to be used as a scientific equivalent of the popular myth of blaming the victim or the naturalistic theory of social problems. In a seemingly humanistic and compassionate manner, the functionalist can argue that some problems seem to be functionally inevitable. For example, consider the following reasoning: Poverty is inescapable, given the nature of the present system. As undesirable as poverty is (and minor reforms should be undertaken to aid the poor), other functional alternatives can be provided in modest ways (why don't they go out and get a decent job?); besides the total system is not bad enough to be severely altered just to resolve this one problem (capitalism's advantages far outweigh its problems). To an extent, this type of reasoning is found in Davis' analysis of prostitution. He dismisses the view that radical change to a socialist or communist society would solve the problem and argues that a kind of enlightened view of the problem, and of sexual freedom generally, is a functional alternative.[27] The appeal for more enlightened views is very much in the tradition of developing humanitarianism in Western thought; furthermore, it requires little, if any, definitive social action in terms of major system changes. Obviously, functionalism's popularity has been "a function" of the need by social scientists to fit the role of modest reformers during the period from the 1940's to the 1960's.

The third and fourth substantive criticisms of the functionalist paradigm are also related to one another. Functionalism has been challenged as being *relevant only to static, closed social systems,* unable to take into account processes of change, especially rapid and radical change. At the same time, functionalists have been accused of *assuming that everything that happens in a society must be fundamental to the survival of that system,* and, therefore, processes of integration, support, and cooperation are desirable. In other words, *the functionalist paradigm tempts one to assume that stability and cooperation are good, whereas change and conflict are bad.* Again, this type of criticism has often been exaggerated by opponents of functionalism and misunderstood by adherents of the paradigm. Coser's analysis of conflict illustrates that conflict behavior could be successfully subjected to functional analysis. However, this, too, tends to be the exception to the rule. Most functionalists have a difficult time arguing in support of change or conflict, though some functionalists have dealt with change and conflict in provocative ways.

Melvin Tumin has identified the way in which functionalism biases academic work in unusually selective ways:

Why is it, one must ask, that while we, i.e., practicing sociologists, seem to be almost uniformly against poverty, mental illness, and racial discrimination, we are somewhat less than uniformly against war, and in some important senses, we are for such things as divorce, adultery, prostitution, crime, delinquency, and inter-racial disorders.[28]

In other words, what the critics of functionalism have done is to point out that ethical and political assumptions within the paradigm lead scientists to view different kinds of problems with different prejudgments, many of which may be inappropriate and unacceptable. On what basis is it appropriate to accept the functional inevitability of prostitution but argue that racial discrimination is always bad? Or to view the problem from another value position, on what basis is it appropriate to accept the functional necessity of war in some cases but argue that mental illness is always unacceptable in any form? Tumin points out that almost all social scientists who work on problems such as mental illness and racial discrimination could not be clearer in their condemnations of these problems, yet many sociologists have become advocates for war, while still others show an uninterested detachment or an implied enthusiasm for sexual freedom, light narcotics use, and black militancy. The point is that functionalists, despite their insistence upon value neutrality, are ideologically motivated, and some of this motivation is inherent within the paradigm they employ.

According to Tumin, social scientists reveal their political and ethical attitudes about a social problem by the kinds of functional analysis they use when dealing with that problem. Events such as illness, discrimination, and extreme poverty are considered to have no *positive functions* by almost all social scientists. Furthermore, if these problems are seen as having some system-maintaining functions, the system being maintained is usually seen as villainous, as part of some unacceptable special interest or power bloc whose members profit from the problem at the expense of others. In contrast, war is often considered to be functionally preferable to some forms of peace. Also, narcotics use, crime, and sexual promiscuity are usually seen as having some positive functions for those involved in the behavior and possibly for larger society as well, while being modestly dysfunctional for others.

Tumin argues that this type of dilemma is a result of the *concept of functional equivalents*, contained within the paradigm. That is, if something that has a function is to be removed from the social system, then an alternative something must be provided to perform the same function. The difficulty is that, on the basis of personal judgments and preferences, not scientific assessment, functionalists cannot accept the apparent functional alternatives for some kinds of behavior. In other cases, functionalists consider the alternatives more desirable or good than the problem behavior. For example, surrender to international Communism might be an alternative to combatting wars of national liberation throughout the world. But surrender seems to imply loss of political and social freedom; therefore, war is often assumed to be preferable. Or, as Bell argued, if large-scale crime were somehow abolished, the government might have to provide alternative means for performing some of the functions of crime, through official dispensation of sex and narcotics or the establishment of satisfactory routes of social mobility for disenfranchised minority group members. If such measures were not taken (and they probably would not be for political and economic reasons), even more undesirable problems might arise. Discontented minorities would turn to revolution out of frustration; the public would massively disregard laws and satisfy their sexual and narcotics appetites in any way possible.

The trouble with the notion of functional equivalency, then, is twofold. First, *it is not necessarily valid*. Tumin asks, what, for example, is the functional equivalency for mental illness? If mental illness is considered to be the result of a retreat from responsibility and daily pressures, the only possible alternatives would be suicide or total retreatism, both probably more undesirable than the original problem. Yet functionalists universally consider mental illness inherently undesirable. Second, and more important, contrary to the insistence by adherents of the functionalist paradigm that theirs is the only true value-free perspective, *functionalism forces value preferences and choices*. It also raises additional value questions, such as: What is equivalent for whom? By whose standards is something judged to be equivalently desirable or undesirable? The answers to these kinds of questions are not always explicit, but their presence, whether they are implicit or explicit, determines the functionalist's bias in his treatment of social problems. Tumin concludes:

The reason our analyses run the way they do, I think, has to do with . . . the doctrine of functional equivalents. Simply, I mean that the possible functional equivalents of the disapproved phenomena either are nonexistent or are even more repulsive than the actual problems themselves, while, by contrast, the functional equivalents of the more approved phenomena are themselves either as tolerable and acceptable as the phenomena, or even morally praise-worthy. . . . In effect, then, I am contending we like some problems more than others because we don't think they're really problems. And we don't think they are really problems because we see them as indirect expressions

*of laudable human spirit and verve and honesty or straightforward-
ness breaking through the hypocritical bounds of our ordinary norms.
. . . It is interesting to note that a major [latent] function of functionalism for sociologists is that it minimizes role strain for them as
they seek simultaneously to play the parts of both concerned citizens
and neutral, value-free scientists.*[29]

Functionalism's Response to the Critics. Functionalists and
others have responded to these criticisms with three major
counterclaims: *critics actually distort the history of the development of functionalism*; *many critics turn out to be latent functionalists themselves*; and *adherents of alternative paradigms
commit the very errors they accuse functionalists of perpetuat-
ing.*[30] However, these attempts to defend the functionalist
paradigm miss the important point and tend to argue about
peripheral issues. If Kuhn's suggestion, that scientific paradigms
are not value-free interpretations of the "real" word, is correct,
then an important issue for social science is the question of
which paradigm best suits the needs of contemporary society
for an adequate resolution of major social problems. Most responsible critics are suggesting that functionalism is like any
other paradigm—it determines how and what will be studied,
thereby implying what should be done in response. The peculiar
biases of the paradigm should be recognized as major difficulties, despite the fact that functionalism is a valuable intellectual perspective for much provocative work. These biases
consist of an abstracted, pretended amorality that makes empirical investigation or acceptance of change and conflict extremely
difficult, and which, in turn, tends to lend support to work that
favors maintenance of the status quo or modest, conservative
responses to social problems. For this reason, some social scientists have begun a search for alternatives to match the popularity
of the functionalist paradigm.

Reflexive Sociology and a New Behaviorism: A Paradigm Revolution?

It is perhaps too early to say whether or not the search for
alternatives to functionalism constitutes a serious paradigm

revolution. Certainly, recent criticisms have been sharp, and sometimes deeply personal, and responses have been similarly heated and emotional. However, the appeals of functionalism and the ability of the paradigm to be adapted to many conflicting views seem to suggest that the battle has been joined but the challenged theory is still in predominance. Nevertheless, as Martindale has indicated, there are a number of competing perspectives that argue for different methodological and substantive approaches to social problems. *These alternative perspectives take one of two forms: those which primarily reject the positivistic and conservative bias of functionalism but accept the need for some holistic view and those which accept the positivism of functionalism but reject the holistic view as inadequate.*

Reflexive Sociology—A Convergence of Classic Functionalism and New Radicalism.   The first alternative has been epitomized in Alvin Gouldner's compelling argument that there is a coming (or present) crisis in social science and sociology.[31] Taking up where C. Wright Mills left off, Gouldner's recent work has become the guideline for a rapidly developing school of radical sociology. Gouldner argues that there are really only two major paradigms in contemporary sociology. One, predominant *"academic or establishment" sociology,* arose in the West from Comptian positivism and is presently embodied in functionalism, especially the work of Talcott Parsons.[32] The alternative paradigm is *radical Marxism,* generally shunned by Western social scientists for political reasons. Academic sociology cannot account for conflict and change, two of the central features of modern society, whereas Marxism can. Academic sociology suffers from a positivistic bias and conservatism, which Gouldner sees as being intimately related. Scientism, with its emphasis upon value-free empirical analysis, has permitted modern sociologists to remain comfortably uninvolved in the central problems of contemporary society and produce knowledge (at rewarding fees) that can be used by vested interests to further their aims while repressing others.

Although Gouldner believes that functionalism's place as the predominant paradigm will be sustained for the forseeable future, he indicates that, at the same time, its inability to meet growing needs for adequate, humane answers to severe social issues will lead to the growth of radical perspectives. These unpopular views will be espoused by the newer and younger members of the social scientific community as they challenge the power and influence of the older ruling elite. Younger members will increasingly question the role of academic sociology as an apologetic for free-market capitalism and statist liberalism in Western history. In so doing, a crisis will be created and a new view, which Gouldner calls a *reflexive sociology*, will emerge, combining elements of the two opposed perspectives.

According to Gouldner, a reflective sociology or social science will call for a recognition that scientific work is not value free and that theorists cannot afford to reify and deify a social system while leaders of that system conduct policies that lead to the military destruction of foreign cultures or the decay and collapse of cities at home. Reflexive sociology will actively involve scientists in public policies designed to change the present system. The new radical (or radicalized) sociologist will seek to transform as well as to understand the world around him, to live in it as well as to live on or from it. The method of the reflexive sociologist, therefore, will depend less upon sophisticated quantitative techniques (the hallmark of positivism) and more upon qualitative judgments and assessments. This new perspective will study values and norms and suggest alternatives. At the same time, it will be more honestly and meaningfully holistic than functionalism, because it will necessitate involvement, action, responsiveness, and value concern by the scientist. Gouldner sees the emergence of a reflexive sociology as a consequence of a steady convergence of elements in classic functionalism and new radicalism over the last several decades.

Applications of Reflexive Sociology—An Analysis of Medicare. The convergence of these two perspectives can also be seen in several recent studies of the impact of Medicare in America, particularly in relationship to the traditional opposition to liberalization of medical benefits by physicians. John Colombotos has studied the impact of Medicare upon the attitudes of physicians.[33] His analysis begins by pointing out that typical liberal philosophy has argued that laws can be used for changing behavior but should never be used to change attitudes, since it would be undemocratic to punish a man for what he thought or believed. He indicates that this view artificially separates behavior and attitudes, when such separation may not be warranted, and the two may be intimately interrelated in reality. The Medicare Law's impact upon physician attitudes and behavior is a good test case. Medicare was Title 18 of the Social Security Amendments Acts of 1965, which established a program of health insurance for people 65 years old or over. Since the 1940's, the medical profession had bitterly opposed such legislation and even threatened a boycott if it were enacted.

Colombotos interviewed over 1,000 physicians in private practice in New York state in 1964 and 1965 before the legislation was enacted, reinterviewed a sample of these physicians ten months after passage but before implementation, and reinterviewed another sample over six months after implementation of the program. He found that despite the decades of almost unanimous opposition, the proportion of his physicians in favor of the act rose from 38 percent before passage to 70 percent less than a year after passage to 81 percent six months before implementation. This compliance behavior contrasted sharply to previous opposition or to the actions of physicians in other contexts (for example, physician strikes in Saskatchewan, Canada, in 1962, and continuing opposition to Medicaid in New York). Colombotos suggests several reasons why this was so. The direct impact of Medicare in New York was relatively less than the Medicaid program, less than 2 million people being covered by the first program and from 3½ to 7 million by the latter. The clients of Medicare were the aged and the program used the insurance principle, whereas the clients of Medicaid were the indigent and the program was based upon the welfare principle. Medicaid provides more services and attempts to control the quality and cost of medical care. In short, Medicare was neither radical nor revolutionary. Furthermore, Medicare had widespread popular support, whereas Medicaid had strong opposition from some special groups (industry, press, farm organizations).

Finally, Medicare is generally the same throughout the country, while Medicaid varies greatly by state and region and is often a confusing mixture of inconsistent and contradictory local, state, and federal laws.

Colombotos concludes by suggesting the implications of this study for legislation in other areas, particularly concerning desegregation. He suggests that the difficulty of legislating racial equality in contrast to the easy acceptance of Medicare could be a function of several things. First, white racism may be more firmly entrenched among large segments of the American public than the traditional fear of government participation in health care programs among physicians. Second, social supports for segregationists are more readily available than social supports for physicians opposed to health care programs. In the case of Medicare, the medical profession was out of step with the public. Desegregationists, on the other hand, seem to be out of step with most citizens. Third, desegregation, like Medicaid, involves a hodgepodge of laws at all societal levels (specific and general laws that apply to schools, transportation, recreation, housing, employment, and/or marriage). Some of these laws *prescribe* segregation. No such situation existed in the case of Medicare. Laws, then, can be used to change attitudes significantly (contrary to traditional liberal myth), though these changes will take place in only very specific circumstances and with regard to particular issues. For example, there is no evidence to suggest that physician acceptance of Medicare is a consequence of more liberal attitudes as a whole on the part of the medical profession.

Extending this type of analysis, which marries older functionalism with a more radical perspective, Theodore Marmor suggests that Medicare actually helped raise doctors' fees.[34] He points out that after Medicare went into effect on 1 July, 1966, the prices of all health services went up. Between December of 1965 and December of 1966, physicians' fees increased almost 8 percent, whereas the yearly increase in fees from 1959 to 1965 had only been about 3 percent. The Bureau of Labor Statistics reported that more than one-third of American physicians raised their fees an average of 25 percent in 1966. Marmor argues that the government's formula for helping to pay the cost of medical services latently functioned to provide an incentive for doctors to raise their fees. Furthermore, the formula was administered with amazing laxness. For example, Medicare would pay 80 percent of the reasonable fee that doctors charged, the patient paying a $50 deductible charge and 20 percent of the remaining balance. A reasonable charge was determined to be one that was customary for that service for typical patients (neither very poor nor very rich); in addition, it could be no more than the prevailing rate in a doctor's locality; and finally, the Medicare payment could be no more than what insurance companies would pay for similar treatment in their private plans.

The basic difficulty was that the Social Security Administration (and private insurance companies) had no way of determining what reasonable, prevailing, and customary fees were. Most physicians had different rates according to different patient abilities to pay; insurance companies had practically no useful data; and many doctors really paid little attention to their own fee schedules (their income had increased since World War II because of increased demand and improved services, not because of elaborate and precise fee schedules). As a consequence, Marmor points out that many physicians were anxious to increase fees. Not only were some probably relatively low in contrast to other doctors, but there also was a fear that government control would tie a physician to past fees for years to come. Furthermore, physicians could charge private patients unreasonable fees, especially the wealthy. The health program allowed physicians to bill patients directly. The patient then sent the bill in for Medicare reimbursement. The reimbursement could be for 80 percent of a reasonable fee, with the result that the patient still had to pay the remaining unreasonable amount to the physician. The functions of the program for the poor were no better. Doctors had commonly reduced their fees for the poor, in some cases charging nothing at all. Medicare meant that the poor could now afford to pay at least something, and some physicians increased their incomes substantially by charging the poor for services for the first time or increasing their charges, assuming that poor patients would receive reimbursement for a proportion and be no worse off than before. The problem for the poor was that they still had to pay a $50 deductible and the remainder of the unpaid proportion (theoretically 20 percent of the reasonable fee).

New Behaviorism—An Interactionist, Social-Processes Perspective. The studies mentioned above indicate the way in which the more reflexive strains have begun to influence traditional functionalist analysis, by rejecting in part its conservative bias while maintaining a holistic view. The second major alternative to functionalism rejects holism and argues for a more elementaristic perspective. This type of early paradigm revolution is exemplified in theories proposing that social problems be viewed as social processes that involve daily interactions between individuals. The perspective has its origins in a natural history approach to the study of social problems and the behaviorism of Charles Cooley and George Mead, discussed in Chapter 4. Richard Fuller and Richard Myers were two of the first scholars to argue that the really common characteristic to all social problems was the fact that they went through stages of development and did not arise full blown at a single moment in history within a social system.[35] Thus, a social problem can always be considered as in a dynamic state of "becoming." *Awareness, policy determination,* and *reform* constitute the three basic stages of this continuous development. Fuller and Myers point out that all problems have their genesis in the realization of people in a given locality that cherished values are threatened by some social condition. Definitions of alarm are communicated, and people come to feel that something must be done. From this initial process, debate over policy alternatives arises. Throughout this stage, various vested interests come to learn that what is considered appropriate policy by some is unacceptable to others. Finally, administrative units are engaged in implementing reform, aimed at the resolution of the identified problem and based upon a consensus concerning policies that have developed from the second stage.

This theory of Fuller and Myers was an attempt to counteract the popular assumption that problems exist because they are some type of objective evil caused by other evils inherent within the system. In contrast, Fuller and Myers suggested that problems exist primarily because of the way in which we identify, define, and attempt to resolve them. Thus, problems are not a result of some condition endemic to the larger society, but rather they are really a function of interaction between concerned and involved individuals in specific contexts and the symbolic responses of these people to one another.

In a recent article, Herbert Blumer has sharpened this view and called for a drastic reorientation of sociological theory and research on social problems.[36] Blumer begins by criticizing the typical approaches to the study of problems. He argues that these typical approaches presume that a problem exists as an objective condition or situation in the social context, and that it has an intrinsically harmful or malignant nature in contrast to a normal or healthy society. Furthermore, a state of dysfunction, pathology, disorganization, or deviance is assumed to result from this problem. The task of the social scientist is seen as one of identifying the harmful condition and describing its essential nature and elements. This information is then placed in the store of scholarly knowledge and/or given to policy makers and the general citizenry. Blumer points out that, as logical as such a view appears to be, it really reflects a misunderstanding of the nature of social problems and, therefore, accounts for the ineffectiveness of many modern attempts to resolve them.

First, contemporary theory does not enable the detection or identification of social problems. On the contrary, Blumer indicates that social scientists discern problems only after they are recognized as such by others in society. For example, a sociological interest in American poverty all but disappeared in the 1940's and 1950's, only to reappear again in the 1960's after the public, politicians, and lay reporters like Michael Harrington[37] discovered poverty in what everyone had thought to be the most affluent society in history. Leonard Reissman has echoed this perspective by pointing out that the Rachel Carsons and Ralph Naders are far more successful than sociologists in calling the public's attention to problems such as the ecology crisis or automobile safety.[38] However, Reissman indicates that social scientists have developed to a fine art the ability to react quickly once a problem reaches the first stage of identification.[39]

Blumer points out that contemporary theory does not enable the detection of problems in another sense as well. The major concepts generated by present-day theory are useless. For example, the notion of "deviance," "dysfunction," or "structural strain" have no benchmarks that enable their positive identification. More seriously, however, sociological theory cannot explain why some social events become defined as problems (thereby achieving the label of deviancy, dysfunction, or disorganization), while other major problematic situations are neither recognized nor defined as problems. For example, why are the following kinds of situations not considered to be major social problems: an overorganized society with repressive potential, the pernicious consequences of the ideology of growth, the unearned increment in land values leading to inequitable distribution of wealth? Why, too, are the following kinds of things considered deviant, dysfunctional, or disorganizational by some but not major problems by most: superpatriotism, life as a hermit or recluse, waste and inefficiency in modern government and industry?

Blumer states that *the second major deficiency of many approaches is the assumption that problems exist only as some objective aspect or condition of society.* Utilizing this assumption some social scientists merely collect and collate rates of deviance, statistics about disorganization, characteristics of deviants, and the like. These types of data are assumed to capture the essence, quality, and character of a problem. What this view and approach ignores is the fact that definitions, labels, and interpretations of problems are crucial. The qualitative nature of a problem resides not merely within the problem but also in the public reaction to that event or situation. For example, political spying and espionage (publically disclosed by the Watergate affair during the 1972 American presidential campaign) is not considered a major problem by many since these acts are "merely politics." Or, traditional petty crime is considered a major problem (as reflected in news coverage, references by politicians, and efforts of law enforcement agencies), while white-collar crime (price fixing, monopoly, graft) receives relatively little attention, and may even be lauded, though figures show the latter to be more severe in its impact upon the economic and social system.

A third, and final, deficiency arises from the first two. Essentially, it lies in *the assumption that the findings that result from an objective study of social problems provides citizens and decision makers with a completely meaningful basis for social action.* Blumer maintains that this conclusion is unwarranted (certainly if recognition of problems and the means of analysis are deficient, the resulting study cannot be completely meaningful). The social scientific description of the allegedly objective characteristics of a problem is often unrelated to, and far removed from, the essential character of that problem. This is a result of the fact that scientific analysis has little relationship to the way in which problems arise and develop, or to the responses they generate. Blumer concludes that social problems are not a result of an intrinsic malfunctioning of society, they are, rather, a consequence of a process of definition and interaction, involving five general stages of development: the emergence of the problem, the legitimation of the problem, the mobilization of action to respond, the formulation of an official plan for action, and the transformation of that plan into some form of administrative implementation. What social scientists really ought to be studying is this process, not the supposed intrinsic character of problems per se. This proposal of Blumer's is closely related to the radical criticism of reflexive sociologists who argue for a social scientific interest in social action, social policy, and value concern.

The importance of the role of social processes and public views in the creation of social problems was recognized by Herbert Spencer at the turn of the century.[40] He argued that when an evil is very great, it seems to attract little or no attention, but when it is mitigated the public definition of it as a problem brings increased efforts to decrease or eliminate it. Finally, when an evil has been greatly diminished, the most pronounced demands for strong measures for its extinction are made. He uses as an illustration the apparent significant decline in drunkenness that took place from the 18th century to 1900 followed by loud advocacy of legislation to suppress this problem. Therefore, if social scientists concentrate upon an analysis of social problems purely by an assumed state of deviance or disorganization always within society *or* merely by what citizens and others determine to be problems at a given moment, they will be misled. This view constitutes both a qualification and a support of Blumer's perspective. For Spencer, social evils were seen to be mitigated by natural processes of social evolution or change. The use and consumption of alcohol became institutionalized; modern industrialization and urbanization made the excessive public use less viable for large numbers of citizens. At the same time, public recognition of the problem and the demand for immediate legal reform came belatedly and was based upon the assumption that society is primarily the result of deliberate actions. Such an assumption, Spencer argued, was incorrect. He believed that society and change were the result of spontaneous processes related to how people play and work in given contexts. What was really important to Spencer for understanding social evils such as alcoholism were daily processes of interaction as they related to the cultural context.

Applications of the New Behaviorism—Alcoholism, Narcotics Use, and Police–Citizen Encounters. An increasing number of analyses and studies of social problems in recent years have utilized this interactionist, social processes perspective in provocative ways. For example, Earl Rubington has argued that when the social definitions of alcoholic deviance and drug-addiction deviance are compared, differences between them can be identified that suggest which rehabilitation techniques might be most helpful under what special circumstances.[41] There are presently an estimated 6 million alcoholics compared to 60,000 narcotics addicts in the United States; ironically, narcotics use is publically defined as a more serious and threatening problem. The use of narcotics, except for those who are seriously ill, is generally forbidden, while, in contrast, the social use of alcohol is approved, even rewarded (the man who can "hold his liquor" is admired). As a consequence, narcotics users become labeled as seriously deviant early in their careers, whereas alcoholics may go undetected for years. Reflecting this dual attitude, criminal punishments for narcotics use are generally far more severe than punishments for excessive alcohol use.

Rubington points out that one way of dealing with the risks of deviance is for the individual to join a group where all members are just as deviant. Narcotics users are more likely to do this than alcoholics. Rubington estimates that only about 100,000 alcoholics are part of the skid-row culture and another 400,000 are in the process of dropping out of their usual roles in society as they become more dependent upon alcohol. In other words, the overwhelming majority of alcoholics are members of the ordinary social world. In contrast, of the estimated 60,000 narcotics addicts, Rubington suggests that some 50,000 participate in drug cultures. The decision to join a drug culture influences an individual's life significantly. A participant spends more time as a drug user, comes to define himself as an addict (or junkie), feels less guilty about his behavior, and, accordingly, becomes more observable as deviant to others in society. Nonparticipants, on the other hand, suffer internal disturbances, rather than external difficulties. They try harder to look normal, feel more guilty about usage, and are more likely to seek help and treatment. Rubington concludes, therefore, that nonparticipants are more likely to profit from individual, one-to-one treatment by a psychotherapist, whereas participants in a drug culture are more likely to profit from group approaches to the problem, since the latter already feel a sense of solidarity and comfort in their group identification.[42]

A final example of a problem area where the developing focus upon interaction and process, rather than upon an abstract larger social system, can lead to provocative conclusions is exemplified by studies of police–citizen encounters that result in friction, hostility, and conflict. The research of James Hudson raises questions about the simplistic notion that white racism, natural antagonisms for the police, or basic police brutality adequately explain problems in these contexts.[43] In an analysis of a study of encounters between police and citizens that resulted in complaints to the Philadelphia Police Advisory Board in 1966, Hudson found that police come into contact with citizens under a number of circumstances that influence the way in which the actors will define one another. The police role involves contacts with informants, with suspects, with law breakers, and with those requesting police assistance. Therefore, multiple demands are made upon the policeman, in terms of the number of responses possible at the start of an encounter; furthermore, the uncertainty about how a situation will ultimately be defined increases the chances of difficulties in police–citizen encounters. This uncertainty is a function of several things. First, Hudson points out that policemen are limited in the ways in which they define situations by the socialization process they have experienced and the milieu of police work. Police departments engage in two roles: law enforcement and maintenance of order. Though these roles are complementary, they are different. Law enforcement focuses upon specific offenses and involves definitive actions (arrest, issuing of a summons, and so on). In addition, law enforcement is more dramatic and heroic. However, policemen more often become involved in maintaining order (quieting a noisy group on a street corner, settling an argument, keeping a parade crowd under control, directing traffic, controlling a family dispute, and so on). One difficulty of this role is that it is the policeman's job to determine whether order prevails, and if necessary, how to reestablish it. As a result, serious disagreement can develop over the definition of a given situation between various actors.

Hudson indicates that, though society has given the police a mandate to enforce law, citizens rarely give active support in the carrying out of this mandate. An arresting officer can encounter hostility from observers of a situation in which he is taking affirmative action. Police are also alienated from the rest of society since they have the unwelcome duty of enforcing the moral norms of the larger society and, as Everett Hughes indicated, doing dirty work for good people. Recruitment plays a role as well. Hudson points to the research that suggests that the police represent a homogenous but unique substratum of larger society—they are mostly lower-middle class, white, and Catholic, but perform their duties in contexts where many citizens may be middle or upper class, nonwhite, and/or Protestant and non-Catholic. Thus, selective recruitment leads to a group whose backgrounds and values fall within a special and narrow range. Socialization of the recruit adds to the feeling of alienation. The symbols of authority (uniform, revolver, night-stick, and shield) mark the policeman off as separate and distinct; even when he is off duty, many citizens continue to regard him as unusual, as one who never stops being a police-man no matter what the context.

Hudson found that an examination of the Philadelphia cases indicated that most police–citizen encounters leading to complaints occurred either in public places or at the subject's residence, where *audiences were present*. Both the police officer and the citizen had to take the situation and the audience into account in confronting one another. The policeman's back-ground, training, and socialization led him to feel that the most important factor was keeping control of the situation. A police-man could not permit his authority to be challenged success-fully, and only he, not a citizen, could take the appropriate actions necessary to ensure this continuing authority. Hudson's analysis of the Philadelphia data disclosed a high number of arrests, suggesting that police use this technique as a means of control whereby the situation is redefined. When a person is arrested, the role relationship dramatically shifts, giving a de-cided advantage to the policeman. Hudson concludes, therefore, that the primary factor in police–citizen encounters is the police-man's authority as determined by recruitment and training, despite the existence of racial, class, or other variables in the particular social situation.[44]

Myths, Paradigms, and Paradigm Revolutions: The Search for New Views of Social Problems

In this section we have considered the three major paradigms used by social scientists, some laymen, and policy makers to analyze, understand, and prescribe solutions for social problems. The discussion of the deviance paradigm analyzed a provocative perspective, one that has spawned much research and theorizing but that also contains major biases. The biases have made it more difficult in recent years for the paradigm to explain the seemingly increasing numbers and nature of social problems and, as a consequence, the new labeling school has raised serious questions about its continued use in social science. In a similar manner, the discussion of the disorganization paradigm disclosed how it has been challenged on moral and political grounds, especially by the work of the new conflict theorists. Of all the paradigms and schools of thought, functionalism is the most popular, widely employed, and seemingly successful. Yet, here too, increasing violations by nature, in Kuhn's terms, have led radical social scientists and new behaviorists to criticize the latent biases inherent within functionalism. What this consideration suggests is that both existing paradigms, with historical roots in popular mythology, and the opposing perspectives and schools of thought have major social and scientific strengths and weaknesses. The relationship between these views of problems and their historical development is summarized in Table 6–3.

Table 6–3
Historical development of popular myths, scientific paradigms, and opposing theories

Historical Period of Greatest Influence	Popular Myth	Scientific Paradigm	Competing and Opposing View
Early	Natural Theory of Social Problems	Deviance	Labeling Theory
Middle	Evil Equals Evil	Disorganization, Social and Cultural	New Conflict Theory
Recent	Blaming the Victim	Functionalism	Radical, Reflexive Social Science and New Behaviorist Perspectives

In the early days of social scientific and lay thinking about social problems, a natural mythology and the social scientific paradigm of deviance became related, the weaknesses of which eventually led to the criticisms of labeling theorists. At the same time, the weaknesses of the natural theory myth and of the deviance paradigm, especially in its older form of a pathology perspective, led to a new myth of evil equals evil and a new paradigm of disorganization. These, in turn, influenced the development of new conflict theory. Finally, blaming the victim in popular mythology has most recently replaced the concept of evil equals evil as a predominant view and has been incorporated into some of functionalist theory about social problems. Weaknesses of these recent views have been harshly criticized by new behaviorists and symbolic interactionists, and by radical social scientists. What this summary suggests is that more meaningful mythology of and paradigm for analyzing problems and proposing resolutions is necessary, one that will respond to the social, political, and scientific criticisms that are being made by the competing and opposing views. However, such a new paradigm, if it is to develop, will probably not be a total rejection of previous perspectives, since many contain valuable strengths. On the contrary, a new mythology and paradigm will most probably be a synthesis of existing and previous views, though the form and the emphasis of the new paradigm will be different. The following concluding section of the book indicates the needs that will have to be met for a new synthesis to develop and the form and emphasis that such a synthesis might take.

Notes to Chapter 6

1. Don Martindale, "Limits of and Alternatives to Functionalism in Sociology." *Functionalism in the Social Sciences: The Strengths and Limits of Functionalism in Anthropology, Economics, Political Science, and Sociology*, Monograph No. 5, Don Martindale, ed. (Philadelphia: American Academy of Political and Social Science, 1965), p. 160. Martindale is referring to Kingsley Davis', "The Myth of Functional Analysis as a Special Method in Sociology and Anthropology," *American Sociological Review*, 24 (December 1959), pp. 757ff.
2. Martindale, *ibid.*, pp. 144–154.
3. Adapted from Martindale, *ibid.*, p. 152.
4. Adapted from Martindale, *ibid.*, p. 161. Martindale includes other types and examples in his article. This table relies upon examples considered in this book.

5. Kingsley Davis, "The Sociology of Prostitution," *American Sociological Review*, 2 (October 1937), pp. 744–755; and "Sexual Behavior," in *Contemporary Social Problems*, 2nd ed., Robert A. Nisbet and Robert K. Merton, eds. (New York: Harcourt, Brace and World, 1966), especially pp. 346–372.

6. Kingsley Davis, "Sexual Behavior," *ibid.*, pp. 352–355.

7. *Ibid.*, p. 360.

8. For example, see the following kinds of references: Kingsley Davis, *ibid.*, pp. 322–372 (contains extensive references to Kinsey and others); Otto Friedrich, "Time Essay: Reflections on the Sad Profession," *Time* (August 23, 1971), pp. 34–35; Laud Humphreys, *Tearoom Trade: Impersonal Sex in Public Places* (Chicago: Aldine Publishing Company, 1970), and the article based upon Humphrey's book in *Transaction*, 7 (January 1970), pp. 8ff.; Ira L. Reiss, "How and Why America's Sex Standards Are Changing," *Transaction*, 5 (March 1968), pp. 26–32; Joseph Slade, "Pornographic Theatres Off Times Square," *Transaction*, 9 (November/December 1971), pp. 35–43, 79; and Mary Lindenstein Walshok, "The Emergence of Middle Class Deviant Subcultures: The Case of Swingers," *Social Problems, 18* (Spring 1971), pp. 488–495.

9. Kingsley Davis, "Sexual Behavior," in *Contemporary Social Problems*, 2nd ed., Robert A. Nisbet and Robert K. Merton, eds. (New York: Harcourt, Brace and World, 1966), p. 372.

10. For a more detailed discussion of the functionalist perspective, see the work of Robert K. Merton; for example, *Social Theory and Social Structure*, rev. ed. (New York: The Free Press, 1957).

11. Robert A. Nisbet and Robert K. Merton, eds. *Contemporary Social Problems*, 3rd ed. (New York: Harcourt Brace Jovanovich, 1971), pp. 1–25, 793–845.

12. Harry M. Johnson, *Sociology: A Systematic Introduction* (New York: Harcourt, Brace and World, 1960), pp. 66–68.

13. Daniel Bell, "Crime as an American Way of Life," *Antioch Review, 13* (Summer 1953); and *The End of Ideology* (New York: The Free Press, 1959), pp. 115–136.

14. See also, Daniel Bell, "From Mafia to Cosa Nostra," *Transaction, 3* (July/August 1966), p. 2.

15. The American-made motion picture "The Godfather," starring Marlon Brando, raised some of these issues. See also Mario Puzo, *The Godfather* (New York: Putnam, 1969); Claire Sterling, "Unhappy 'Godchildren': U.S. Hoods in Italy," *International Herald Tribune* (October 10, 1972), editorial page.

16. Arnold M. Rose, "Law and the Causation of Social Problems," *Social Problems, 16* (Summer 1968), pp. 33–43.

17. *Ibid.*, p. 37.

18. This discussion is adapted from an unpublished paper by Stuart Palmer, "On the Unintended Consequences of Social Control," delivered at the annual meeting of the American Sociological Association in San Francisco (September 1969).

19. See, for example, Eliot Freidson and Buford Rhea, "Processes of Control in a Company of Equals," *Social Problems*, 11 (Fall 1963), pp. 119–131; Freidson, "The Impurity of Professional Authority," in *Institutions and the Person: Papers Presented to Everett C. Hughes,*

Howard S. Becker *et al.*, eds. (Chicago: Aldine Publishing Company, 1968), pp. 25–120; Friedson, "The Professional Mind," *Arts and Sciences* (Winter 1966); and Freidson, *Unprofessional Consequences of Professionalization*, unpublished paper delivered at the annual meeting of the American Sociological Association in San Francisco (September 1969).

20. C. Wright Mills, *The Sociological Imagination* (New York: Oxford University Press, 1959). See also the criticisms by Alvin W. Gouldner in *The Coming Crisis of Western Sociology* (New York: Avon Books, 1970).

21. For example, see I. C. Jarvie, "Limits of Functionalism and Alternatives to It in Anthropology," *Functionalism in the Social Sciences: The Strengths and Limits of Functionalism in Anthropology, Economics, Political Science, and Sociology*, Monograph No. 5, Don Martindale, ed. (Philadelphia: American Academy of Political and Social Science, 1965), pp. 18–34.

22. *Ibid.*, pp. 22–24.

23. Melvin Tumin, "The Functionalist Approach to Social Problems," *Social Problems, 12* (Spring 1965), pp. 379–388.

24. Talcott Parsons, *The Social System* (New York: The Free Press, 1951); and Talcott Parsons and Neil Smelser, *Economy and Society* (New York: The Free Press, 1956), pp. 16–19.

25. William Flanigan and Edwin Fogelman, "Functionalism in Political Science," *Functionalism in the Social Sciences: The Strengths and Limits of Functionalism in Anthropology, Economics, Political Science, and Sociology*, Monograph No. 5, Don Martindale, ed. (Philadelphia: American Academy of Political and Social Science, 1965), pp. 111–136.

26. See Melvin Tumin, "The Functionalist Approach to Social Problems," *Social Problems, 12* (Spring 1965), pp. 379–388, for a summary of these criticisms.

27. For an example of the use of functionalism to support a conservative perspective, see Edward C. Banfield, *The Unheavenly City* (Boston: Little, Brown, 1970).

28. Melvin Tumin, "The Functionalist Approach to Social Problems," *Social Problems, 12* (Spring 1965), p. 383.

29. *Ibid.*, pp. 385–388.

30. For example, see Harry C. Bredemeier, "Banfield, Gouldner, and Social Problems," *Social Problems, 18* (Spring 1971), pp. 554–568; Murray L. Wax, "Letter to the Editor—More on Gouldner," *Social Problems, 19* (Fall 1971), pp. 279–280; and the letters from Wilburt E. Moore and Robert A. Feldmesser, with a response from Robert H. Lauer, *American Sociological Review, 37* (June 1972), pp. 376-379.

31. See Alvin W. Gouldner's *The Coming Crisis of Western Sociology* (New York: Avon Books, 1970), and the reviews of this book by Guy Swanson, Steven E. Deutsch, and Richard A. Petersen, "Review Symposium," *American Sociological Review, 36* (April 1971), pp. 317–328. Also see the following references: Stanley Aronwitz, Roy Bennett, Bennet M. Berger, and Edgar Z. Friedenberg, "A Symposium—Strategies for Radical Social Change," *Social Policy, 1* (November/December 1970), pp. 9–23; J. David Colfax and Jack L. Roach, eds., *Radical Sociology* (New York: Basic Books, 1971); Lewis A. Coser, "Unanticipated Conservative Consequences of Liberal Theorizing,"

Social Problems, 16 (Winter 1969), pp. 263–272; "Editorial—It's Time for Theory in America," *Social Policy, 2* (March/April 1972), pp. 2–3; Alvin W. Gouldner, "Toward the Radical Reconstruction of Sociology," *Social Policy* (May/June 1970), pp. 18–25; Jack L. Roach, "The Radical Sociology Movement: A Short History and Commentary," *The American Sociologist, 5* (August 1970), pp. 224–235; Marion K. Sanders, "The Professional Radical, 1970," *Harper's Magazine* (January 1970), pp. 35–42; and "Some Radical Perspectives in Sociology," *Sociological Inquiry, 40* (Winter 1970), pp. 3–165.

32. See Talcott Parsons, *The Social System* (New York: The Free Press, 1951).

33. John Colombotos, "Physicians and Medicare: A Before–After Study of the Effects of Legislation on Attitudes," *American Sociological Review, 34* (June 1969), pp. 318–334.

34. Theodore R. Marmor, "Why Medicare Helped Raise Doctors' Fees," *Transaction, 5* (September 1968), pp. 14–19.

35. Richard C. Fuller and Richard R. Myers, "The Natural History of a Social Problem," *American Sociological Review* (June 1941), pp. 321ff.

36. Herbert Blumer, "Social Problems as Collective Behavior," *Social Problems, 19* (Winter 1971), pp. 298–306.

37. Michael Harrington, *The Other America: Poverty in the United States* (New York: Macmillan, 1962).

38. Rachel L. Carson, *Silent Spring* (Boston: Houghton Mifflin, 1962); and Ralph Nader, *Unsafe at Any Speed* (New York: Grossman, 1965).

39. Leonard Reissman, "The Solution Cycle of Social Problems," *The American Sociologist, 7* (February 1972), p. 7.

40. Herbert Spencer, "Spontaneous Reform," *Facts and Comments* (New York: D. Appleton and Company, 1902), pp. 29–34.

41. See Earl Rubington, "Of Drunkards and Junkies," *Transaction, 6* (July/August, 1969), pp. 5–6.

42. Also see Howard M. Bahr, "Institutional Life, Drinking, and Disaffiliation," *Social Problems, 16* (Winter 1969), pp. 365–375; and Howard Moody, "Narcotics Addiction in an Addicted Society," *Christianity and Crisis, 25* (June 14, 1965), pp. 128–131. Both of these analyses of alcohol and narcotics use employ an interactionist and societal reaction perspective to generate unusual and new views of these problems.

43. James R. Hudson, "Police–Citizen Encounters That Lead to Citizen Complaints," *Social Problems, 18* (Fall 1970), pp. 179–193.

44. For a provocative case study of a militant black response to white force and police repression; see Harold A. Nelson, "The Defenders: A Case Study of an Informal Police Organization," *Social Problems, 15* (Fall 1967), pp. 127–147.

Part III

The Search for New Social-Problems Myths and Paradigms

Reston, Virginia: Model for future communities or wasteful and repressive social experimentation?
(Dennis Brack, Black Star)

7. Old Views Versus New Needs

We have seen that those who study, think about, or try to plan programs to resolve social problems have been influenced, often unknowingly, by three kinds of popular myths and three associated kinds of scientific theories. Most of the contemporary crisis in our apparent inability to resolve problems such as war, pollution, crime, narcotics use, sexual deviance, alcoholism, and the like is a result of the fact that public policy leads to programs based upon these myths and theories. Since the myths and theories do not adequately deal with the changing nature of modern society, the programs often create more problems than they resolve.

We Mean Well But . . .

Inadequacies of Popular Myths and Major Scientific Paradigms. In historical sequence, the three popular myths have been a natural theory of social problems, the idea that evil equals evil, and the tendency to blame the victim. The natural theory emerged early in American history as a result of reformist Puritanism, the desire to do good, and prevailing social and scientific theories of the time (for example, Freudianism and Darwinism).

It argued that problems were the natural, inevitable, unavoidable, and expected results of man's more evil nature, his imperfectability, and the like. At the turn of the century, more humanistic and compassionate views, plus the impact of relativism, made this myth less applicable and acceptable, and it was replaced by the notion that evil equals evil. The emphasis, however, remained upon reforming the person who performed the evil acts. This second myth saw evil as being the result of and leading to other evils; for example, if one smoked pot he might eventually take heroin and, therefore, have to steal or kill to support his addiction. In the last several decades, much social science research has shown the inaccuracy of this concept in many contexts.

As a consequence, the third popular myth became predominant in the 1940's and 1950's. Blaming the victim was a way in which citizens and decision makers could show humanitarian concern for the victims of social problems without necessarily challenging or threatening the existing social system and vested interests. For example, people were thought to become criminals because they lived in terrible slumlike conditions; therefore, if only decent surroundings and adequate jobs could be provided, these people could be moved from such a corrupting environment, thereby solving the problem. In this way, blaming the victim built upon the early evil-equals-evil concept. Such a theory rarely questioned why slums arose in the first place (thus reflecting the initial natural myth), and it put the solution emphasis upon the need for individual victims to improve themselves and their habits. Aspects of all these myths can be seen in present welfare programs, views of poverty, explanations for crime and delinquency, concern for pollution and war, programs for combating narcotics use, and so on.

At the same time, three major scientific paradigms—deviance, disorganization, and functionalism—developed that were influenced by and, in turn, had an impact upon these popular myths. Adherents of the deviance paradigm argued that a certain amount of deviant behavior had to be expected in any society. Indeed, at times, this deviance was even seen as serving useful purposes for either or both the deviants and society as a whole. Disorganization adherents argued that some people lived in disorganized contexts, which led to understandably disorganized personal behavior. More recent functionalists argue that social problems exist because they function to maintain some necessary manifest or latent purpose within the prevailing social system. The difficulty is that each of these views can explain only a part of reality when specific problems are studied, and often the part explained is the least important analytically, the safest politically, and the most misleading from the standpoint of social action. Deviance can be used to support a naturalistic myth, disorganization to prove that evil equals evil, and functionalism to blame the victim. Since these three paradigms are the only ways in which most social scientists have looked at problems during the last century, they have become increasingly inadequate, even undesirable, because of their inherent political and moral biases.

As a result, paradigm revolutions have begun to take place. Labeling theory challenges not only the methodology and philosophy of deviance but also the tacit moral and political assumptions behind the paradigm. New conflict theory similarly challenges the disorganization paradigm. Functionalism is being challenged by two schools of thought: a new radical social science with roots in Marxism and a new behaviorist perspective, which argues against the reified and deified social system approach of functionalism. In short, the study of social problems is in a state of turmoil and revolution. Popular attitudes are undergoing major changes, and disillusionment prevails as most programs of action do not seem to work well. The irony is that everyone, both layman and scientist, from the early reformists to the new cynics, has meant well. The consistent desire has been to do something helpful for the victims of social problems, to identify and take action against the perpetrators of the problems, and to reform or reorganize society as necessary. But most often the myths and paradigms have resulted in anything but good deeds. The natural myth of problems explains everything away by explaining nothing at all. The myth of evil equals evil employs tautological reasoning and is simply not correct in many cases. Blaming the victim seems humanitarian but avoids raising universalistic questions and issues. The deviance paradigm has generated useful concepts but is often seriously biased by the assumption that anything that does not adhere to accepted norms is deviant—therefore, bad or undesirable. The disorganization paradigm commits some of the same errors as the popular myth of evil equals evil. Functionalism, while it seems to be the most adaptable paradigm, still has difficulty accounting for change and conflict, and for deviation from the societal values and goals assumed to be appropriate.

The Resulting Conservative Disillusionment and Radical Cynicism.   The contemporary intellectual and policy consequences of this disillusionment with old theory and the developing search for alternatives have been summarized by S. M. Miller as follows:

The conservative 1950's were characterized by the American Celebration; the first three Nixon years might be called the American Resignation. Two decades ago, as social problems festered beneath the surface of the national consciousness, many (ex-left) intellectuals proclaimed that America had matured into an untroubled, affluent society that had ended ideology. Now, after the experience of the 1960's, when national administrations tried to solve the problems ignored during the 1950's, a new school of commentators (containing some of the celebrators of the 1950's) declares that these problems are less serious than they seem. Combining optimism about the status quo with pessimism about change, they conclude that nothing is wrong with America that lowering our objectives won't solve. *The country will be in worse shape, runs the logic of the American Resignation, if we keep trying to solve our problems. In the pages of* Commentary, The New York Times, Atlantic, *and the* Public Interest, *commentators like Harvard's Nathan Glazer, Edward Banfield, Richard Herrnstein, and Daniel P. Moynihan, and N.Y.U.'s Irving Kristol and Sidney Hook, demand the abandonment of the liberal reformist spirit of the early 1960's and the embracing of the society that the decade left us. They shape the outlook of a large group who once considered themselves liberals and radicals and now think of themselves as moderates, centrists, and even conservatives.*[1]

Miller points out that the attack of the new, *conservative resignationists* is based upon four types of assumptions, which are

reflected in recent research and theories. First, some resignationists have become disillusioned with social and cultural perspectives and are looking for biological and genetic determinants of
social problems. The persistence of many problems despite massive public and private programs of action seems to suggest that
more intractable variables than social and cultural ones account
for most problems. The conclusion, therefore, is that there must
be something in the very nature of man that accounts for our
inability to resolve most problems. Herrnstein and Jensen are
examples of these types of theorists.

Second, other new resignationists argue that cultural and
social factors are determinant and that they create almost irre-
sistable barriers to change. For example, Edward Banfield has
argued that the inability of the poor to defer gratifications until
later periods in life makes it impossible for them to achieve.
Even if the poor were given greater opportunities, they would
be culturally unable to use them in the most appropriate way.
(The popular myth of poor people buying Cadillacs with welfare money illustrates this view.) Therefore, since attempts to
aid the poor and eliminate poverty cannot succeed, it is best to
leave the whole business alone.[2] Concepts such as a culture of
poverty also contribute to this second type of resignationist
perspective.

The third type of assumption, according to Miller, is the
automatic acceptance of the American Puritan work ethic.
Welfare is seen as a form of disorganization because it erodes
this ethic. Black families are seen as deviant because they do not
resemble the white, middle-class "ideal" of a strongly motivated
father authority. In part, the new resignationists relate this commitment to the Puritan ethic to prior assumptions. It is assumed
that the Puritan ethic most closely reflects the true inherent
nature of man. Furthermore, programs that latently undermine
the ethic are doomed to failure, not only because they run counter to man's basic nature, but also because they run counter to
the basic traditions of American society and culture.

Finally, the new resignationists see rising conflict and
confrontation as evil and threatening. Specifically, Miller points
out that the resignationists are most fearful of backlash resentment from working-class white ethnics and the prevailing

meritocratic elite, especially in response to more liberal and radical programs of change. Thus, the new resignationists have difficulty taking into account the possible meaningful role of rapid change and conflict in contemporary society. Again, ironically, their concern is based upon seemingly humanitarian impulses. They argue that if radical programs lead white working men and elites to rebel against change, then oppression and repression will certainly result, with the consequence that both the victims of social problems (blacks, women, the poor, deviants) and liberal social thinkers will be persecuted and punished.[3]

In addition to resignation by conservatives, modern disillusionment has also resulted in an alternative response as we have seen: *the radical perspective*, which totally rejects all prevailing views and theories, assumes an inherent pathology in most if not all existing social forms, and seeks completely new views, techniques of analysis, and solutions to problems. However, in extreme form, this out-with-the-old, in-with-the-new perspective contains its own special bias and weakness. Ironically, many new radical theorists are not proposing total rejection of previous assumptions. In some cases, new radical perspectives merely express older views in a somewhat different form or often, though quite appropriately, remind us of important historical polarities that have characterized the study of problems by social science since its inception. For example, new pathology is based upon many of the same types of assumptions as older pathology perspectives, merely changing the essential focus from a search for the source of problems as inherent within individuals to a search for the source as inherent within deviant, disorganized, or pathological social systems, elites, or institutions. Also, radicals using a functionalist paradigm, run many of the same risks as the conservative theorists who employ this paradigm (reifying the system, the assumption of functional equivalents, and so on). Finally, new radical criticisms of older perspectives have frequently reminded social scientists of the traditional and *as yet unresolved* dichotomies: positivism versus humanism and holism versus elementarism. A good deal of radical criticism is elementaristic questioning of holistic theory, humanistic questioning of pragmatism, or other variations of these polarities.

Strengths and Weaknesses of Competing Views—Three Requirements for a New Paradigm. In some ways, contemporary conservative resignation and radical rejection of the existing system suggest that social theory has come full circle since the early days of social science: from a natural theory arguing that problems were an unavoidable part of man's life to conservative assumptions that things are not really that bad after all or to radical assumptions that things are so bad that nothing short of a major revolution will work. Furthermore, such a situation is not conducive to an adequate resolution of prevailing problems, since both prevailing perspectives and criticisms of these perspectives frequently contain special weaknesses, as well as strengths, often unrecognized by the adherents of the views. Table 7–1 summarizes and compares these strengths and weaknesses.

What such a summary and comparison illustrates is that social scientists and policy makers have meant well, but. . . . No existing theory or paradigm is wholly satisfactory, although some seem more applicable and adaptable to understanding and resolving social problems. A new paradigm and perspective, combining usable elements of earlier views, is required, and the comparison below indicates what will be needed to develop such a new paradigm. All of the prevailing, traditional paradigms tend to suffer from three common weaknesses: (1) the inability to generate knowledge particularly applicable to *policy-oriented and applied research;* (2) the lack of *future perspectives* or a concern with *alternative social systems;* and (3) the inability to accommodate the concepts of *change* and *conflict.* Indeed, the emerging schools of thought, as incipient paradigm revolutions, attack the deviance, disorganization, and functionalist paradigms on these three bases. New pathology and labeling theory criticizes deviance for its inability to consider alternative interpretations and, therefore, its inability to lead to innovative programs of meaningful action for deviants themselves. New conflict theory criticizes disorganization for its inability to conceive of alternative types of social systems. Radical views and the new behaviorism criticize functionalism for its inability to deal with practical policy issues and questions. Therefore, the reasons why we have failed are not only what the new resignationists or many radicals assume them to be; they are also a consequence of an absence of

Table 7–1

Strengths and weaknesses of major social scientific paradigms and schools of thought

Paradigm and School of Thought	Strengths	Weaknesses
Old Pathology	Humanitarian concern	Conservative bias; individualistic determinism; assumption of objective pathology
Deviance	Can be used in particularistic or universalistic ways; can be used in a value-free fashion; all kinds of puzzles to be solved; encourages much theory and speculation	Latently conservative and status quo oriented; assumption of objective nature of deviance
New Pathology	Universalistic; attacks biases of older views	Radical bias; social determinism; assumption of objective pathology
Labeling Theory	Attacks biases of deviance paradigm; emphasizes subjective aspect of deviance; creates new puzzles to be resolved	Usefulness limited to special circumstances and kinds of deviance; denies objective deviance
Disorganization	Lends itself well to empirical analysis; all kinds of puzzles to be solved; encourages much theory and speculation	Latently conservative and status quo oriented; assumption of objective nature of disorganization
Conflict Theory	Attacks biases of disorganization paradigm; creates new puzzles to be solved	Reification and deification of conflict, even in extreme forms
Functionalism	Strongly rooted in sociological views of man and society; can be used in a value-free fashion; encourages much theory and speculation; potential for radical and critical perspectives	Inherently conservative; difficult to account for change and conflict; difficult to apply to empirical analysis
New Radical Perspectives	Attacks biases of older paradigms; universalistic	Radical bias; strongly moralistic
New Behaviorism	Attacks universalistic bias of older views	Tends to be particularistic

theories and perspectives that fulfill these three new requirements.

Why We Fail: Policy-Oriented and Applied Research

The first reason why we have failed in resolving social problems is because the available paradigms do not generate policy-oriented knowledge or applied research of the kind required. According to Howard Waitzkin, social scientists have avoided action- and applied-oriented research because of several major dilemmas inherent within the social sciences and in the relationship of social scientists to policy makers and men of power.[4]

The Difficulty of Policy-Oriented Research—Four Dilemmas of the Social Scientist. The first dilemma lies in the conflict between *positive* versus *normative* statements. Positive statements involve declarations of fact concerning relationships between variables. Normative statements involve descriptions of what ought to be. Both kinds of statements lead to a form of prediction but in markedly different ways. Positive statements tell policy makers what will happen if they manipulate certain kinds of social and cultural variables. For example, labeling theory would argue that if meaningful definitions are provided to deviants by institutional authorities, then improved self-definitions will result. In contrast, normative statements advise actions based on personal judgments. In this case, a labeling theorist might argue that meaningful self-definitions *should* be provided to deviants by institutional authorities.

Waitzkin states that this distinction creates problems. *Social scientists who cling to a completely value-free perspective and feel they can make only positive statements, yet at the same time want their work to be instrumental in the solution of social problems, face a very special difficulty.* Often these scientists assume that action implications are sufficiently inherent in their findings, though they realize that normative statements do not logically derive from positive statements. As a consequence, two patterns of behavior tend to develop. Either scientists withdraw from involvement in the world of social action (merely hoping their discoveries will be used to better the human condition), or they mask normative statements as positive statements. Scientists who choose the latter response run the risk of seriously biasing their studies. As a result, policy makers and the general public, who eventually discover this bias, become skeptical of the reliability of social scientists as men committed to impartial truth.

A second and related dilemma is *the conflict between value-free research and the demands of civic responsibility*. Early in the history of social science, Max Weber suggested that scientists should not allow values to influence their work, though, obviously, they might possess strong personal values and commitments.[5] It is evident, however, that the problem of separating one's judgments from one's work is almost impossible. As a consequence, many scientists have tended to live two distinct and separate lives: one as a model value-free researcher, the other as an active supporter and espouser of social causes. The problem here is the "either/or" character of most of the argument about value freedom versus value commitment of social scientific work —the misleading assumption that the scientist must be either completely free of value or totally committed to specific views. The final chapter to follow will indicate how studies might incorporate both characteristics in a controlled and productive way.

Waitzkin points out, however, that the problem goes beyond values and ideals—it involves as well the personal relationships of the social scientist. A third dilemma is *the inherent conflict between career advancement and social-problem solving*. Career advancement depends upon producing knowledge that is applicable to the needs and requirements of accepted paradigms. In contrast, knowledge useful for the resolution of social problems may require research and theory that is in direct contradiction to prevailing paradigms. Furthermore, the scientist who commits himself to solving problems may find himself in a different context far removed from the type of environment that would encourage traditional research and study. He may work for a public or private agency where he has no colleagues with whom to communicate. Indeed, his very involvement with action and policy may make him susceptible to charges of a lack of basic competence or ability by his colleagues in more traditional academic environments.

Related to this conflict is a fourth dilemma, *the problem of consultation versus cooptation.* When scientists are asked to act as consultants to those in power, the relationship that develops can often result in the scientist's supporting or enhancing prevailing policy, regardless of other value or policy concerns. For example, Waitzkin refers to the manner in which anthropologists advised the military during World War II about cultural patterns in occupied areas. The purpose of this consultation was to facilitate American military control by managing tensions and conflicts resulting from cultural differences. Anthropologists, however, did not limit themselves to examining foreign contexts:

In his book The Governing of Men, *Alexander Leighton describes the "human relations" approach in relocation camps operated by the American government to house Japanese-Americans evacuated from the West Coast during the war. By identifying the belief system and social organization of the Japanese-Americans in these camps, these social scientists were able to advise administrators about policies which would relieve tensions.*[6]

This happened despite the fact that postwar judgment has seen the relocation of Japanese-American citizens as undemocratic and unconstitutional, and, therefore, tensions should probably not have been lessened. Indeed, social scientists might have sided with the internees and studied the undemocratic aspects of the internment. In a similar manner, social scientists have for many decades produced studies aiding industrial managers to adapt workers to the tensions of assembly-line jobs, to obtain higher output without adjusting pay, or to handle grievances without the necessity of radical unionization.[7] In other words, representatives of the establishment tend to be the sponsors of applied research, and these sponsors easily coopt scientists, often without their knowledge or complicity. As a result, many scientists tend to eschew applied or action-oriented research altogether.

Possible Responses to the Dilemmas.   As formidable as these dilemmas may seem to be to the development of paradigms and theories applicable to policy-oriented and applied research, there are specific kinds of actions and perspectives that could begin to resolve the difficulties in contemporary problems research. Albert Reiss argues that applied research must have a special character, much of which is absent in present work.[8] For example, with the exception of some economic theory, social explanations of problems generally do not specify the consequences of various actions or behavior. This means that contemporary theories cannot predict social change and cannot forecast the consequences of intervention by authorities to bring about desired changes.[9] One of the reasons for this inability is that prior research on deviance and disorganization has tended to focus upon individuals rather than upon aggregates, populations, or social organizations and institutions. As a consequence, theories about change depend upon psychological rather than sociological, or social system, explanations. They are particularistic rather than universalistic, as William Ryan put it.[10]

Strategies for action, therefore, turn out to be attempts to change individuals (as Etzioni pointed out, the least effective action that can be taken[11]), not attempts to change or alter social systems. Reiss suggests, for example, that to know how to reduce births is not to know how to reduce the birth rate; to know that smoking causes lung cancer is not to know how to reduce either smoking or cancer; to know how to influence an individual through psychotherapy is not necessarily to know how to reduce mental illness in society at large.[12] Reiss wonders whether modern society would have invested so heavily in the training of psychologists and psychiatrists if applied sociological research had predicted the kinds of political problems discussed by Szasz[13] (discussed in Chapter 4) or the fact that the costs of individual therapy would exceed the capacity of the system to bear it. Reiss indicates that:

A policy relevant to sociology might concern itself less with what causes people to behave the way they do than with how they can be changed by manipulating systems. To investigate the latter is no simple matter. Yet I find it curious that much of the research on deviant behavior is about how people get into rather than on how they get out of deviant behavior. It is a striking fact, for example, that most delinquents and criminals pass out of deviance; yet there are almost no studies on how they pass.[14]

Reiss also points to the participation of social scientists on recent commissions reporting upon crime, civil disorder, and domestic violence. For example, most of the scientific effort in the reports of the National Commission on Violence was applied to documenting that Americans are violent (and to a great degree), the types of violence, as well as discussions of what factors tend to cause violence. Reiss states that while violence among men was treated as problematic, civility was not. In the same manner, the report of the National Advisory Commission on Civil Disorders emphasized the necessity to reduce "American racism" but did not mention those social and cultural factors or programs of action that might make tolerance problematic. In other words, there is a great need for applied research that utilizes a sociological imagination, focuses upon crucial social issues, is universalistic in nature, and deals with the consequences of various programs and actions.

An Example—Rex Hopper's Study of the Impact of Cybernation. These needed types of perspectives can be seen in a provocative analysis by Rex Hopper of the impact of cybernation upon postindustrial society.[15] Hopper's previous research led him to the conclusion that orthodox conceptions of revolutionary upheavals were inadequate. He identified the common variable in all prerevolutionary contexts as the emergence of a numerically significant, economically powerful, and intellectually informed marginal group. By a *marginal group*, Hopper referred to people who were only partially related to the prevailing structure of political power and social prestige—those who receive some benefits from the system but are not in major positions of control. In the United States, such a sizable, economically influential, and intellectually capable marginal group has never emerged. Hopper indicates that historically the ranks of labor might have been expected to furnish such a potential. However, the early and complete incorporation of organized labor into the power and prestige structure of America negated a tendency towards marginality for the workingman. Hopper hypothesizes, though, that when one examines the near future, it appears that cybernation may bring the type of change that could create such a marginal group. He indicates that if this situation should come about, American society might well be faced with another instance of the classical historical dilemma where warfare is employed to divert attention away from internal problems and conflicts to stave off revolutionary propensities. War would be selected over revolution because society's leaders could use a totally militarized economy to control and eliminate an emerging marginal group. Hopper's theory, proposed in the mid-1960's, remarkably "predicted" some of the revolutionary and rebellious confrontations of the late 1960's and the most consistent economic problem of the 1970's—the economic impact of demilitarization—involved in ending the Vietnam War and demobilizing American society.

Hopper begins his analysis by pointing to the research that indicates that the cybernation revolution may be of far greater magnitude than the revolution that extended the labor of man's muscle power with the use of machine. Where the industrial revolution replaced human physical powers with machines, the cybernation revolution is replacing human mental and intellectual powers with machines. Hopper points out that the most obvious immediate effect of this process upon the population will be increased *displacement through unemployment*. This unemployment will occur in subtle, sometimes latent, ways. For example, Hopper refers to one of the early results of selective cybernation in some industries—the decision not to hire rather than to fire. In other words, new additions to the work force are simply not hired. At the same time, cybernation strikingly increases productivity while requiring fewer people to produce more. Yet, all estimates indicate that the population will continue to grow and continue to add newcomers to the employment market.

Of special importance is the fact that cybernation no longer restricts job displacement to blue-collar workers. The employment victims of cybernation will include (and already have), in addition to blue-collar adults, service workers, middle management, professionals, and untrained adolescents. These groupings will not only be displaced in actual employment opportunities, but they will also be displaced in a more fundamental and serious sense. Displacement will occur through obsolescence, since as machines replace the power provided by men's brains, man becomes more useless, unnecessary, and even undesirable. For example, the petroleum and chemical industries run refineries and processing plants by machinery programmed with computers and monitored by a few men. Eventually, the few men may be replaced since they are subject to human error and cannot operate as quickly as the machines they monitor. Furthermore, it is estimated that the telephone company would have to employ all the women in the labor force plus 20 percent to maintain the present level of service if computerized line markers were not available. In other words, cybernation makes obsolete the human intellect and the human nervous system.

Hopper also refers to a third type of displacement, which could turn out to be the most disruptive of all. Cybernation is latently undermining the basic cultural values of society without adequate substitutes being provided. Man is unaware of this process and has yet to start the search for adequate values in a cybernetic age. Hopper calls this process a type of *cultural displacement*. The American economy has essentially rested upon the concepts of property and work. However, increasingly in recent years, property has become less the source of economic power, and ownership no longer determines the relationship between people and the amount and types of things they consume. The nature of property, that which is owned, has changed from land to machines. At the same time, work occupies fewer hours in the lives of the population. Yet as people work less, the total national product grows more, further defying old values and beliefs. Hopper summarizes the cultural impact of these kinds of changes as follows:

With the subversion of the institutions of poverty and work we are left with the illusion that we are "working," with old habits and compulsions as supports for the social edifice. In other words, the old cultural values are no longer functional and, in such circumstances, some very basic (and revolutionary) questions become crucially relevant: If a fraction of the labor force is capable of supplying an abundance of everything the population needs and wants, then why should the rest of the population have to work for a living? If production cannot be maintained at a profit under such circumstances, then why should a profit be made? Does profit remain a useful standard of accounting in a propertyless society? Is full employ-

ment (in the usual sense of unemployment to the extent of 4 percent of the labor force) any longer an attainable objective (unless war or other unacceptable alternatives are utilized to artificially maintain a low rate of unemployment)? Is the very concept of full employment outmoded? What takes the place of wages in a workless society? [16]

Hopper's central thesis is that such changes, brought about and supported by cybernation, can create a *numerically significant, economically powerful, intellectually informed marginal group.* That such marginality has already started to occur is evident by a number of processes: unemployment in war-related professions, declining opportunities in many services (especially education), rising blue-collar unemployment, lack of adequate opportunities for youth, and the like. These diverse groupings could coalesce to form a numerically significant constellation. Furthermore, these groupings would still remain financially influential, since they constitute the foundation of an affluent, consumer-based economy. Finally, these groupings are educated and intellectually aware. Whether or not the revolutionary potential thus created develops further will depend in part upon a recognition by society of the possible problem, the degree to which these groups feel a common context of marginality, and the responses of public leaders.

As this analysis by Hopper indicates, then, the concept of applied research implies a great deal more than merely working on practical problems. The kinds of problems selected for study, the particular perspective employed, and the relationship of social scientists to their subject matter are crucial. Hopper's research indicates how social scientists can utilize a sociological imagination for applied- and action-oriented studies. It also shows how analyses can deal with the consequences and implications of particular kinds of policies or changes for the larger social system—in this case, the cybernation revolution's impact upon other revolutionary social movements. This kind of research need must be met in order to generate a new social science paradigm, and it leads to a consideration of a second need—the necessity to develop a future and alternative systems perspective.

Why We Fail: Future Perspectives and Alternative Systems

The absence of a future perspective—the second major reason why contemporary perspectives of social problems lead to programs that fail—implies more than a lack of simple predictions. An oft-repeated shibboleth of science, that knowledge is produced for the purpose of prediction and control, is frequently used by social scientists. Yet, ironically, just as frequently it is difficult, if not impossible, to find social scientific examples of adequate prediction or of the effective use of research findings for purposes of controlling social problems. It is the prediction-and-control aspect of scientific knowledge that makes such knowledge applicable to specific social problems and issues. Therefore, the almost total absence of this aspect in social science may account for the paucity of meaningful applied research. A possible exception to this general lack can be found in economics, which has generated paradigms of the social system suggesting present trends and future consequences. At the same time, it is significant to note that no social scientist really "predicted" the black urban revolution in America or the worldwide liberation movements (for racial, sexual, and economic minorities) of the 1960's. In science, the notions of prediction and control depend upon one another. If a social problem is to be adequately controlled, scientifically derived statements must be made that will indicate the possible consequences of various types of problem-solving programs. We have already seen the reluctance of many scientists to engage in applied or action-oriented research, which results in the seeming lack of predictive social science. At the same time, however, many social scientists are also reluctant to engage in prediction. This further reluctance is a function of several things.

Hindrances to Futurist Perspectives. Howard Waitzkin suggests that social scientists use a kind of *rationalistic optimism* which argues that accurate data about social problems will naturally contribute to social change when the data are integrated into some rational plan of action.[17] He calls this view a consequence of the dilemma of comprehensive planning versus bargaining. In other words, social scientists assume that once a comprehensive plan of action is developed, it will be implemented by rational men wishing to do good. This type of assumption has been prevalent in the social sciences since the earliest period, when August Comte suggested that a natural science of man and society could be constructed and used in deliberate ways to improve the human condition, much as natural and physical science is applied to resolving the problems of nature for the benefit of man. The problem, as Waitzkin sees it, is that, in reality, such linear processes toward reform and improvement do not occur in this altruistic and idealistic manner. Rational plans are often the result of political or personal needs, not conscious and logical desires to resolve problems. For example, most contemporary cities have long-range master plans, based upon sophisticated techniques of gaming or future planning, because the federal Housing Act of 1954 required such a plan before urban renewal and other funds could be made available. Thus, most communities make decisions about urban problems (land use, renewal, action projects, and so on) because of the need to receive funding, not because of the desire for rational planning. In addition, what goes into a plan, particularly its implementation, is a result of political and personal bargaining and compromise, not the result of the logical outcome of a rational predictive process. Waitzkin suggests, therefore, that there is a gap between scientific assumptions and expectations and social reality, and when this gap is realized many social scientists prefer to eschew prediction and planning altogether.

A second reason for the absence of future-oriented social research, especially in America, relates to the traditional predisposition of many scientists, citizens, and decision makers alike toward preconceptions about what is required for such research. For example, though Americans like to think of themselves as innovators and experimenters, in reality their tendency is to *avoid unusual or deliberately daring experiments* in social relations, especially at the public level. Traditional values emphasizing individual freedom and independence are often cited as reasons why major programs of experimentation should not be undertaken. To this extent, a kind of natural theory of social problems, leading to the belief that one should do as little as possible and merely hope for the best, is predominant. Where other countries, notably Israel and the Scandinavian nations, frequently undertake fundamental programs of change, America has depended upon education, advertising, or propaganda as a means of persuading individuals to alter their personal habits, rather than trying to manipulate social contexts in significant ways. This is obviously a consequence of the understandable American emphasis upon individualism and the accompanying distrust of organizational or institutional control. The distinction between the harsh and successful drunk-driving laws in Scandinavia and Britain and the American tendency to forget the connection between alcohol use and automobile safety is an example.

At the same time, however, Americans, as well as citizens in other cultures, also tend to *embrace uncritically* and unthinkingly *new programs* or fads. As a consequence, large-scale changes in welfare, narcotics treatment, the processing of criminals, education for the disadvantaged, and the like may be brought about spontaneously without adequate rational planning and certainly without consideration for possible future consequences. As a result, a paradox is created. Conservatism may interpret rational social experimentation as radical and, therefore, to be avoided; at the same time, the desire for the new and different, for the daring and unusual, can lead to the embracing of ill-conceived attempts to rectify fundamental social problems. In such a context, it is not surprising that we often fail in attempts to resolve social problems in the modern world. Failure is also a consequence of the *unresolved conflict between the wish to look experimental and the reality of being prudent and cautious.* As Daniel Moynihan has pointed out, the current American resignationist myth maintains that social programs failed from the time of the New Deal through Lyndon Johnson's Great Society because great amounts of public money were thrown irresponsibly into ill-conceived programs.[18] Moynihan presents evidence to support the conclusion that programs during the Great Society and War on Poverty era were oversold in promise while simultaneously being underfinanced, so much so that failure was almost assured. In other words, Richard

Nixon and other Americans listened to the promises of government planners and assumed that futuristic declarations of intent to eliminate poverty, racial degradation, poor housing, and the like were being supported by more than adequate resources. In actual fact, they were not, partly because the Vietnam War took needed funds and effort away from social programs and partly because of the American penchant for aspirations to often overreach American willingness to spend money and human resources on unusual forms of social experimentation. This dichotomy in relation to resolving social problems contrasts strikingly with the almost limitless funding and effort devoted to the development of the atomic bomb in World War II and the space explorations of the 1960's, and the resultant success of these hard science programs. Yet, the desire to predict future options and to control social events for good purposes remains, as exemplified by the extent to which many citizens honor and reward soothsayers, astrologists, magicians, and fortune tellers who claim to be able to foretell the future with absolute certainty.[19]

Responding to These Hindrances—The Distinction Between Natural and Constructed Systems. There is, however, an important distinction between predicting the actual future and the kind of future-oriented social science research that is needed to resolve social problems. Richard Henshel quotes Dennis Gabor's statement that "the future cannot be predicted, but futures can be invented"[20] and points to the difference between predicting actual reality or imagined systems, or between natural and constructed social systems.[21] *Natural systems* are those that emerge from the basic processes of daily life, whereas *constructed systems* are those that are fashioned strictly in accordance with the requirements of the scientist. Prediction can be attempted in both cases, but, as Henshel points out, the results will be considerably different. The difficulty is that natural and physical science has been successful in predicting constructed systems; these predictions, in turn, have some limited validity when applied to natural systems. However, social scientists and decision makers have tended to reverse this procedure when viewing social problems. They have demanded that social science be used to predict natural events and have been reluctant to accept the validity of constructed systems.

Illustrations of this dilemma abound. Henshel points out that prediction is weak in most social science (again, with the exception of some economic theory) because social scientists think in terms of piecemeal modifications of ongoing systems rather than in terms of creating completely new alternative systems. Anders Boserup's study of conflict in Northern Ireland (discussed in Chapter 5), which proposed an alternative political system for institutionalizing religious conflict, is a marked exception in contemporary social science. In addition, where physical science is used to predict reactions within systems constructed and controlled by decision makers and scientists (for example, a laboratory experiment in biology or a space-travel experiment in a vacuum chamber), social science is expected to predict uncontrolled and uncontrollable phenomena. For example, Henshel points to the fact that social scientists are expected to produce reformed criminals in an institutional framework created by nonscientists, with aims other than reformation in mind, and run by nonscientific personnel for other than reform purposes. Sometimes physical science attempts to deal with the natural world, as in the case of weather prediction in meteorology or earthquake and oil deposit identification in geology. The lack of success experienced by the physical sciences in these cases is similar to the apparent lack of predictive ability in social science.

Henshel concludes by arguing that the seeming absence of adequate social engineering in social science has resulted in a widespread misconception, shared by social scientists, that there is a difference in predictive powers by various disciplines (especially physical versus social sciences). The physical sciences seem to have been far more successful and useful than the social sciences because of the intrinsic nature of their procedures and subject matter. Henshel suggests, however, that social science deficiencies are really a result of the failure to conceptualize and deal with constructed systems and the tendency to attempt prediction of occurrences in real systems. He suggests that the predictive power of social versus physical science may be a lot closer than many expect, if the correct types of perspectives are generated—that is, the proposal of alternative social systems based upon the analysis of prevailing systems.[22] Thus, what is needed is not crystal-ball gazing, the common accusation by those who oppose a futurist orientation, but rather the logical construction of alternatives to prevailing institutional and organizational forms. Furthermore, a study of the future consequences of particular actions aimed at remedying prevailing social problems is necessary, not the assumption that we are better off doing nothing or that anything done for good is better than nothing done at all. This type of research does not necessarily mean that the social scientist must bias his research or force his preferences upon decision makers and the public. On the contrary, Roy Amara and Gerald Salancik describe such research in the following way:

In its broadest terms, "future research" is any activity that improves understanding about the future consequences of present developments and choices. One of its goals is to examine systematically what can be, as contrasted with what will be, or what should be. Implicit in the use of "can" is the notion of choice or possibility, whereas the use of "will" implies deterministic prediction, and "should" connotes an interplay of values and choice—a province more properly of ethics and politics.[23]

Amara and Salancik suggest that the roles of scientist and futurist research can be naturally joined. The scientist's goal is to test specific paradigms and theories about human behavior. Anything that threatens this test must be controlled by elimination, experimental manipulation, or statistical manipulation. The futurist's goal is to suggest through discovery or logic a model for the human world that extends our perception of reality sufficiently to permit reasoned choices and decisions.[24] Therefore, the futurist perspective is not at odds with the scientific perspective; rather it is a natural extension of that role.[25]

Examples of the Futurist Perspective—Population Studies. Except for some economic theories, the single example of a consistent futurist concern in social science is the area of population studies. The work of men such as Frank Notestein are indications of the extent to which scientific analysis in classic forms and future orientation can be joined for the purposes of applying knowledge to the resolution of problems.[26] Notestein's concern is with the typical population problem of economically undeveloped countries—the overproduction of people in relation to the resources available for sustaining them. He points out that most of the newly developing nations have populations that are growing by at least 2.5 percent per year. Compounding the problem is the fact that those as-yet-to-develop nations with slower rates of growth have almost no health protection and will quickly and suddenly experience rapid population increase whenever rudimentary health services are implemented. A 2.5 percent growth rate doubles the population in 28 years, while higher rates, experienced by some countries, can double a population in 20 years or less. Unless growth rates in these contexts are slowed, the developing and yet-to-be-developed nations will have to deal with twice their present population size even before the children born this year have completed their own childbearing.

As Notestein points out, the causes of this crisis are obvious. Birth rates remain high, while death rates drop dramatically. In some cases, birth rates in developing nations are higher than the rate was in Western Europe during 19th-century modernization:

Whereas in Europe there tended to be about 35 births a year per 1,000 population, in today's newly developing countries birth rates generally range from 40 to 55. . . . Death rates differ even more spectacularly. In 19th-century Europe, death rates of 25 per 1,000 population were common and a rate as high as 30 was not unusual. In today's newly developing countries a rate of 25 is very high, 20 is common and the rates go as low as 6 per 1,000 population.[27]

Notestein suggests two major reasons for this situation: *low death rates* due to the modern efficiency in disease control and to the production of an ever younger population encouraged by *high birth rates*. The latter factor causes, for example, Taiwan to have a lower death rate than the United States, and Ceylon a lower death rate than France or England. The population pressures created are exacerbated since the economic product of a new nation may be growing at only 5 percent a year. If population is growing at around 3 percent, the per capita income rises at a rate of 2 percent. At this rate, it takes over 30 years for incomes to double, but, as we have seen, only 20 years or less for the population size to double. In modernizing nations this could mean a per capita income rise from $100 per year to only $200 per year. In summary, even an excellent economic performance, without any unanticipated problems, would result in over twice as many people continuing to live in almost abject poverty, with only minimal increases in the resources for the improvement of education and productive equipment.[28] Finally, two long-term consequences could result—these consequences are *political instability* followed by extended war, revolution, or repression and/or catastrophic *loss of life* as a result of widespread famine and epidemic diseases.

As grim as this prospect seems to be for some countries, Notestein suggests that the future could hold out other options, if the appropriate actions and programs are undertaken. He sees four hopeful signs: the development of national policies favoring family planning; the demonstrated public interest in limiting childbearing; the improvement in contraceptive technology; and in some countries, governmental adoption of birth control programs.[29] Notestein points out that a decade ago, India alone had adopted a national policy to promote family planning, while today more than half the people of the newly developing world live under governments that have begun such programs. These include China, Nepal, Pakistan, India, Ceylon, Malaysia, Indonesia, Singapore, Hong Kong, Taiwan, South Korea, Iran, Turkey, Egypt, Tunisia, Morocco, Kenya, Barbados, Jamaica, and Honduras. Other countries are developing programs in either public and/or private spheres (Colombia, Chile, Thailand, Philippines, Venezuela). Though a governmental policy does not necessarily guarantee effectiveness in birth control, the growth of awareness of the problem in many nations is encouraging.

At the same time, despite traditional studies indicating cultural resistance to birth control in agrarian societies, evidence is accumulating to suggest growing public interest in limiting family size. These attitudes seem to be found in villages as well as in cities, and among illiterates as well as among the educated. Notestein hypothesizes that attitudes are changing because undeveloped areas actually have a great deal more modernization than initially strikes the eye. Even in a context of what seems to be overwhelming poverty to the affluent Westerner, the native villager has motion pictures, a transistor radio, and a desire to educate his children. He is increasingly aware that more surviving children mean greater difficulty in providing enough food, and that in the modern world a medium-sized family is sufficient to provide adults with protection in their old age. Related to this change is the improvement in contraceptive technology:

During the past decade we have gained two methods which are safe, cheap and highly effective and that for the first time make no demands on the couple at the time of coition. One is the new plastic intrauterine device (I.U.D.) that, once inserted, remains indefinitely in place for those who tolerate it. . . . The oral steroids offer the other most promising method. Until recently, they were too expensive to meet the needs of the majority in the developing countries. Recently, however, prices for bulk orders have dropped to about 15 cents per cycle, which permits their use in governmental programs, at least for those patients who cannot use the U.I.D. When the pill is systematically taken it is absolutely effective.[30]

Thus, the villager wishing to limit his family size has available to him easy, quick, and inexpensive means.

Finally, Notestein points out that some countries have already experienced dramatic reductions in their birth rate or employed family planning techniques to reduce population pressures significantly. Therefore, the possibility of effective programs or spontaneous public response has been tested and found to be feasible. South Korea, Taiwan, Hong Kong, and Singapore are examples, though one of the most dramatic illustrations is the case of a modernized nation, Japan:

Japan's birth rate, for example, had dropped by last year [by 1966] from a postwar high of 34 per thousand to 14; Japan now shares with Hungary the lowest birth rate in the world. The decline was not the result of a governmental birth control program; it was mainly due to abortion rather than contraception, and came almost in spite of the government. The public took such enthusiastic advantage of abortion permitted by the "Eugenic Protection Law" that it was politically impossible to interpret the law narrowly. At present there is a marked trend away from abortion and toward contraception, but Japan has shown that population growth can be drastically reduced by a prosperous people having few inhibitions against abortion and served by a competent medical establishment. The Japanese medical community's enthusiasm for abortion has seeped into Taiwan, South Korea, Hong Kong and Singapore, though it remains illegal. Abortion is legal in the U.S.S.R. and all of Eastern Europe except East Germany and Albania.[31]

Moreover, Notestein indicates that, for those countries opposing these methods of birth control on moral grounds, the problem of population might be attacked from the standpoint of institutional change. The age of marriage might be altered, states could reward parents for small families (for example, reversing the present American tax schedule that gives higher deductions for more children), or parents of large families might be penalized. He feels that such changes are farther off in the future than simple acceptance of family planning (or the more "radical" embracing of abortion). Nevertheless, what his analysis does indicate is that there is nothing inevitable or deterministic about the population problem, so long as nations and societies are willing to adopt the techniques necessary to combat the problem, and to consider alternative types of social systems and institutions.

Why We Fail: Accounting for Change and Conflict

The final reason why contemporary perspectives of social problems often lead to programs that fail is the general social scientific difficulty in accounting for change and conflict, except as an assumed pathological or deviant phenomena. We have seen the most obvious examples of this inability in the case of the conflict theory criticism of the disorganization paradigm and the radical criticism of functionalism. However, this difficulty is actually endemic to all prevailing myths and paradigms. The implication here is not that social scientists should suddenly and enthusiastically embrace change and conflict of all types, forms, and degrees in an uncritical manner, but rather that social scientists must reformulate their perspectives of these phenomena. They must generate views that can interpret change and conflict, even in many extreme forms, as sometimes functional, desirable, or normal.

The Fallacies of Deviance and Trauma.   For example, Robert Lauer argues that two major fallacies, inherent within social scientific paradigms, seriously distort the ability of social scientists to assess the actual nature of social change.[32] Lauer points out that conservative functionalism is not the only problem. He maintains that all scientific paradigms contain assumptions, rather than scientific truths, which make it difficult to account for the actual nature of social change. These assumptions, according to Lauer, are often treated as facts based upon observation and common sense, and, as such, they gain legitimacy and become pervasive in social scientific thought. The two most common misconceptions about change are the *fallacy of deviance* and the *fallacy of trauma.* Lauer describes the fallacy of deviance in the following way:

A considerable amount of sociological thinking has viewed change as in some sense a violation of the normal. . . . This reflects a conservative strain which has pervaded sociology throughout its history. . . . The focus on stability and concomitant neglect of change assumes that static analysis can be made without coming to terms with change, and that an understanding of social change demands a prior and thorough understanding of social statics. Sociologists, then, have been far more concerned with structures than with processes. . . . Persistence and regularities have been viewed as the normal state of affairs; change has been viewed as a kind of social deviance.[33]

According to Lauer, not only does such a perspective seriously bias one's work, particularly in the area of studies of social problems (events that often signify or bring about important social change), but it provides a distorted picture of reality. He suggests that it would be far more meaningful to see change as inherent in the very nature of things, as integral to the basic fabric of social life. It is ironic that many social scientists have identified change with deviance and stability with normality, when the history of man, the evolution of societies, and the socialization of the individual are all processes characterized by upheaval, transition, and movement. Change, therefore, is normal at both the individual and societal level. As Lauer puts it, society (and man) must grow and change or it will decay. What really should be of interest to social scientists is the question of the *rate, degree,* and *quality* of change, rather than its absence or presence.

Lauer points out that the idea of change as abnormal is also frequently associated with a second fallacy: the notion that change is traumatic. Social scientists have called change an ordeal, a crisis, and even a foreign and unwanted agent. Some evidence seems to support this view; mental illness is sometimes related to change insofar as social and cultural stress can lead to emotional stress. Many people seem to resist change tenaciously and aggressively, as those who attempt to introduce new ways of thinking, behaving, and living so often recognize. Supporters of the status quo emphasize the need for uniformity and tradition; when social and cultural values are threatened, they disparage the habits and ways of those who are different. A variety of factors inhibit change, especially in less modern contexts:

. . . rigid stratification systems, a high degree of social inequality, community fragmentation, vested interest, and cultural motor patterns. Finally, there are social psychological factors; the government, for example, is generally conceded to be crucial to much change in the contemporary world, yet the peasants' perception of that government often involves considerable suspicion and distrust. . . . And the argument could be clinched by citing the numberless concrete instances of resistance to change, including resistance to railroads, the automobile, the typewriter, alternating current, tractors, umbrellas, street lighting, and even potatoes.[34]

A closer examination of the nature of these types of reactions to change discloses that people usually resist in three specific cases: *when change threatens basic security, when change is not understood*, and *when change is imposed*. The seeming trauma of change can really be accounted for in these terms. For example, the apparent conservatism of a peasant community, according to Lauer, may actually be a natural process of weighing risks, since these people continually live on the very edge of survival in a subsistence economy. In addition, change may be resisted because it interferes with more highly valued changes. Lauer refers to the example of the Barbadians rejecting agricultural diversification, as recommended by both British and American experts, because they prized another kind of change more highly—upward mobility: "The Barbadian who goes into full-time agriculture forfeits his chances for cultural success; the potential change in personal status, therefore, is the basis for rejecting a change in agricultural economy."[35]

There are, therefore, a variety of reasons why a particular change may be resisted and none relate to any intrinsic trauma or tendency to resist all changes. The assumption of trauma is a negative value judgment that leads a social theorist to posit that persistence and stability is the normal state of affairs in society. Once again, Lauer suggests that the really crucial issue is not change per se; rather it is the rate of change that can be related to stress (thereby, apparently, to trauma). For example, research suggests that change or adaptation that is too slow can cause as much stress and strain as too rapid change. Slow change or the inability to change at all can sometimes threaten the very survival of individuals and societies, particularly in the modern world where new and different types of crises and problems continually demand innovative responses.[36] Theories unable to support these kinds of perspectives of change are particularly inappropriate when analyzing contemporary social problems.

A Criticism of Consensus and Cohesion as Stabilizing Social Elements, by Michael Mann. In a similar manner, Michael Mann criticizes the tendency of modern theory to view consensus and cohesion as normal, and conflict and dissensus as deviant. He points to the fact that there is still agreement between almost all theorists that some minimal degree of value consensus is necessary to maintain liberal democracies. This consensus theoretically allows these societies to handle conflict and remain stable. Ironically, Mann points out that this view is even apparent in the work of contemporary conflict theorists, who admit the existence of consensus but question its validity.[37] In other words, many studies argue that the stability and success of democratic societies is a result of the sharing of general political values. Great Britain and the United States are characteristically pointed to as examples of this success and are frequently contrasted to less successful democracies or presumably unstable nondemocratic states. This view is based upon the assumption that Americans usually agree on the basic issues that often polarize the citizenry into antagonistic groups in other societies. One reason given for the underlying consensus is the fact that political contests in America do not usually involve serious threats to the way of life for most citizens. Politicians and journalists in the United States have picked up this myth and constantly refer to the need to appeal to the "mainstream of thought," the "middle American," or the "middle of the road."

Mann questions whether this perspective is a valid picture of reality, or whether it merely reflects underlying political biases untested and unexamined in empirical data. He begins his critique by identifying the various ways in which consensus has been defined. Some scholars argue that consensus deals with ultimate values—equality and achievement, for example. Other scholars stress the importance of commitment to social norms, the agreement that individuals should adhere to the democratic rules of the game. Still other scholars have pointed to the commitment to beliefs concerning how a society should be organized. For example, most Americans apparently agree upon the need for harmony and cooperation (and oppose class conflict), while others stress the essential benevolence of elites and decision makers (though admitting that these leaders sometimes make bad mistakes). Mann points out that in all of these views the major problem is an assumed link between some type of consensus (or the absence of conflict) and social cohesion.

In reality, there are four criticisms that can be made of the view that shared understandings integrate and legitimate social structures.[38] *First, most general values, norms, and be-*

liefs that supposedly integrate society are vague and therefore could be used to legitimate almost any social structure. For example, both conservatives and revolutionaries appeal to common values such as social justice, peace, or democracy, as do antagonists in contemporary international conflicts. Yet integration obviously does not exist between such diverse and conflicting groups.

Second, even when a value is stated precisely, it may lead to conflict rather than to cohesion. Though some values necessarily unite men, others almost inevitably divide them. Peace, honor, justice, and social order are all concepts that have seriously divided Americans, according to various political persuasions, for the last several decades. What looks like "peace with honor" to some appears to be repression and inhumanity to others. What looks like justice to some appears to be a lack of social order to others.

Third, Mann points out that *it is difficult for the absolute standards embodied in values to co-exist without conflict.* For example, "achievement" and "equality," two of the most highly honored Western values, tend to limit the scope of one another. Total equality would delimit achievement for some; total achievement potential for all would negate the possibility of equality for others. Mann suggests that this type of natural value conflict is inherent in all societies. As a result, social systems develop ways in which various values can be insulated from other competing values. The existence of cohesion or consensus, therefore, is not a consequence of the values themselves, but rather it is a result of the success of the insulation process.

Finally, where insulation processes work well, cohesion is achieved because there is no common commitment to core values, contrary to prevailing liberal democratic mythology. For example, Mann points to the society that values achievement, yet contains a sizable lower class incapable of attaining anything approaching meaningful success and status. Such a society can maintain cohesion only if the lower class is likely to acquiesce in its inequality and place less emphasis upon achievement aspirations than upon other values (immediate gratification). This type of perspective is also an excellent response to scholars like Edward Banfield (discussed in the first section of this chapter) who argue that the poor are inherently unable to achieve or to defer *gratifications*. On the contrary, willingness to *defer achievement* can be seen as a functional necessity to manage the inherent conflict that would otherwise threaten the cohesion of the system. The moral question of whether or not this type of resolution is more desirable than open conflict (since the resolution permits basic inequalities to remain) must then be openly confronted.

Conflict and Change as Positive Social Forces—Two Studies by Charles Loomis. An example of the use of these newly emerging perspectives of change and conflict can be seen in the work of Charles Loomis. He argues that all social action can be analyzed in terms of conflict, since this phenomenon is not so much an unhealthy state needing treatment as it is a common fact of social life. His studies are also an example of the way in which other new requirements for social-problems theory (applied research, alternative systems, and a future perspective) can be utilized.[39] Loomis' two studies of Latin American cultures and societies and of change in Indian communities, are an illustration of the sociological imagination at its best.

The first project drew populations to be examined from five sources: the general public of the United States, rural persons in Michigan, Spanish-speaking people of the Southwestern United States, rural Mexicans, and urban Mexicans. About 2000 individuals each were interviewed in Mexico and 2000 in the United States. Questions were asked to obtain measures of two major variables: actual contacts or linkages with people across the border, and attitudes that tended to further or hinder these linkages. *Actual linkages* were identified by visits to the other country, friends there, encounters in church, encounters in other organizations, relationships with relatives and neighbors, contacts among work associates, and second-hand contacts through a relative, close friend, or spouse. *Attitudinal linkages* were identified by questions seeking sentiments of the following kinds: Should the leaders cooperate more? Should the nations have closer connections? Would the informant like to have some friends or more friends across the border? How would you rate the other nation?

This study disclosed that the greater the behavioral linkage or contact the greater the desired linkage and/or the higher the regard. In other words, the extent to which Mexicans and North Americans liked one another was positively correlated with their interaction with one another. However, of special interest were the factors that might lead to disliking. Paralleling the basic finding, Loomis found that the proportion of informants who said they did not want the other nationals or their descendants as citizens, co-workers, neighbors, or relatives in marriage was twice as large among those who reported no contact across the border than among those who reported linkages. Religion was a significant variable:

More than half the Mexicans rejected both Protestants and Jews. . . . North Americans in the various samples were more tolerant, no more than one-third ever rejecting both Jews and Catholics for these status-roles. In all samples for the United States, Catholics have higher linkages manifest both in interaction with Mexicans and in liking for them than do Protestants. In Mexico, the few Protestants interviewed have higher interaction and liking scores for United States nationals than do Catholics. Atheists, agnostics and informants who reported themselves as having no religion, in both countries manifest relatively high desire for linkage or liking of the people across the border.[40]

The applied significance of such research becomes apparent when Loomis discusses *the unique characteristics of a linking population*—the Spanish-speaking people of the Southwest who link both societies and cultures together. Their scores on scales measuring both behavioral and attitudinal linkages proved to be exceptional. Their exposure to both societies was so complete that regardless of formal education, their identification with both United States and Mexican nationals was high. This finding leads Loomis to hypothesize that a linking population completely immersed in more than one society and partaking of the characteristics of both societies can become a vehicle for a nation to create and maintain linkages and, thereby, avoid potential conflict. Ironically, therefore, linkages among nations through other ethnic groups have the potential for both the generation and resolution of conflict.

Furthermore, educational attainment was more highly

and negatively correlated with ethnocentrism and more positively correlated with the desire for linkage and liking in Mexico *than in the United States.* As Loomis puts it:

If our aim is to resolve conflict between the two countries and among groups, these findings indicate that inputs into education in Mexico will bring higher yields than similar inputs in the United States. On the other hand, we found educational attainment to be more closely and negatively correlated with measures of authoritarianism in the United States than it is in Mexico. . . . Suppose we have the wherewithal to do what it takes to add two years to the schooling of every student just ready to drop out of school, in both countries. In Mexico, we would reduce prejudice and increase liking of the across-the-border people more than we would in the United States. However, we would decrease authoritarianism more in the United States.[41]

The second research project that Loomis conducted dealt with the special role of *leaders of change* within rural villages in India. Over 300 villages were selected and from these 5800 adult males and females and key influential leaders were interviewed. Questions dealt with the villagers' interest in, knowledge of, and actual adoption of chemical fertilizer, improved seeds and better tools, vaccination for smallpox, vaccination for typhoid and cholera, and birth control.

As expected, the influential leaders were found to have adopted, or were in the process of adopting, more of the new practices than the general population. They were more actively linked with official change agents (representatives of public and private agencies) and were more cosmopolitan and rational. In short, they were modernizing more quickly. For example, whereas three-fourths of the influentials had adopted chemical fertilizer on their farms, less than one-half of the general population of males had done so. Over half of the influentials used insecticides, 86 percent had smallpox vaccinations, and about 10 percent practiced family planning, while the percentages of the general population were about 25 percent, 75 percent, and 4 percent, respectively. Nevertheless, Loomis found that the paradoxical situation, where the traditional thrives alongside the modern, was typical. For example, over half of the general informants believed that evil spirits caused disease or said they would go to a religious leader or temple for treatment of small-pox. Three major factors seemed to account for the striking differences between influentials and the general population. First, an *aspiration for education* was correlated with the tendency to be an innovator or early adopter of new techniques and knowledge. Second, the strength of a villager's *linkage with extension workers and agents* (such as professional health and agricultural specialists, lesser trained village level workers, and elected local officials) was correlated with the acceptance of change. Finally, *exposure to mass media* such as movies and radio seemed significant. In other words, in the process of modernization in India, as in the case of desired linkages between Mexico and the United States, education, contact with mass media, and behavioral linkages were important.[42]

The significance that such research holds for the development of new perspectives of change and conflict and for the proposal of alternative forms of social systems for the resolution of conflict is introduced by Loomis in the following way:

Various studies of disaster—which combines force, though not always from human sources, and sentiment—show that at a certain point after a social organization has been stricken there develops a level of integration and communication of sentiment unknown to members before. It has been called the "halo effect" and usually occurs at a predictable stage in the sequence of events after the intense rescue and salvage activities. Members who, in pre-disaster days, were relatively isolated and insulated from each other, come out of their shells, take part in a meaningful enterprise, cooperate in rescue work, help to rebuild, and find in the work that they have an increased understanding of and liking for one another. A fund of good will is begotten. During this period actors communicate sentiments which produce community or system morale, making the community an end in and of itself. Perhaps some would say that a therapeutic community emerges.[43]

Essentially rapid change or conflict can create the same type of conditions as those surrounding a natural disaster and can lead to community cohesion and the resolution of internal conflicts. In this sense, conflict can be praised, or prized, in those contexts where it functions to maintain and enhance ongoing social relationships.

Loomis applies this view to the problem of governmental assistance to bring about modernization changes. He points out thàt his experience with traditional societies in Asia, Latin America, and Africa has led him to be impressed by the lack of impact of huge outlays (of funds, facilities, and personnel) devoted to the resolution of social problems. In contrast, he proposes the following types of programs as alternatives:

Within our own country, we might think of setting up a pilot city. Why does not the Federal government offer funds and resources on a competitive basis to the one *city which would agree to make the most changes and effort toward bringing social justice and freedom from poverty to its citizens? The demonstration could be located in* the one *city most willing and able to make the great changes necessary. As sociologists, we know such changes would bring crises and conflict. These would be used in leap-frogging ahead. . . . Such a demonstration would be highly visible. Right away some industries suffering from unstable conditions might want to move there. Since a chief aim of this demonstration would be ideal race relations, many Negroes might be expected to go there.*[44]

Such a "radical" experiment would be designed to utilize the resulting change and conflict to create a halo effect, bringing about significant alteration in prevailing forms of social interaction and giving rise to a means for resolving traditional forms of interethnic conflict. Furthermore, such an experiment would be subjected to intensive analysis for application elsewhere, and social and cultural linkages could be utilized to transmit the changes and to adopt them to other contexts. Loomis indicates that such an experiment is not without international precedent. For instance, the nation of Israel employed unique experimentation in the case of the kibbutz to bring about rapid and needed changes in its early period of development. However, the willingness of other nations to contemplate such experiments depends upon significantly altered perspectives of the nature of both change and conflict.

In summary, most social scientific and popular thinking about social problems has been motivated in the past by the desire to do good, for all affected by problem behavior. At the very least, there has been an attempt to remove the consequences of the problem for society, or to modestly reform the system or those involved in the problem behavior. At the same time, however, the kinds of scientific paradigms generated to date have more often than not led to the failure of recent public and private programs of action, or they have led to the creation of seemingly more severe problems for both society and those involved directly in the problem behavior (both victims and perpetrators, plus the innocent). The common inadequacies of existing paradigms can be seen in the general lack of policy-oriented or applied social research, the absence of future perspectives and speculation about alternative social systems, and the difficulty in accounting for change and conflict. If a more adequate scientific paradigm, one that reflects the nature and needs of contemporary society, is to be developed, these inadequacies will have to be remedied. Otherwise, attempts to resolve contemporary social problems will continue to create frustration, anger, and disillusionment among citizens, decision makers, and those most intimately influenced by the resulting unwise decisions and actions. The current ferment and argumentation in social science, as exemplified by competing schools of thought and theories, suggests the beginnings of a search for alternative paradigms, a possible preparadigm revolution in Kuhn's terms. The following concluding chapter considers several cautions that should be kept in mind during this search and tentatively indicates the general emphases a new paradigm might develop to fulfill the requirements discussed in this chapter.

Notes to Chapter 7

1. S. M. Miller and Ronnie Steinberg Ratner, "The American Resignation: The New Assault on Equality," *Social Policy*, 3 (May/June 1972), p. 5.
2. *Ibid.*, p. 8; and Edward C. Banfield, *The Unheavenly City* (Boston: Little, Brown, 1970).

3. See S. M. Miller, *ibid.*, pp. 5–14, for a fuller discussion of these four resignationist assumptions.

4. Howard Waitzkin, "Truth's Search for Power: The Dilemmas of the Social Sciences," *Social Problems*, 15 (Spring 1968), pp. 408–419.

5. Max Weber, "Science as a Vocation," *From Max Weber: Essays in Sociology*, H. H. Gerth and C. Wright Mills, trans. (New York: Oxford University Press, 1958); and *The Methodology of the Social Sciences*, E. A. Shils and H. A. Finch, trans. (New York: The Free Press, 1949).

6. Howard Waitzkin, "Truth's Search for Power: The Dilemmas of the Social Sciences," *Social Problems*, 15 (Spring 1968), p. 416.

7. See, for example, Howard Waitzkin, *ibid.*, p. 416; and Robert K. Merton and Edward C. Devereux, Jr., "Practical Problems and the Uses of Social Science," *Transaction*, 1 (July 1964), pp. 18–21. See also Ralph L. Beals, *Politics of Social Research* (Chicago: Aldine Publishing Company, 1969).

8. Albert J. Reiss, Jr., "Putting Sociology Into Policy," *Social Problems*, 17 (Winter 1970), pp. 290–293.

9. See also Gwen Andrew, "Some Observations on Management Problems in Applied Social Research," *The American Sociologist*, 2 (May 1967), pp. 84–89, 92.

10. William Ryan, *Blaming the Victim* (New York: Pantheon Books, 1971).

11. Amitai Etzioni, "Human Beings Are Not Very Easy to Change After All," *Saturday Review* (June 3, 1972), p. 45.

12. Albert J. Reiss, Jr., "Putting Sociology Into Policy," *Social Problems*, 17 (Winter 1970), pp. 290–293.

13. See Maggie Scarf's interview with Szasz: "Normality Is a Square Circle or a Four-Sided Triangle," *The New York Times Magazine* (October 3, 1971), pp. 16ff.

14. Albert J. Reiss, Jr., "Putting Sociology Into Policy," *Social Problems*, 17 (Winter 1970), p. 291.

15. Rex D. Hopper, "Cybernation, Marginality, and Revolution," *The New Sociology*, Irving L. Horowitz, ed. (New York: Oxford University Press, 1964), pp. 313–330.

16. *Ibid.*, p. 320.

17. Howard Waitzkin, "Truth's Search for Power: The Dilemmas of the Social Sciences," *Social Problems*, 15 (Spring 1968), pp. 418–419.

18. Daniel P. Moynihan, *The Politics of a Guaranteed Income: The Nixon Administration and the Family Assistance Plan* (New York: Random House, 1972).

19. See Peter Andrews, "The Prediction Game," *Saturday Review* (January 15, 1972), pp. 14–16.

20. Dennis Gabor, *Inventing the Future* (London: Secker & Warburg, 1963).

21. Richard L. Henshel, "Sociology and Prediction," *The American Sociologist*, 6 (August 1971), pp. 213–220.

22. *Ibid.*, p. 215.

23. Roy C. Anara and Gerald R. Salancik, "Forecasting: From Conjectural Art Toward Science," *The Futurist*, 6 (June 1972), p. 112.

24. *Ibid.*, p. 113.

25. For a further discussion of this type of issue and examples of the futurist perspective, see Durnham P. Beckwith and Dennis L.

Meadows, "The Future of Man: Optimism vs. Pessimism," *The Futurist*, 6 (April 1972), pp. 62–66; Wendell Bell and James Mau, eds., *The Sociology of the Future* (New York: Russell Sage Foundation, 1971); Harvey Brooks and Raymond Bowers, "The Assessment of Technology," *Scientific American*, 222 (February 1970), pp. 13–20; Joseph F. Coates, "The Future of the U.S. Government," *The Futurist*, 6 (June 1972), pp. 104–108; Peter F. Drucker, "The Surprising Seventies," *Harper's Magazine* (July 1971), pp. 35–39; "137 Innovations Are Foreseen" (an editorial), *The Futurist*, 5 (October 1971), p. 207; Andrew Hacker, "Questions for 1968," *Saturday Review* (January 6, 1968), pp. 102–103; and Mark Wynn, "Who Are the Futurists?" *The Futurist*, 6 (April 1972), pp. 73–77.

26. Frank W. Notestein, "The Population Crisis: Reasons for Hope," *Foreign Affairs*, 46 (October 1967), pp. 167–180; and in *Comparative Perspectives on Social Problems*, Vytautas Kavolis, ed. (Boston: Little, Brown, 1969), pp. 259–271.

27. *Ibid.*, p. 260.

28. *Ibid.*, p. 261.

29. *Ibid.*, pp. 262–267.

30. *Ibid.*, p. 264.

31. *Ibid.*, p. 267. In 1967 the city of Aberdeen, Scotland, began providing the pill and other contraceptive devices without cost. In 1973 the city reported a birth rate of 14.1 per 1,000 compared to 17.4 in the rest of Scotland, and a drop of illegitimate births to 7.7 percent of all births, compared to 10.6 percent for all of Scotland.

32. Robert H. Lauer, "The Scientific Legitimation of Fallacy: Neutralizing Social Change Theory," *American Sociological Review*, 36 (October 1971), pp. 881–889.

33. *Ibid.*, p. 881.

34. *Ibid.*, p. 883.

35. *Ibid.*

36. See Warren Bennis and Philip Slater, *The Temporary Society* (New York: Harper & Row, 1968), for a detailed development of the perspective that the inability to change can lead to trauma and crisis, particularly in the contemporary world.

37. Michael Mann, "The Social Cohesion of Liberal Democracy," *American Sociological Review*, 35 (June 1970), pp. 423–439.

38. *Ibid.*, pp. 424–425.

39. Charles P. Loomis, "In Praise of Conflict and Its Resolution," *American Sociological Review*, 32 (December 1967), pp. 875–890.

40. *Ibid.*, p. 879.

41. *Ibid.*, p. 881.

42. *Ibid.*, p. 886.

43. *Ibid.*, p. 889.

44. *Ibid.*, p. 889.

Do social programs resolve problems or merely help the powerful?
(Franklynn Peterson, Black Star)

8. Toward Alternative Paradigms

The major argument of this book has been that both popular myths about and scientific paradigms used to analyze social problems create difficulties because of their inherent biases. This does not imply, however, that myths or paradigms should be abandoned. As we have seen, popular myths about problem behavior give citizens a way of understanding and making some sense of what might otherwise constitute either threatening or unrecognizable events—events that have serious consequences for society. In a similar manner, paradigms give scientists a way of identifying appropriate subjects for study, an indication of what methods of study should be employed, and a guide to the importance of specific studies in terms of the scientific, political, and moral goals and values of their profession and the larger society. In other words, without myths, citizens could not respond to problems, or they would respond with unorganized, random hysteria and fright. Without paradigms, scientists could not recognize problems or organize their work in rational, planned ways. Therefore, both myths and paradigms are needed. The difficulty is that, as preconceived ways of viewing the world, both tend to arise within specific kinds of social and historical contexts, but when these contexts change, older myths and paradigms tend to be retained. Citizens and scientists are understandably resistant to adaptations and changes in what they consider to be valuable and desirable views of the world. Therefore, a discontinuity may rapidly develop between the old beliefs and assumptions and a new reality, new political and moral needs, and new social requirements. This discontinuity becomes more pronounced as increasing numbers of citizens and scientists feel it necessary to defend their perspectives adamantly against an increasing amount of criticism from adherents of completely new and, therefore, radical and revolutionary views. Such a situation characterizes modern social science and explains the present crisis in theory and action concerning social problems.

Because of the old myths citizens fail to distinguish problems in a changed context, often identifying the sources of the problems incorrectly. They then support inappropriate actions to resolve the problems. We have seen examples of this process in the way in which the older natural, evil-equals-evil, and blaming-the-victim myths make meaningful responses to contemporary problems, such as the ecology crisis, crime in the streets, and changing sexual behavior, all but impossible. Old paradigms can function the same way to make current social scientific research identify the wrong causes, sources, and/or consequences for various forms of new problem behavior. Looking for sources of social disorganization cannot adequately explain the extent and character of modern militancy and protest, unless one adopts an antisociological view that most of modern society is completely disorganized. Looking for the causes of war only in terms of the assumptions of deviance cannot explain the prevalence and persistence of this problem, unless one assumes an inherent, inescapable deviance in man, a kind of functional equivalent to "war will always be with us." We have seen how these alternative views lead nowhere in terms of problem resolution, since the implication is that nothing can, nothing should, or nothing need be done about the situation.

At the same time, though, old beliefs may help to explain and, therefore, to develop responses to some special forms of modern problem behavior. Some crime results from the teaching and learning of deviance; some urban turmoil is a consequence of disorganization. This dual character in prevailing myths and paradigms which contain *some particularistic utility*, as well as *increasing universalistic disutility*, has created the crisis in social problems theory and action.

The Place of New Paradigms in Contemporary Social Science: Two Cautions

The recent rise of competing schools of thought within social science suggests a general search for alternatives, particularly for more adequate and useful paradigms. What directions this search should take is a major question for all students of social problems. The search, however, should initially take into account and hence be based upon two important cautions.

The Importance of Traditional Paradigms. The first caution arises from the recognition that *old beliefs and assumptions are far from worthless.* The difficulty is that they may come to represent only a very small part of contemporary reality, a part that is increasingly less typical because of rapid change. In Chapter 1, Table 1–1 suggested four basic types of social-problems theory according to whether the theory was basic, applied, supportive, or change oriented. The discussion of the various paradigms in Part II disclosed that most previous work has been supportive in character, basic in orientation, and, for the most part, of only limited use in generating knowledge for direct application to social problems. For example, traditional functionalism is an illustration of a paradigm that primarily encourages basic–supportive research. Disorganization is also a perspective that tends to generate mainly basic–supportive analyses of problems. Somewhat differently, deviance theory has led to applied research and action, but it has been almost always within a supportive perspective. The new criticisms of prevailing paradigms, in contrast, characteristically argue for more applied and/or change emphases. A possible representation of the classification of paradigms and critical schools of thought by these kinds of research is given in Table 8–1.

In other words, prevailing paradigms are almost totally committed to a supportive point of view, to theories and concepts of problem behavior that reflect accepted and public per-

Table 8–1
The types of social science research associated with major paradigms and schools of thought

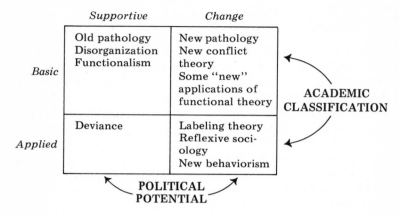

	Supportive	Change
Basic	Old pathology Disorganization Functionalism	New pathology New conflict theory Some "new" applications of functional theory
Applied	Deviance	Labeling theory Reflexive sociology New behaviorism

ACADEMIC CLASSIFICATION

POLITICAL POTENTIAL

spectives and generate knowledge that does not threaten the status quo. At the same time, prevailing paradigms, with the exception of deviance theory, encourage mainly basic research —that is, the study of social problems allegedly free from value commitment or involvement and of little direct use for application. The only partial exception is the deviance paradigm, which has produced some applied knowledge. However, this knowledge has been utilized in a supportive fashion to return the deviant to predefined normality through education, punishment, or rehabilitation. In contrast, new criticisms uniformly argue for a change orientation, and the most radical of the new schools of thought also stress the need for applied research that intimately involves the social scientist in action. In summary, the prevailing paradigms have not been nor are they now worthless. However, they have produced only certain kinds of knowledge about social problems, and these kinds of knowledge are less universalistically applicable to a world where the demand for an immediate resolution of problems and the amount and character of change have become pronounced.

When it comes to knowledge that can be applied or deals with change, social science does not yet possess adequate paradigms—only critical schools of thought or, as Kuhn calls them, preparadigmatic views or expressions of discontent. Therefore, most social scientists and decision makers return to the familiarity and comfort of older paradigms, which are inadequate, at best, when challenged to take action to meet contemporary problems. The main point of this book, then, is one of emphasis. We need basic, supportive, applied, *and* change-oriented research, but we tend to get primarily basic, supportive, and some limited applied research. The search for alternative paradigms that could encourage and sustain applied-change research, therefore, is mandatory.

Social Research as Both Value Relevant and Value Free. The second major caution that must be taken into account in the search for alternative paradigms is related to another major theme of this book. In several chapters, the classic notion of value-free research, especially in social science, has been shown to be a persistent myth. Functionalists who have produced basic knowledge in an assumedly neutral fashion can be seen to have generated theories about social problem behavior with marked biases and value implications. The same is true for those deviance theorists who have argued that the pragmatic application of rigidly scientific methods leads to value-free results. However, *although* absolute *value-free research is a myth, it is not totally unrealistic as a model for science.* In reality, all good social research is *both* value free and value relevant, especially research that deals with applied knowledge and an orientation toward change. In other words, the polarized belief that all scientists can or must choose either complete value freedom or total value relevance is misleading. Prevailing paradigms have generally viewed them as mutually exclusive, thereby avoiding attempts at resolving the problem of how social scientists can be committed to relevant social applications, while remaining value free. Adherents of the paradigms have, therefore, tended to opt out of the dilemma by clinging to the assumptions of pure, basic, value-free research. In addition, some of the recent critics tend to perpetuate the false polarity by stressing the need for complete, total, and continuous value involvement by scientists. At the same time, however, other recent criticisms of prevailing paradigms point the way to possible answers to this dilemma, which suggests that the issue might be resolved by new paradigms in the near future.

First, the mere development of more radical applied-change research would provide an adequate balance and counterpoint to the present dominance and transcendence of basic–supportive research. The difficulty is that many supporters of the old views tend to label this new kind of research as fraudulent, incompetent, and polemical, since that sort of perception is integral to the paradigms they are employing. One who does not conform to prevailing views must be a fraud, an incompetent, or a dangerous political radical using the guise of science to put forth mere political opinion. However, the discussions in Parts I and II of this book disclosed that the production of schlock and the presentation of scientian knowledge is by no means confined to the political left or to the critics of prevailing paradigms. At the very least, one might hope for a more ecumenical view within social science that would encourage the study of social problems from new, presently absent, or presumably unacceptable perspectives.

Second, some critics have suggested that the value-free debate can be partially resolved by understanding the essential role of the social scientist qua critic and intellectual. That is, a social scientist is by his very nature a questioner and critic, and, as pointed out at the beginning of this book, he does his most provocative and meaningful work when he produces research that is myth breaking. For scientists, then, to produce knowledge that is used only by elites to perpetuate the established order is a fundamental corruption of the academic and intellectual role. As Howard Becker puts it: "Whose side are we on?" [1] What Becker and others are arguing for is a conscious choosing of sides. Instead of research that only makes it easier for prison officials to control institutionalized populations, the scientist should also conduct studies from the perspective of the prisoner, with the purpose of producing knowledge that could be used to humanize and deinstitutionalize the prison context. Instead of research that merely makes it easier for society to attempt controls of sexual deviance through harsher laws, the scientist should conduct additional studies from the perspective of the deviant, with the purpose of producing knowledge that might lead to the modification and liberalization of laws. Instead of research that simply makes it easier for national leaders to wage wars, the scientist should conduct other studies from the perspective of the citizen, with the purpose of producing knowledge that could be used to make it difficult for nations to mobilize and sustain military forces for waging war. In other words, Becker and other new critics have argued that the issue of value relevance becomes critical in the first step of a scientist's research, when he decides precisely for whom he works and determines who the recipients and primary consumers of his knowledge will be. These critics argue that adherents of prevailing paradigms fool themselves and others when they maintain that they are value free, since they at least latently chose to side with the established order. In addition, the critics point out that making a value choice at the beginning of one's work, in terms of deliberately selecting some kinds of problems to study in particular ways, does not necessarily imply that values must bias or distort the remainder of the study. Scientific controls, rigorous data-collection techniques, and value-free methods of testing findings can still be employed. Therefore, the issue is not really one of being totally value free or totally value relevant.

This last qualification by some critics of prevailing paradigms suggests the third manner in which the issue might be resolved in a future paradigm. *Value-free research* can be defined as research whose approach, methods, and techniques of analysis are employed, *free from value judgments made by the scientist or by outside influences. Value-relevant research*, in contrast, is research that *deals with important value issues, with universalistic, social system problems of fundamental importance*. If such definitions are accepted, then both types of research obviously are not incompatible; on the contrary, they are necessarily interrelated. Value-free research without value relevance can result in the production of trivia or, worse, knowledge that deliberately avoids raising fundamental questions. Value-relevant research without value freedom can result in mere polemics without scientific or social validity or utility. In other words, the two must go hand in hand if social science is to respond to the contemporary crisis in theory, particularly as it relates to the study of social problems.

When one examines an idealized depiction of the steps employed by scientists to conduct a study, a way in which both value-free and value-relevant perspectives might be used together becomes apparent. The scientific approach to a social problem assumes that commonsense notions about the problem need to be tested rigorously, because public hunches and feelings about an issue may be incorrect or inappropriate. Furthermore, the testing process is the accepted mode of research. The major steps in the research procedure might be depicted as follows[2]:

1. Statement of purpose for the study and selection of an important problem.
2. Collection of preliminary data from a universe or samples in the universe, related to the kind of problem selected. Examination of the data to suggest relationships between different types of phenomena.
3. Formulation of scientific hypotheses that suggest relationships between social phenomena and might explain the problem being studied.
4. Testing of the hypotheses by rigorous and controlled collection of data. Conclusions are reached as to the accuracy of the hypothetical guesses, whether they were true, false, or difficult to determine as either true or false.
5. Explanation of the findings. Theories are formulated as explanations of why the hypotheses turned out to be true, false, or inconclusive.
6. Implications for further research that is needed and/or social action that might be taken.

For example, a scientist might become interested in the problem of suicide, defined by society as serious because of the extreme nature of the act and its apparent increase in modern contexts. He feels that public views and interpretations of the problem are not appropriate or adequate. He, therefore, rejects the view that the major cause is organic or psychic propensities within individuals. To say that someone commits suicide because he is sick or disturbed leads nowhere in terms of either understanding or social action. Instead, the scientist assumes that social and cultural factors in the environment are crucial. Preliminary data collection substantiates this perspective. Examination of case histories of suicides and of national statistics discloses that both the mentally ill and the sane commit suicide, that other problem behavior (like alcohol use) is not necessarily related to suicide, that suicide does not seem to vary by hereditary characteristics (race, age, or sex), and that suicides seem to vary essentially by social and cultural environmental circumstances (religion, marital status, employment, prosperity versus depression, and the like).

The scientist then proposes the hypothesis that the determinants of suicide are social variables. Data are rigorously collected to disclose the social characteristics of suicides compared to those of nonsuicides in various contexts. The findings show that suicides are higher among Protestants and lower among Catholics, higher among unmarried and widowed and lower among those in "complete" family units, higher in periods of crisis such as revolution and depression but lower during periods when a society is mobilized for war, higher in the military (especially among officers) but lower in civilian society. The conclusion is reached that suicide varies with *the degree of integration* in a society. When integration is generally *absent* (broken families, lost employment), suicide (anomic or egoistic) may result because the individual feels alienated and lonely. At the same time, some societies and cultures or sectors of the society, such as the military, demand ritual or altruistic suicide for reasons of honor after a defeat; therefore, in this context, a *high* degree of integration can lead to other forms of suicide. What such a study suggests is the need for further research not only on suicide but also to examine the consistent human dilemma: How much social integration is too much? How little social integration is too little?

This brief example of the use of the scientific method is taken from the classic study by Emile Durkheim, discussed in

Chapter 4.[3] It illustrates the use of both value-free and value-relevant perspectives throughout in the following manner:

1. Statement of purpose	Value relevant.
2. Preliminary data analysis	Value free.
3. Formulation of hypotheses	Value relevant.
4. Testing hypotheses	Value free.
5. Explaining findings	Value relevant.
6. Further research suggested	Value free.

In other words, both perspectives were used in a cyclical manner throughout the study. The statement of purposes involved a conscious recognition and subsequent rejection of public values and opinions. Collection of preliminary data involved the examination of the widest amount of information possible, free from personal judgment, in order not to bias results. The formulation of the hypothesis took into account not only the results of the preliminary data, but it also deliberately rejected popular views, or to some extent, in Becker's terms, it took sides. Then, once again, data collection to test the hypothesis was free of value preference or distortion to provide ample opportunity for disproving the hypothesis. Finally, the explanation of the findings involved human judgment about the importance of too much or too little social integration in a society, both of which could lead to suicide, and the suggestions for further research came from a value-free assessment of the entire study and its implications for society and the profession.

This brief use of Durkheim's classic study, as an idealized depiction of the scientific method, suggests that both value relevance and value freedom are necessary if social research on problems is to be provocative and useful. In reality, most social scientists use these approaches and techniques, although they rarely follow the steps in precise order and they may often argue that they do not make value judgments. However, it is not only possible to be both value free and value relevant, it is also possible to handle these kinds of emphases in research rigorously and in an ordered fashion by employing the steps in the scientific method in special ways. As with all the typologies and classifications suggested throughout this book, this discussion is an ideal model and a simplification of what happens in the daily activities of scientists. For example, having once committed himself to reject certain explanations of a particular form of problem behavior, the scientist may find it difficult, as an involved citizen, not to manipulate his data in such a way that his assumptions are proven to be true and the rejected assumptions are proven to be false. Nevertheless, the ideal model does suggest that, to be more useful, a future paradigm will have to incorporate in this or similar fashion the needs for both value-free and value-relevant work.

This discussion of the necessary cautions that qualify the search for new paradigms indicates that new successful paradigms cannot be sought as total rejections of existing perspectives or assumptions. The search for knowledge about and resolutions to social problems requires the full spectrum of different types of research: basic or applied, and supportive or change oriented. The difficulty is that applied–change research is relatively undeveloped and basic–supportive research, with its inherent biases, tends to be predominant. At the same time, the argument over values and their proper (or improper) presence (or absence) in scientific analysis has been artificially polarized by both adherents of old paradigms and advocates of new schools of thought. The development of new paradigms is necessary, paradigms that build upon existing views, encourage work with new perspectives, and possess the appeal, status, and influence of predominant paradigms. The final objective of the present analysis is to determine what sources in present theory about social problems seem to provide the most promising direction for this search for new paradigms.

Potential Sources for New Paradigms

Kuhn argues that one major paradigm tends to predominate in a scientific discipline at particular periods of time, and his historical analysis of the natural and physical sciences seems to support this single paradigm view.[4] There is a question, however, of whether Kuhn's conclusion represents a generality true of all scientific disciplines, whether it is an ideal model that is valid for most sciences, or whether it applies only to the hard sciences.

The Multiparadigmatic Nature of Social Science. In other words, it is obvious that contemporary social science does not possess the *single, major paradigm character* that has typified the history of the natural and physical sciences. In contrast, throughout its history social science has been characterized by the existence of several equally predominant, and somewhat competing, paradigms. Again, a possible exception is economics, where Keynesian theory briefly arose to undisputed eminence for several decades. However, even in economics this unified approach was achieved only in some limited kinds of political and historical contexts, and some economists in other contexts (for example, socialist societies) often utilized other competing paradigms. The multiple paradigm nature of social science, simply because it does not conform to the model for the hard sciences, cannot be assumed to be an inherent sign of weakness or "unscientific" stature. On the contrary, the multiple paradigm model may be a function of the unique nature of the subject matter of the social sciences. In addition, the predominance of single paradigms in scientific disciplines can actually inhibit change and innovation, or at least delay it, when new perspectives may be required by rapidly changing conditions and demands. The argument of this book, therefore, assumes that social science will and should remain multiparadigmatic in character, especially in the study of social problems. However, an assessment of the present criticism of prevailing paradigms is required to determine which might be most successfully adapted to and developed into competing paradigms.

Probable and Improbable Sources of New Paradigms. Which among the competing schools of thought (new pathology, new conflict theory, labeling theory, reflexive social science and related radical perspectives, new behaviorism, and functionalism) might best be adapted to provide the basis for new paradigms? The strengths and weaknesses of each, discussed in Chapter 7 and summarized in Table 7–1, is a basis for such an assessment.

New pathology views, arguing that deviance and disorganization may be inherent within the prevailing social system rather than within individuals, enhance a universalistic view of problems and directly attack the biases of prevailing paradigms. At the same time, however, these same views have their own special kinds of biases. The assumption of systemic sources for problems can result in a form of radical determinism—that is, crime, ecological crises, drug use, and sexual deviation are seen to be a function of weaknesses and disadvantages in existing institutions only. Therefore, the answer to resolutions must lie in either wholesale revolution and change or resignation in the form of retreat and apathy, neither of which is realistic or likely to lead to resolutions. New pathology also stresses the objective character of problems and fails to recognize the possible role of subjective interpretations, either by those involved in the problem behavior or by citizens as a whole. In other words, something is assumed to be fundamentally wrong with modern society, rather than with the way in which we tend to define, identify, and correct problems. It is doubtful, therefore, that new pathology alone could become the basis for useful paradigm, although new pathologists have raised important questions about prevailing views.

New conflict theory, in contrast, adapts important elements of one prevailing paradigm—functionalism—to criticize the assumptions of the other paradigms—deviance and disorganization. It argues that conflict, in addition to cooperation, consensus, or maintenance of orderly processes, can be as justifiably viewed as playing important roles in the social system. Therefore, drug use, crime, revolution, and militancy can be important to both those involved in these forms of behavior and to the larger society. Rather than being merely disruptive and threatening, they may be the means by which individuals adapt for survival in threatening situations, and they can lead to necessary changes in attitudes and modes of response to what are considered to be problems. There are, however, two major unresolved weaknesses in new conflict theory. First, its proponents run the risk of reifying and deifying conflict, even in its most extreme forms. Just as functionalists tend to accept the existence of the prevailing system as natural, new conflict theorists can accept the existence of conflict as natural and, therefore, as desirable, largely inescapable, and never really disruptive or disorganizing. This weakness, however, might well be met with a stress upon the manifest versus the latent functions of conflict, the particularistic versus the universalistic consequences of conflict, and the functional versus dysfunctional aspects of conflict. A second major weakness is that not all forms of problem behavior are necessarily amenable to a conflict perspective. For example, some aspects of the ecology crisis and the problem of alcohol abuse do not seem to reflect the characteristics of open and significant conflict between two or more contending groups within society. Conflict may result as the problem is discovered, but the concept of conflict may not explain the reason for the problem in the first place, nor the manner in which the problem might be resolved. New conflict theory, then, also stresses the objective aspect of problem behavior and has difficulty accounting for subjective, behavioristic (elementaristic) characteristics.

The major contribution of labeling theory has been the emphasis upon subjective, behavioristic elements as they relate to social problems. Together with the new behaviorists and symbolic interactionists, labeling theorists have pointed to the way in which one's definitions of what constitutes a problem, the manner in which self and social definitions may influence one another, and the particularistic context of daily interaction between those engaged in problem behavior can be fundamentally important. As Blumer pointed out, problems are really processes, and processes involve definitions, values, and interaction. Therefore, definitions, values, and interaction cannot be ignored, and older prevailing paradigms, especially deviance and disorganization, tend to ignore or take for granted society's definitions and values. As Becker and others pointed out, a great deal of problem behavior may be mislabeled or falsely labeled by larger society, and a mere change in the label (through modification of laws, attitudes, or responses to deviants) may resolve the problem. The weakness of labeling theory, together with the new behaviorism, is its focus essentially upon particularistic, subjective aspects of problem behavior, as an understandable corrective to the biases of prevailing paradigms. When this focus becomes extreme, these new theories tend to be applicable only to some problems in very limited circumstances (for example, the work of Alcoholics Anonymous or the treatment of inmates in mental institutions). Therefore, the tendency for these views to reject a good deal of what previous perspectives have offered and not to build upon or incorporate earlier assumptions suggests that they alone do not provide a basis for new paradigms, though they are excellent vehicles for criticizing earlier views.

Finally, new reflexive social science and radical perspectives, similar to conflict theory, tend to adopt a functionalistic perspective of problems in a somewhat different way than that of older paradigms. To this extent, these new competing schools of thought are universalistic and action oriented at the same time. In addition, reflexive and radical perspectives demand a future concern and an interest in the possibility of alternative social systems. However, the perspectives have yet to resolve satisfactorily the issue of a commitment to total value relevance versus the need to retain some value freedom at specific places in the research procedure. As a result, much new radical analysis does often tend to be more polemical and less scientific, and, as a consequence, limited or unrealistic in its possible application to contemporary problems.

In summary, it is important to note that the most likely possibilities for new paradigms, which could stand as equally influential competitors to prevailing paradigms, are to be found within new conflict theory and reflexive and radical perspectives. In addition, significant contributions will be made by labeling theory and behaviorism, though these perspectives alone are unlikely to lead to new paradigms. Interestingly, new conflict theory and radical views seem to incorporate many elements of functionalism. This implies several possibilities for the immediate future. First, functionalism may begin to attain the status of a single predominant paradigm while social science merely maintains a multiparadigmatic appearance. An intellectual confrontation might then occur between two major schools of thought within the one paradigm—between those who are committed to more conservative, modestly reformist views and those who are espousing more radical, change-oriented perspectives. Second, a new paradigm might develop that takes the form of a radical, reflexive functionalism. Such a paradigm could not only represent a much needed counterpoint to prevailing paradigms, but it could also provide scientists and citizens with new ways of viewing problems, conducting study and research, and seeking solutions. If the contemporary crisis in social-problems theory and action is to be meaningfully confronted, several of these developments must be encouraged and sustained within modern social science.

Notes to Chapter 8

1. Howard S. Becker, "Whose Side Are We On?," *Social Problems*, 14 (Winter 1967), 239–249.
2. For a more complete discussion of the ideal scientific research method, see Delbert Miller, *Handbook of Research Design and Social Measurement* (New York: David McKay Co., 1964); Claire Selltiz, Marie Jahoda, Morton Deutsch, and Stuart W. Cook, *Research Methods in Social Relations*, rev. ed. (New York: Holt, Rinehart and Winston, 1959); and Ralph Thomlinson, *Sociological Concepts and Research* (New York: Random House, 1965). This kind of issue is also discussed in Ritchie P. Lowry and Robert P. Rankin, *Sociology: Social Science and Social Concern*, 2nd ed. (New York: Charles Scribner's Sons, 1972), pp. 15–19.
3. Emile Durkheim, *Suicide*, G. Simpson, ed., J. A. Spaulding and G. Simpson, trans. (New York: The Free Press, 1951). A detailed discussion of Durkheim's analysis by various steps of the scientific method can be found in Ritchie P. Lowry and Robert P. Rankin, *Sociology: Social Science and Social Concern*, 2nd ed. (New York: Charles Scribner's Sons, 1972), pp. 10–15.
4. Thomas S. Kuhn, *The Structure of Scientific Revolutions*, 2nd ed. (Chicago: University of Chicago Press, 1970).

References

Publication References by Paradigms, Critiques, and New Views

The following is a listing and categorization of some recent and general publications dealing with social problems. It is not meant to be inclusive and, therefore, does not represent an exhaustive reference to all possible sources. For example, books and articles discussing specific problems are obviously excluded for purposes of brevity. This listing is presented as a suggestive guide to the reader. It indicates the kinds of references available in the general area of concern for all social problems, according to major paradigms, criticisms of these paradigms, and new schools of thought as discussed throughout this book. In addition, classification of an author under one particular category does not imply that this author avoids the use of other perspectives. Categorization is by basic or essential orientation only. As indicated previously, most contemporary social scientists employ a sophisticated mixture of the many available perspectives. The difficulty is that they sometimes do not make these perspectives manifest either to themselves or to their readers, and rarely do they assess the influence of these perspectives upon their conclusions. In this sense, the following listing suggests the major influences inherent in various references. Finally, this listing gives a general indication of where most recent work on social problems has been theoretically concentrated and, thereby, shows where additional work may be needed in order to develop a new, more effective paradigm for the future.

Applied and Action-Oriented Social Science

The following includes references that generally argue against traditional, value-free, abstract social research and insist instead upon the necessity for value concern, futurist perspectives, and activist involvement by social scientists. As such, these references often fall within new conflict theory, new radical perspectives, and the like.

Adrian, Charles R., ed. *Social Science and Community Action.* East Lansing, Mich.: Michigan State University, 1960.

Gouldner, Alvin W., and S. M. Miller, eds. *Applied Sociology: Opportunities and Problems.* New York: The Free Press, 1965.

Harris, Fred R., ed. *Social Science and National Policy*. Chicago: Aldine Publishing Company, 1970.

Heidt, Sarajane, and Amitai Etzioni, eds. *Societal Guidance: A New Approach to Social Problems*. New York: Thomas Y. Crowell, 1969. "Selected Studies in Social Problems" Series.

Shostak, Arthur B., ed. *Sociology in Action: Case Studies in Social Problems and Directed Social Change*. Homewood, Ill.: The Dorsey Press, 1966.

Sjoberg, Gideon, ed. *Ethics, Politics, and Social Research*. Cambridge, Mass.: Schenkman Publishing Co., 1967.

United States Department of Health, Education, and Welfare. *Toward a Social Report*. Washington, D.C.: U.S. Government Printing Office, 1969. Also available as Wilbur J. Cohen, ed. *Toward a Social Report* (Ann Arbor, Mich.: University of Michigan Press, 1970).

Zurcher, Louis A., Jr., and Charles M. Bonjean. *Planned Social Intervention: An Interdisciplinary Anthology*. San Francisco: Chandler Publishing Company, 1970.

Conflict Theory

Binkley, Luther J. *Conflict of Ideals: Changing Values in Western Society*. New York: Van Nostrand Reinhold Company, 1969.

Coser, Lewis A. *The Functions of Social Conflict*. New York: The Free Press, 1956.

Coser, Lewis A. *Continuities in the Study of Social Conflict*. New York: The Free Press, 1967.

Cuber, John F., William F. Kenkel, and Robert A. Harper. *Problems of American Society: Values in Conflict*. New York: Holt, Rinehart and Winston, 1964. Also influenced by social processes and disorganization approaches to social problems.

Loomis, Charles P. "In Praise of Conflict and Its Resolution," *American Sociological Review*, 32 (December 1967), pp. 875–890.

Simmel, Georg. *Conflict*. Kurt H. Wolff, trans. New York: The Free Press, 1955.

Deviance Paradigm

Berg, Irwin A., and Bernard M. Bass, eds. *Conformity and Deviation*. New York: Harper & Row, 1961.

Clinard, Marshall B. *Sociology of Deviant Behavior*, 3rd ed. New York: Holt, Rinehart and Winston, 1968.

Feldman, Saul D., and Gerald W. Thielbar, eds. *Life Styles: Diversity in American Society*. Boston: Little, Brown, 1972.

Gerson, Walter M., ed. *Social Problems in a Changing World: A Comparative Reader*. New York: Thomas Y. Crowell, 1969.

Gibbs, Jack P. "Conceptions of Deviant Behavior: The Old and the New," *Pacific Sociological Review*, 9 (Spring 1966), pp. 9–14.

Rushing, William A., ed. *Deviant Behavior and Social Process*. Chicago: Rand McNally, 1969.

Disorganization Paradigm (Social and Cultural)

Bernard, Jessie. *Social Problems at Mid-Century: Role, Status, and Stress in a Context of Abundance*. New York: The Dryden Press, 1957. Also influenced by the theory of role deviance.

Bredemeier, Harry C., and Jackson Toby, eds. *Social Problems in America: Costs and Casualties in an Acquisitive Society*. New York: John Wiley & Sons, 1960. Also influenced by value conflict theory and a focus upon individual responses.

Elliott, Mabel A., and Francis E. Merrill. *Social Disorganization*, 4th ed. New York: Harper & Row, 1961.

Faris, Robert E. L. *Social Disorganization*. New York: The Ronald Press, 1955.

Hauser, Philip M. "The Chaotic Society: Product of the Social Morphological Revolution," *American Sociological Review*, 34 (February 1969), pp. 1–19. Also influenced by functionalism and pathology perspectives.

McDonagh, Edward C., and Jon E. Simpson. *Social Problems: Persistent Challenges*, 2nd ed. New York: Holt, Rinehart and Winston, 1969.

McGee, Reece. *Social Disorganization in America*. San Francisco: Chandler Publishing Company, 1962.

Nordskog, John Eric, *et al.*, eds. *Analyzing Social Problems*. New York: The Dryden Press, 1956. Also includes references to deviancy, functionalist, and social processes approaches.

Ogburn, William F. *Social Change*. New York: Huebsch, 1922. Develops the theory of cultural lag, which plays an important role in most disorganization approaches.

Petersen, William, and David Matza, eds. *Social Controversy*. Belmont, Calif.: Wadsworth Publishing Company, 1963.

Winter, J. Alan, Jerome Rabow, and Mark Chester, eds. *Vital Problems for American Society*. New York: Random House, 1968. Value conflict approach.

Functionalist Paradigm

Bryant, Clifton D., ed. *Social Problems Today: Dilemmas and Dissensus.* Philadelphia: J. B. Lippincott, 1971. Also includes references to deviancy, labeling, and disorganization perspectives.

Davis, Kingsley. "The Myth of Functional Analysis as a Special Method in Sociology and Anthropology," *American Sociological Review, 24* (December 1959), pp. 757ff.

Martindale, Don, ed. *Functionalism in the Social Sciences: The Strengths and Limits of Functionalism in Anthropology, Economics, Political Science, and Sociology.* Monograph No. 5. Philadelphia: American Academy of Political and Social Science, 1965.

Merton, Robert K., and Robert A. Nisbet, eds. *Contemporary Social Problems,* 3rd ed. New York: Harcourt Brace Jovanovich, 1971. Also influenced by deviancy and disorganization paradigms.

Nisbet, Robert A. *The Social Bond.* New York: Alfred A. Knopf, 1970.

Parsons, Talcott. *The Social System.* New York: The Free Press, 1951.

Petersen, William, ed. *American Social Patterns.* Garden City, N.Y.: Doubleday, 1956.

Sykes, Gresham M. *Social Problems in America.* Glenview, Ill.: Scott, Foresman, 1971.

Tumin, Melvin. "The Functionalist Approach to Social Problems," *Social Problems, 12* (Spring 1965), pp. 379–388. A critical appraisal of functionalism as it has been used in the past.

Labeling Theory

Becker, Howard S. *Outsiders: Studies in the Sociology of Deviance.* New York: The Free Press, 1963.

Becker, Howard S., ed. *The Other Side: Perspectives on Deviance.* New York: The Free Press, 1964.

Becker, Howard S., ed. *Social Problems: A Modern Approach.* New York: John Wiley & Sons, 1966.

Becker, Howard S. "Whose Side Are We On?" *Social Problems, 14* Winter 1967), pp. 239–249.

Kitsuse, John I. "Societal Reaction to Deviant Behavior: Problems of Theory and Method," *Social Problems, 9* (Winter 1962), pp. 247–256.

Rubington, Earl, and Martin S. Weinberg, eds. *Deviance: The Interactionist Perspective.* New York: Macmillan, 1968. Influenced by social processes theory of problems.

Mixed Theoretical Approaches

Dentler, Robert A. *Major American Social Problems.* Chicago: Rand McNally, 1967. Tends toward deviancy and disorganization paradigms.

Gold, Harry, and Frank K. Scarpitti, eds. *Combatting Social Problems: Techniques of Intervention.* New York: Holt, Rinehart and Winston, 1967. Combines interest in applied social science and functionalism.

Merrill, Francis E., *et al. Social Problems.* New York: Alfred A. Knopf, 1950. Utilizes deviancy and disorganization paradigms.

Raab, Earl, and Gertrude Jaeger Selznick. *Major Social Problems.* New York: Harper & Row, 1959. Essentially influenced by the functionalist approach.

Rosenberg, Bernard, gen. ed. *Selected Studies in Social Problems Series.* New York: Thomas Y. Crowell. Includes:
    Korn, Richard R., ed. *Juvenile Delinquency* (1968).
    Sagarin, Edward, and Donald E. MacNamara, eds. *Problems of Sex Behavior* (1968).
    Seligman, Ben B., ed. *Aspects of Poverty* (1968).
    Silverstein, Harry, ed. *The Social Control of Mental Illness* (1968).

Rubington, Earl, and Martin S. Weinberg. *The Study of Social Problems: Five Perspectives.* New York: Oxford University Press, 1971.

Scanzoni, John, ed. *Readings in Social Problems: Sociology and Social Issues.* Boston: Allyn & Bacon, 1967. Includes references to deviancy, disorganization, functionalism, labeling theory, conflict theory, and so on.

Schur, Edwin M. "Recent Social Problems Texts: An Essay-Review," *Social Problems, 10* (Winter 1963), pp. 287–193. Influenced by the new radical perspective.

Pathology Perspectives (New and Old)

Henderson, Charles R. *Introduction to the Study of the Dependent, Defective, and Delinquent Classes and of Their Social Treatment.* Boston: D. C. Heath, 1909. Old view.

Ibrahim, Azmy Ishak. "Disorganization in Society, But Not Social Disorganization," *The American Sociologist, 3* (February 1968), pp. 47–48. New view.

Kavolis, Vytautas, ed. *Comparative Perspectives on Social Problems.* Boston: Little, Brown, 1969. New view.

Lemert, Edwin M. *Social Pathology.* New York: McGraw-Hill, 1951. Also an early reference to labeling theory.

Rosenberg, Bernard, *et al.*, eds. *Mass Society in Crisis: Social Problems and Social Pathology*, 2nd ed. New York: Macmillan, 1971. New view.

Smith, Samuel. *Social Pathology*. New York: Macmillan, 1911. Old view.

Radical and Revolutionary Perspectives

Editors. "Radical Perspectives in Sociology," *Sociological Inquiry, 40* (Winter 1970), pp. 3–165.

Gouldner, Alvin W. *The Coming Crisis of Western Sociology*. New York: Avon Books, 1970.

Hamalian, Leo, and Frederick R. Karl, eds. *The Radical Vision: Essays for the Seventies*. New York: Thomas Y. Crowell, 1970.

Lindenfeld, Frank, ed. *Radical Perspectives on Social Problems*. New York: Macmillan, 1968.

Mills, C. Wright. *The Sociological Imagination*. New York: Oxford University Press, 1959.

Perrucci, Robert, and Marc Pilisuk, eds. *The Triple Revolution: Social Problems in Depth*. Boston: Little, Brown, 1968.

Roach, Jack L. "The Radical Sociology Movement: A Short History and Commentary," *The American Sociologist, 5* (August 1970), pp. 224–235.

Ryan, William. *Blaming the Victim*. New York: Pantheon Books, 1971.

Saxton, Lloyd, and Walter Kaufman, eds. *The American Scene: Social Problems of the Seventies*. Belmont, Calif.: Wadsworth Publishing Company, 1971.

Social Problems as Social Processes

These types of references are also closely related to the concept of social problems as a form of collective behavior, labeling theory, and to an interactionist perspective.

Blumer, Herbert. "Social Problems as Collective Behavior," *Social Problems, 18* (Winter 1971), pp. 298–306.

Davis, F. James. *Social Problems: Enduring Major Issues and Social Change*. New York: The Free Press, 1970. Also utilizes the deviancy paradigm.

Fuller, Richard C., and Richard R. Myers. "The Natural History of a Social Problem," *American Sociological Review* (June 1941), pp. 321ff.

Reissman, Leonard. "The Solution Cycle of Social Problems," *The American Sociologist*, 7 (February 1972), pp. 7–9.

Schur, Edwin M. "Reactions to Deviance: A Critical Assessment," *The American Journal of Sociology*, 75 (November 1969), pp. 309–322.

Author and Researcher Index

Subject Index

Note: For specific types of social problems, some separate listings are included. Also see the entry **Social problems areas of study.**

Accidents and disasters. *See* Automobile safety; Social problems areas of study: pollution and the environment

AFDC welfare program, 83, 84

Aged, problems of the, 155–156. *See also* Social problems areas: health

Aggression, 12, 40, 163, 216

Alcoholics Anonymous and the American Temperance Movement, 121, 128–130, 299

Alienation and anomie, 5, 152–155, 174–176

American Association of Suicidology, 154

American social problems, 7–9, 19, 21–27, 29–31, 33–38, 40–43, 50, 56–63, 70, 82–92, 94–95, 100–102, 108–112, 121–126, 128–130, 140–146, 149–150, 153–160, 162–168, 170–171, 177–178, 198–203, 207–212, 225–229, 230–232, 233–236, 248–250, 255–260, 262–264, 270, 273–278. *See also* listings for other countries

American Sociological Association, 8

American sociology, 8–9

Animal and animal-like behavior, 12, 19–20, 39

Applied and action-oriented research and theory. *See* Social theories and social research, types of

Argentina, social problems in, 168–169

Aristotle, 4

Authority *vs.* power, 144, 181

Automobile safety, 41, 100–102, 230, 263

Barbados, 268, 273

Behaviorism. *See* Paradigm revolutions

Belgium, 29, 189

Berrigan, Daniel, 94

Biologically *vs.* socially determined behavior, 12, 39, 55–63, 195, 206

Birth control and birth rates. *See* Social problems areas: population

Black-white relations, black family, black solidarity, etc. *See* Social problems areas: race and ethnic relations

Blaming the victim. *See* Popular myths

Boundary-maintaining functions, 94, 211

Britain, social problems in, 28–30, 103, 115, 150, 178, 182, 263, 274

Bureaucracy, 7, 89

Capitalism, 4, 7, 17, 217

Careers of sociologists and social scientists, 8–11, 64–68, 257

Catholics. *See* Religion and social problems

Ceylon, 268

Chance, the use of the concept in social science, 26, 58

Change, social and cultural, 9–10, 67–68, 148–149, 220, 251–252, 259–260, 270–276, 287–288, 296

Chicago School of Sociology, 140, 192

Child abuse, 156–157

Chile, 113, 268

Chinese-American families and China, 162–163, 203, 268

Christianity, 4. *See also* Religion

CIA, 34–35, 53

Civil liberties, 22

Civil rights. *See* Social problems areas: race and ethnic relations

Colombia, 268

Communism, 4, 180, 198, 201, 203, 219

Conflict, social and cultural, 9–10, 53–54, 71–72, 186, 220, 251–252, 270–276

Conflict theory. *See* Paradigm revolutions

Conformity, 31, 96–98, 112–116, 119–121, 172. *See also* Paradigms: deviance